Douglas MacArthur

Biographies
IN AMERICAN FOREIGN POLICY
Joseph A. Fry, *University of Nevada, Las Vegas*
Series Editor

The Biographies in American Foreign Policy Series employs the enduring medium of biography to examine the major episodes and themes in the history of U.S. foreign relations. By viewing policy formation and implementation from the perspective of influential participants, the series humanizes and makes more accessible those decisions and events that sometimes appear abstract or distant. Particular attention is devoted to those aspects of the subject's background, personality, and intellect that most influenced his or her approach to U.S. foreign policy, and each individual's role is placed in a context that takes into account domestic affairs, national interests and policies, and international and strategic considerations.

Volumes Published

Lawrence S. Kaplan, *Thomas Jefferson: Westward the Course of Empire*
Richard H. Immerman, *John Foster Dulles: Piety, Pragmatism, and Power in U.S. Foreign Policy*
Thomas W. Zeiler, *Dean Rusk: Defending the American Mission Abroad*
Edward P. Crapol, *James G. Blaine: Architect of Empire*
David F. Schmitz, *Henry L. Stimson: The First Wise Man*
James E. Lewis Jr., *John Quincy Adams: Policymaker for the Union*
Thomas M. Leonard, *James K. Polk: A Clear and Unquestionable Destiny*
Catherine Forslund, *Anna Chennault: Informal Diplomacy and Asian Relations*
Lawrence S. Kaplan, *Alexander Hamilton: Ambivalent Anglophile*
Andrew J. DeRoche, *Andrew Young: Civil Rights Ambassador*
Jeffrey J. Matthews, *Alanson B. Houghton: Ambassador of the New Era*
Clarence E. Wunderlin, Jr., *Robert A. Taft: Ideas, Tradition, and Party in U.S. Foreign Policy*
Howard Jablon, *David M. Shoup: A Warrior against War*
Jeff Woods, *Richard B. Russell: Southern Nationalism and American Foreign Policy*
Russell D. Buhite, *Douglas MacArthur: Statecraft and Stagecraft in America's East Asian Policy*

Douglas MacArthur

Statecraft and Stagecraft in America's East Asian Policy

Russell D. Buhite

ROWMAN & LITTLEFIELD PUBLISHERS, INC.
Lanham • Boulder • New York • Toronto • Plymouth, UK

ROWMAN & LITTLEFIELD PUBLISHERS, INC.

Published in the United States of America
by Rowman & Littlefield Publishers, Inc.
A wholly owned subsidiary of The Rowman & Littlefield Publishing Group, Inc.
4501 Forbes Boulevard, Suite 200, Lanham, Maryland 20706
www.rowmanlittlefield.com

Estover Road
Plymouth PL6 7PY
United Kingdom

British Library Cataloguing in Publication Information Available

Library of Congress Cataloging-in-Publication Data

Buhite, Russell D.
  Douglas MacArthur: statecraft and stagecraft in America's East Asian policy / Russell
D. Buhite.
    p. cm.—(Biographies in American foreign policy)
  Includes bibliographical references and index.
  ISBN-13: 978-0-7425-4425-3 (cloth: alk. paper)
  ISBN-10: 0-7425-4425-7 (cloth: alk. paper)
  ISBN-13: 978-0-7425-4426-0 (pbk.: alk. paper)
  ISBN-10: 0-7425-4426-5 (pbk.: alk. paper)
  1. MacArthur, Douglas, 1880–1964. 2. MacArthur, Douglas, 1880–1964—Political
and social views. 3. United States—Foreign relations—East Asia. 4. East Asia—
Foreign relations—United States. 5. United States—Foreign relations—1933–1945.
6. United States—Foreign relations—1945–1953. 7. United States—History,
Military—20th century. 8. East Asia—History, Military—20th century. 9. Generals—
United States—Biography. 10. United States. Army—Biography. I. Title.
  E745.M3B78 2008
  355.0092—dc22
  [B]

                                                                                2007052729

Printed in the United States of America

∞™ The paper used in this publication meets the minimum requirements of
American National Standard for Information Sciences—Permanence of Paper
for Printed Library Materials, ANSI/NISO Z39.48-1992.

~

Contents

~

MacArthur Chronology

1880
January 26
Douglas MacArthur born at Little Rock, Arkansas

1893
Enrolls at West Texas Military Academy

1899
Enrolls at U.S. Military Academy at West Point

1900
Father, General Arthur MacArthur, becomes military governor of the Philippines

1903
Graduates from West Point

1904
Promoted to First Lieutenant

1905
Parents take Douglas on East Asian tour

1906
Becomes aide to President Theodore Roosevelt

1908
Reprimanded for insubordination—twice

1911
Becomes captain

1912
General Arthur MacArthur, father, dies

1913
Named to general staff

1915
Becomes major

1917
Becomes colonel, chief of staff of Rainbow Division

1918
Decorated for bravery in WWI
Becomes general and commander of Rainbow Division

1919
Named superintendent at West Point

1922
First marriage—to Louise Brooks
Assignment to Philippines

1929
Divorce from Louise Brooks

1930
Becomes chief of staff of army

1932
Leads rout of Bonus Army

1935
Mother, Pinkie Hardy, dies in Manila

1936
Appointed field marshal of Philippine armed forces

1937
Marries second wife Jean Faircloth

1938
Son, Arthur, born

1941
President Franklin D. Roosevelt appoints MacArthur U.S. Far East com-
mander
Allows Japanese to destroy his air force
Retreats to Corregidor

1942
Taken to Australia
Receives Congressional Medal of Honor

1944
Meets with FDR in Hawaii
Promoted to five star general

1945
Returns to Philippines
Accepts Japanese surrender
Appointed supreme commander in Japan

1950
Korean War begins
MacArthur named UN commander
Inchon landing
Crosses 38th parallel
Meets President Harry S. Truman at Wake Island
Chinese enter Korean War

1951
Opposes President Truman on Korean War strategy and tactics
Sends letter to Rep. Joseph Martin
Truman fires MacArthur
MacArthur testifies at Senate hearings

1952
MacArthur speaks at GOP convention
Opposes Eisenhower nomination

1961
Travels to Philippines

1962
Last speech at West Point

1964
April 5
MacArthur dies at Walter Reed Army Medical Center

~

Preface

Several observations are in order about this biography of General Douglas MacArthur. First, in his memoir published in 1969 former Secretary of State Dean Acheson, displaying palpable biliousness, refers sardonically to MacArthur as the "oracle."[1] Acheson was calling attention to the general's frequent imperious and grandiloquent pronouncements about the importance of East Asia to the United States, opinions with which the secretary often disagreed. Whether or not "oracle" accurately describes the general is open to question. What I have suggested in my title is that MacArthur engaged in both statecraft and theater in his behavior. I intend nothing profoundly pejorative in my use of the term "stagecraft."

Secondly, although the book takes its place in a series of biographies in American foreign policy, it deals with a controversial military figure, one who played a role in foreign policy and whose recommendations and behavior created tension between himself and his commanders-in-chief. Both Presidents Franklin D. Roosevelt and Harry S. Truman found MacArthur troublesome not only because of his political connections to powerful Republicans in the United States but also because of his inclination to flout presidential authority. Truman eventually fired the general after finding him insubordinate. The line between legitimate and insubordinate military behavior is not always clear. There are times when moral imperatives may require that military officers speak up, undertake moves contrary to orders, or resign. That is a philosophical question this book does not seek to answer. There are numerous times, as during President George W. Bush's war in Iraq, when, in a strategic or tactical sense, military officers in retrospect seemed right and civilian authority wrong. Many critics of Truman have believed that, MacArthur's insubordinate action aside, the general's military advice was sound. Truman's supporters and most scholars believe the opposite. This is an issue the book does address.

Thirdly, no study of MacArthur and American foreign/military policy can fail to evaluate the general's mind and personality. Those contemporary civilian officials who dealt with him on a regular basis—President Truman, Secretary of State Acheson, Secretary of Defense George Marshall, presidential adviser Averell Harriman and countless others—speak frankly about MacArthur's egocentric behavior. Military officers who knew him or worked with him, such as Generals Dwight D. Eisenhower, Robert Eichelberger, Omar Bradley, J. Lawton Collins, and Matthew Ridgway, became openly contemptuous of MacArthur's publicity-seeking self-aggrandizement. Eichelberger in letters to his wife referred to the general as "Sarah" after the actress Sarah Bernhardt.[2] Biographers D. Clayton James, Carol Petillo, Michael Schaller, William Manchester, Stanley Weintraub, Bernard Duffy, Geoffrey Perret, and others, in one way or another, address the importance of MacArthur's overweening ego. Petillo in particular makes a strong case for a psychological explanation of the general's early years. In other words, those who knew him or have studied him have posited psychological explanations of his behavior.

I am neither a psychologist nor a psychiatrist, nor have I ever been drawn to psychobiography. But after discussion with numerous academic psychologists and extensive reading on ego-related disorders, I have come to the conclusion that merely to identify MacArthur's egocentrism is not sufficient. It is necessary to see in him a pathology that some psychologists call narcissistic personality disorder. I have spelled out the components of this disorder in the final chapter and shown how I think it helps define the general. If readers find my suggestions unconvincing they are obviously free to come up with their own conclusions. Someone once noted that models are always wrong but they are sometimes useful. The model, in any event, does not suffuse my narrative or the story of MacArthur's role in American foreign and military policy.

Finally, I wish to thank several individuals who have made the book possible. My good friend Richard Hopper, former vice president and editor at Scholarly Resources Inc., asked me several years ago to undertake the project. I am grateful to him, in the first instance, for giving me the opportunity. Professor Joseph "Andy" Fry of the University of Nevada, Las Vegas, the biographies' series editor, not only offered encouraging words along the way but applied his editorial expertise to the manuscript. His efforts have proven enormously helpful. Professor Howard Jablon of Purdue University, North Central read the manuscript with a critical eye. Suzie Fairman of Virginia Commonwealth University helped prepare the manuscript for the press and completed the index. She has been a fine friend and invaluable "word processor." Robin Collier of the history department at the University of Missouri, Rolla is not only the best administrative assistant in the world; she is also a wonderful typist and has been an all-around facilitator of my work. Professor Larry Gragg, a talented and considerate department chair, helped me immensely, most especially in freeing me from my regular teaching duties during the spring semester of 2006. The faculty and staff of the library and history department at Clemson University, in particular Amy Matthews, Trish Nigro, and professors Roger Grant and Tom Kuehn, assisted in ways too numerous to mention during a recent visiting professorship at Clemson. To all of the above I must state the obvious: the book would have been much more difficult to complete without their time and energy.

Notes

1. Dean Acheson, *Present at the Creation: My Years in the State Department* (New York: Norton, 1969), 430.
2. Robert Eichelberger, *Dear Miss Em* (Westport, Conn.: Greenwood, 1972), 20.

CHAPTER ONE

⌒

The Measure of the Man

He bounced on his toes to reach his full five feet eleven inches in height—his hawk nose accentuated by his seventy-two years; his pasty complexion enhanced by the white glow of the klieg lights; his shoe-polished hair swept across his balding pate from a part an inch or two above his right ear; his fame fading; his message largely ignored by the noisy throng below. He was the keynote speaker at the 1952 Republican National Convention, the political cats-paw of right-wing Texas oilmen and financial backers, H. L. Hunt and Clint Murchison. He was General Douglas MacArthur, the insubordinate military officer fired a year earlier by his commander in chief. He did not put on an impressive performance. It may not have been his last hurrah but it was close.

MacArthur desperately wanted to become president of the United States. His chance in 1952 could come only if the convention reached a deadlock between Senator Robert Taft of Ohio and General Dwight D. Eisenhower. Eisenhower, toward whom MacArthur held equal amounts of contempt and envy, possessed the delegates. MacArthur skulked off to New York where he remained incommunicado for weeks. He knew the inadequacy of his speech, and he knew Eisenhower had locked up the nomination. He would not endorse his fellow general.

This was not MacArthur's first run at the presidency. He had hoped that successful oversight of the occupation of Japan, culminating in a treaty of peace with the former World War II enemy, would provide a base for his nomination in 1948. For a variety of reasons that plan did not succeed. He had hoped that his exaggerated military achievements and contrived press reports would result in a draft in 1944. That move got nowhere. In both of those instances, as in 1952, he expected a draft; it always came to a draft. He could not risk his fragile ego with an open announcement of his candidacy for the office. What he most desired was unattainable: an enormous groundswell of support within the Republican Party, a glorious return to the adulation of his grateful countrymen, and, finally, like George Washington, nomination and election with an overwhelming mandate.

Douglas MacArthur was no George Washington. One of his biographers has said that "he was a great thundering paradox of a man, noble and ignoble, inspiring and outrageous, arrogant and shy, the best of men and the worst of men, the most protean, most ridiculous and most sublime."[1] He was, in fact, a deeply flawed personality whose behavior throughout his career, on both military and diplomatic matters, and in whatever capacity he served, clearly reflects those flaws. That is not to say he was without complexity, without intellectual talent, without insight, without some of the qualities of greatness.

He was the product of an ambitious, domineering, recognition-seeking mother and an ambitious, domineering, recognition-seeking, military-hero father. His mother was Mary Pinkney Hardy, a daughter of the Confederacy and the seventh child—among fourteen—of a Norfolk, Virginia cotton broker. His father was Arthur MacArthur Jr., the son of a prominent judge from Milwaukee, Wisconsin and later Washington, D.C. Arthur Jr. had become a Civil War officer, a colonel before the age of twenty, who achieved distinction for leading the 24th Wisconsin Regiment at the battle of Missionary Ridge. For his acts of valor and after some political maneuvering by Arthur Sr., he won, some twenty-seven years after the fact, the Congressional Medal of Honor. Disdaining a legal career for the military, he served for many years in frontier outposts in the American West, his rank in the regular army becoming second lieutenant and, soon, captain. It was during a temporary assignment in New Orleans that Captain MacArthur met and later married Mary Hardy, known throughout her life as "Pinkie."

Douglas was born in Little Rock, Arkansas, on January 26, 1880, the third and youngest son. His oldest brother Arthur became a distinguished naval officer; his next older brother Malcolm died of measles at the age of five. Young Douglas spent his formative years in a succession of western forts where he apparently experienced a comparatively happy childhood, riding the desert or prairie on easily available horses, listening to the soldiers' embellished adventure stories, imbibing his father's legendary past. He was especially drawn to the elaborate ceremony and parades, the saluting and bugling, the flourishes of martial spirit over which his father presided at these posts. During his father's many absences, his mother inculcated in him his duties to country, to God, to family, to her, and, more specifically, to her husband's honor. So far as anyone can determine, he never rebelled. He wanted to become a soldier from his earliest memory onward.

Young Douglas received an elementary school education fragmented by the family's frequent moves. Though his performance in school may have had little to do with the skirts and long curls he wore until age five (one biographer suggests gender confusion derived from his mother's imposition of this hair and clothing) one thing is certain: he was not a good student.[2] In fact, he did not become successful in school until the family moved to San Antonio in 1893, when he was thirteen, and he enrolled in the West Texas Military Academy. There he took a smattering of mathematics, ancient languages, and history, and he began to excel. Whether his performance derived from the poor academic quality of this school, which was at best a repository for delinquent boys, or his intellectual coming of age, is impossible to determine—probably a little of both. What we do know is that he graduated as valedictorian of his class in 1897, after achieving some distinction not just in the classroom, but as a cadet and on the playing fields as well. He tried his hand at football but did better at baseball, a game he always loved but played with only moderate proficiency. The sports competition at West Texas Academy may have been greater than the academic, but not by much. He tried hard but was never a good athlete.

As he completed his high school years, his mother and father called upon his politically connected grandfather to secure a presidential appointment for him at the United States Military Academy. He failed to get in via that route. Pinkie then took him back to Milwaukee where she enrolled him in a preparatory program and pulled more strings, while his father, whose most recent assignment had put him in St. Paul, Minnesota, did the same. There were academic deficiencies and a physical one; he had scoliosis. He overcame both—one with intensive study and the other with intensive exercise to strengthen his back muscles to compensate for the curvature. He was admitted to West Point with the plebe class of 1899.

What he received at West Point beyond more God and Country is difficult to say. The Military Academy was no better and probably not as good as many of the technical schools springing up across the country. The education there was not the equal of that provided at the nation's best universities, or even its indifferent ones. But he attained a rudimentary technical preparation for his career, studied more language, some history, and graduated at the head of his class in 1903. For three of the years he also played sports, once again performing better in baseball than anything else. If it needed proving, he demonstrated that he had a good, retentive mind, and he showed his gift for leadership. He did not, however, become a well-educated man. Indeed, it is doubtful if he ever became well educated, despite his posturing and portentous rhetoric, laced with classical, or better put, antique references. As Eisenhower would later put it, MacArthur left West Point to begin his acting career. Not insignificant to his psychological and emotional development during his West Point years was the fact that his mother accompanied him to the Academy, ensconcing herself in Craney's Hotel, within easy viewing distance of the campus and her boy. She saw him and counseled him and advised him daily. If it bothered him that his mother took him to college and then stayed on for four years, he never betrayed his embarrassment.

Pinkie used that time to hammer home her lessons. During a particularly difficult period in Douglas's life, as he nervously prepared to testify before a congressional committee investigating hazing at the Military Academy, she sent him a poem that speaks volumes about her and her relationship with her son. It may also provide a window on his personality over the next sixty plus years. Part of that poem reads as follows:

Like mother, like son, is saying so true
The world will judge largely of mother by you.
Be this then your task, if task it shall be
To force this proud world to do homage to me.
Be sure it will say, when its verdict you've won
She reaps as she sowed: "this man is her son!"[3]

The question that any psychological assessment would ask is, could he ever do enough to satisfy his domineering mother? A further question was whether he could ever live up to the accomplishments of his imperious father, now a general officer in charge of American forces in the Philippine Islands.

To say that the United States was not entirely at peace with itself, upon young MacArthur's graduation from the Academy in 1903, would be a serious understatement. The nation had just come through a war with Spain that resulted in a colonial possession halfway around the world. Despite a century of continental expansion, a great many Americans considered overseas imperialism antithetical to longstanding national principles. Differences with the William McKinley and then Theodore Roosevelt administrations on the issue caused a major debate at the turn of the century. The Populist movement of the previous decade identified serious strains in the social, cultural, economic, and political fabric of the country. Progressivism, the reform crusade that crossed party boundaries and lasted for the next two decades, focused on the limitations imposed by monopoly and special privilege. There were huge disparities in wealth and opportunity that reformers set out to address. The new second lieutenant was not insulated from this popular reform sentiment, and his most important scholarly biographer has argued that this intellectual baggage affected him in his post–WWII assignment in Japan.[4]

Meanwhile, the Philippines became the focal point of his early military life, and an area of the world to which he repeatedly returned. Douglas's first intimate knowledge of the islands came during his father's assignment there during the Spanish-Cuban-American War. Brigadier General Arthur MacArthur arrived in the Philippines on August 4, 1898, and quickly saw action in one of the few serious skirmishes in that theater of the war. He won recognition from his superiors for that battle and not long thereafter received promotion to major general of volunteers. After the peace was concluded with Spain on December 10, a new phase of the war began as American troops battled with the forces of an insurgent nationalist group led by Emilio Aguinaldo, who were no more anxious for American domination than Spanish. This was a much more difficult war, costly and marked by brutal American atrocities against the Filipino "brown brothers." Eventually MacArthur became commander of all American troops in this conflict and, in May 1900, military governor of the Philippines. Although he fought ferociously against Aguinaldo's uprising and did much to subdue it, Arthur MacArthur held an enlightened view of his enemy, and his role as military governor represented a first step toward bringing reform to the islands: he began elementary schools, instituted habeas corpus, and insisted, when possible, that his men treat the Filipinos with respect.

Douglas learned several "lessons" from his father's experience in the Philippines, and benefited in one important way. In June 1900, President McKinley sent William Howard Taft, later secretary of war and president of the United States, to the islands as head of a Philippine commission to begin instituting civil government in the new colony. He and MacArthur quickly clashed. MacArthur resented Taft's presence (Taft later said that in the general's company his sweat glands always seized up) and treated him coolly. He would not abide civilian interference in his affairs. Taft, who had the support of Roosevelt and Secretary of War Elihu Root, could not tolerate MacArthur's behavior and soon engineered his recall. MacArthur had become an opponent of the early transition to civilian rule in the Philippines as well as a petty, outspoken critic of Taft. His next assignment was oblivion and, before long, retirement. He became a vocal critic of Root for his military reforms and for his choices for chief of staff; and he simply could not accept civilian authority or keep his mouth shut. Douglas also drank in his father's belief in colonies and projection of American power into Asia and the Pacific. The most important contribution Arthur Jr. made to Douglas's career, however, came in the form of his support and cultivation of a group of young officers, subordinates to him in the Philippines, who would later be in position to assist his son: Peyton March, William Mitchell, Charles Summerall, Enoch Crowder, and, not least, John J. Pershing.

It is exceedingly interesting that Douglas MacArthur and many of his military colleagues would become assertive proponents of individualism, self-reliance, small government, free enterprise, and committed members of the Republican Party, because the military establishment that young MacArthur joined and benefited so immensely from was nothing if not a welfare state. Indeed, his early assignments were hardly assignments at all but rather make-work projects in the manner of Franklin D. Roosevelt's later Works Progress Administration (WPA). His superiors, it seems, did not know where to send him or what to have him do. He spent his first two months of active duty on leave; he then took up an engineering corps assignment in northern California in which his "job" was to do inspections, secure supplies, and write occasional reports. He lived a privileged life that did not end when he was sent to the Philippines in October 1903. In fact, it never ended. His parents used their connections to get him promotions and attractive posts. Later he used those connections and new ones that he established to advance his career and his comforts. Because the army had so little for its talented young officers to do, it made use of the new Philippine colony. At first MacArthur did tasks around Manila. Then he was sent to the southern coast of Panay, just one of over 7,000 Philippine islands, mainly to oversee the building of a wharf and retaining wall. While in this assignment, he accompanied an engineering unit into the jungle of the small island of Guimaras on a search for building timber, where, according to MacArthur's account, he was ambushed by a couple of guerrillas whom he quickly shot and killed with his pistol. It made a good story. It may have happened as he told it, or it may not have, though no one questioned the existence of two dead Filipinos at the end of the episode.

In October 1904, MacArthur returned to San Francisco from his tour in the Philippines and spent the next eight months overseeing engineering projects in northern California. Much of that time he was ill from malaria, which he had contracted in his recent assignment in the islands, so, understandably, he did not do his best work during this period. When his immediate superior officer was not happy with his performance, his parents came to his rescue. His father, after his removal from the Philippines, had become for a time, perhaps as a sop from President Roosevelt, U.S. military attaché in Japan. Arthur arranged the dismissal of his aide-de-camp and the appointment of his son to the post. The appointment enabled Douglas to accompany his parents on a lengthy tour of several Asian and Pacific countries. The reasons for the tour remain unclear to this day—it was probably an important-sounding though meaningless junket to keep General MacArthur quiet.

Douglas arrived in Japan on October 29, 1905, ready to assume his duties as "aide" to his father. He and his parents began their tour of Asian and Southeast Asian countries three days later, the trip to be completed by boat, rail, and horse-drawn coach. So far as can be determined, Douglas looked after vouchers and travel arrangements, attended ceremonial functions, and studied colonial military outposts in the region. The tour, which consumed eight months, took the MacArthurs first to Japanese bases and briefly to Shanghai and Hong Kong, then in turn to Malaya, Singapore, The Dutch East Indies, Burma, India—where they spent two months—on to Siam, to China, and back to Japan. Douglas described the trip later as a defining time in his life whereupon he came to see Asia and the Pacific islands as critical "to the very existence" of America. His father's report, such as it was, stressed the growing strength of the Japanese and the importance of the American control of the Philippines. Both MacArthur men would claim throughout their lives, and probably in great measure because of this trip, that they possessed unique and special knowledge of the "Oriental mentality."

Some measure of the kind of army in which Douglas served in those early years was the absence of orders upon his return to San Francisco in August 1906; he spent the first five weeks lingering aimlessly with his parents. After that, he undertook a series of assignments in which he performed poorly, so poorly in fact that had it not been for his father's connections he might have been drummed out of the service. But based on experience to that point, there was little reason for assuming that he could not do pretty much as he pleased, with impunity. Through the remainder of 1906 and into 1907 Douglas's main assignment was to complete the course at the army's engineering school at Washington, D.C. Though he finally finished the course in absentia, he did not do well, either out of lack of interest, which was likely, or because he held a simultaneous appointment to work for President Roosevelt in arranging social functions at the White House. The latter post, almost certainly secured by his father, accorded with his predispositions toward power and influence, and he claims to have supplied Roosevelt with vital information about Asia and the Pacific. Whatever the case, once again his superior officer was not pleased: "Throughout the time Lieutenant MacArthur was under my observation, he displayed, on the whole, but little professional zeal." The same was true in MacArthur's next assignment as an engineer with the district office in Milwaukee, Wisconsin, where his job was to assist in deepening and improving harbors along Lake Michigan. His demand for special consideration, time off to be with his parents, and his generally poor work habits, led Major William Judson to submit a devastating report on the young lieutenant. "I am of the opinion," Judson wrote, "that Lieutenant MacArthur, while on duty under my immediate orders, did not conduct himself in a way to meet commendation, and that his duties were not performed in a satisfactory manner."[5] Once again, his father bailed him out, this time securing him a transfer to Fort Leavenworth, Kansas.

For the first time since assuming active duty MacArthur blossomed, as he took command of troops. He took over Company K, the lowest ranking company on the post and made it into an efficient unit, one that drew praise from his superiors. He also participated in the post's active social life, particularly in the athletic part of that life, as a player-manager of the baseball team. The assignment at Leavenworth also brought him into contact with a number of contemporary officers with whom he was to serve through the remainder of his career. One was Robert Eichelberger, later a general officer who over time became disdainful of the preening, posing MacArthur. Another was George Marshall, who could not abide him from the start of their long relationship. The duty at Leavenworth saved MacArthur's military career, probably because for the first time he realized he had to apply himself in order to get ahead. His parents could only help him; they could not guarantee his future. A significant development during his three years at Leavenworth was his promotion from first lieutenant to captain, formal evidence of upward progress.

Following completion of his tour in Kansas, MacArthur's career took a fortuitous turn. His family connection brought another plum assignment. His father Arthur died of a heart attack on September 5, 1912, while delivering a speech to his old Wisconsin unit. General MacArthur, still aggrieved from what he considered ill treatment at the hands of William Howard Taft (at that time President Taft) and former Secretary of War Root, had expressly refused to allow any military recognition upon his death, but his influence lived on. Douglas wrote later that his father's sudden death was a major turning point in his life, shaking him to the core, forever placing his father's career before him as an exemplar for his own. The death also exacted its toll on Pinkie, who suddenly fell ill and demanded the lion's share of her two sons' time. She often took to her bed at times of stress, or most particularly when she wanted Douglas's attention, declaiming loudly that she was near death while living on until 1935. The result of this family crisis was Douglas's transfer, through the intervention of old family friend General Leonard Wood, then chief of staff, to the office of the chief of staff. This assignment was another make-work duty to allow him to move his mother to Washington, D.C., where she could get the best possible medical care. It also led within a year to young MacArthur's appointment to the general staff, something that absolutely would not have occurred had his father and mother not developed the relationship with Wood.

During President Woodrow Wilson's fracas with Mexico in which he sought the overthrow of the murderous regime of Victoriano Huerta, American troops occupied Vera Cruz in the spring of 1914. General Wood sent MacArthur on a reconnaissance mission to the city to secure information about Mexican deployments in the area and to identify locomotives to transport U.S. troops and equipment. This mission, conducted south of the city, which in the main took place during the night of May 7, resulted in MacArthur's skirmishing with Mexican forces and "bandits" and, according to his own account, shooting two of them. He came away, he said, with five bullet holes through his clothing—a near fatal experience. He tried hard in the aftermath of this affair to get the Congressional Medal of Honor and was disappointed mightily when it was denied him. Whether or not he was seeking to emulate his father's bravery is unclear; what appears obvious is that the denial of the medal confirmed his father's lesson that superior officers could not be trusted to impart well-deserved honors. This was but one early manifestation of MacArthur's lifelong paranoia.

"Statesmen" must successfully navigate their way through crises to gain historical attention. "Leaders" are created through circumstance, through a confluence of events that brings the most important component of leadership: followers. Military officers need wars or armed conflict if they are to achieve promotion and recognition. Back in Washington during the period of American neutrality after war erupted in Europe in August 1914, Major MacArthur worked on preparedness issues, cultivated contacts within the Wilson administration, and displayed skill as a representative of the army's Bureau of Information in dealing with the press. The latter experience proved extremely valuable later, particularly during WWII. It was American intervention into WWI, however, that brought the breakthrough in MacArthur's career.

His association with the winning side in a serious military policy dispute led to his active participation in the war, to his heroism and decoration for valor—and, in short, made him known to many of his countrymen. A major question at the time of American intervention was whether to use draftees or national guardsmen as the primary U.S. force to engage the Germans. MacArthur sided with Secretary of War Newton Baker, who soon became his benefactor, in convincing President Wilson that the Guard should be used. Then MacArthur convinced Baker to create a division composed of men from Guard units across many states; a "rainbow" would stretch across the country for the selection. The so-called Rainbow Division, which Baker chose MacArthur to lead, thus came into existence. Baker also promoted MacArthur from major to colonel. In October 1917, MacArthur led the Rainbow Division ashore in France.

Over the next year and a half MacArthur participated in eight battles, in which he deliberately exposed himself to danger, refused to take precautions against gas attacks, and often disdained even the use of his helmet. For these acts of bravery he received numerous decorations and the undying loyalty of his men. He shared their sacrifices and their successes, and his natural superciliousness seldom manifested itself. In short, he made friends on a scale that he was never able to duplicate before or after. Most knowledgeable observers of his later career would argue that he was nearly totally friendless. That was not true in his WWI experience. His men not only seemed to like him, they tolerated his posturing and his affectations of dress—his riding crop, his rumpled hat, his cane, his absurdly colorful, flowing muffler. He was not entirely free of controversy, however, as he fought a verbal and ultimately political battle with superiors who at one point sought to break up his division for use as replacements for other units. He earned the enmity of officers who did not look kindly upon his direct appeal to Congress and the American press to keep his division intact. These officers saw him as a show-off and self-promoter. The lessons were not lost on MacArthur, who skillfully used the press and congressional connections to advance his career, and who always thereafter harbored an unhealthful paranoia about those "jealous" desk officers out to thwart his advancement.

After the war, MacArthur held a command position in one of the rural occupation zones of Germany, one immune from the revolutionary activity sweeping the rest of the country. In April of 1919 he returned to the United States. With the assistance of his mother who called upon old loyalties to her husband, he received the appointment of superintendent at West Point. This post was attractive because it not only carried recognition as a plum assignment but also allowed him to keep his rank from WWI, which had risen to brigadier general. His mother's fawning letters to Secretary of War Baker and General Pershing had assisted with the promotion. He also found the position appealing because it provided a chance to modernize the Academy's curriculum.

His tenure at West Point lasted a little over two years. He was only partially successful in updating the curriculum, which was controlled by the fac-

Figure 1.1.   West Point Superintendent MacArthur. Reprinted Courtesy of the General Douglas MacArthur Foundation.

ulty, and in this case by a reactionary group of men who wanted no change. But his tenure was also limited by his social activity. He met and in 1922 married Louise Cromwell Brooks, a wealthy socialite divorcée from Baltimore, with two children, who, rumor had it, was also sleeping with General Pershing, then a widower. According to one biographer who has completed a successful psychological portrait, MacArthur's first sexual experience came at age forty-two with Mrs. Brooks. The marriage did not have Pinkie's approval; she refused to attend the wedding. And the marriage did not last long because, according to Louise, who was herself experienced and something of a libertine, MacArthur was sexually dysfunctional: he had erectile deficiency and, though a general, was "a buck private" in bed.[6] Pinkie, who had moved into the superintendent's mansion (a huge step up from Craney's hotel), now had competition from another woman and was furious with her "boy." Pershing, as chief of staff, was more of a problem. He quickly transferred MacArthur to the Philippines.

That assignment did not last long, but it lasted too long for Louise. Ensconced in a comfortable house in Manila and surrounded by the American colonizing elite, whose parties she frequented as often as possible, she could have and probably should have found excitement in the tour. Instead, she found Manila boring and oppressive. She longed for the good times back home. Douglas's absences, which took him among other places to Bataan, where he undertook an extensive survey of the peninsula in consonance with War Plan Orange (a contingency plan to hold the peninsula and the island of Corregidor in the event of a future Japanese invasion), fostered her resentment. His fondness for and good relations with Filipino officials left her baffled. Occasionally at parties she vented her wrath, as when she once referred to him sarcastically as "Sir Galahad" and, after she joined a cycling club, when she rhetorically asked, "can you imagine Douglas on a bicycle?"[7] In February 1923, the couple and her children sailed for home in response to a plea from Pinkie. Douglas's brother Arthur, the admiral, had died of appendicitis in December 1922. The death of her eldest son and the absence of her youngest were too much to bear; she had become critically ill.

MacArthur's arrival in the United States led to three major developments. The first was an immediate improvement in Pinkie's health. The second was his promotion to major general. The third was the gradual dissolution of his marriage. Louise and Pinkie, though not in agreement on much of anything—Louise later blamed her interfering mother-in-law and her husband's mamma's-boy psychology for the break up of the marriage—did agree in 1923 that Douglas was due a promotion. He had been a brigadier for five years, and he and they, if for no other reason, thought it was time. Louise contacted an influential lawyer friend of hers in Washington, who also happened to be a former member of the Rainbow Division, to see what he could do. She offered to pick up the check for whatever his efforts cost. Pinkie wrote to "old friend" Jack Pershing. She told "dear Jack" how "handsome" he still was and beseeched him to help her boy. Though Pershing cared little for

MacArthur, he did his best, and in January 1925 Douglas received the promotion.

Following the promotion, MacArthur assumed command of the III corps in the Washington-Baltimore area and participated halfheartedly in the social life of the capital, while living at Louise's Baltimore County estate. During these years his most important duties involved sitting as one of thirteen judges in the court-martial of Billy Mitchell, who had disobeyed orders and allegedly brought dishonor on the army for aggressively promoting air power. Specifically, he showed how airplanes could sink battleships. MacArthur always claimed he voted for acquittal but how he voted remains unclear; Mitchell apparently did not think MacArthur had supported him. MacArthur also gained national attention as head of the American Olympic Committee, an appointment given him by the committee because of his enthusiastic promotion of sports at West Point. The U.S. team won medal after medal in the 1928 games at Amsterdam.

Despite the attention he gained from these duties, and attention and fame were what he always relished more than anything else, the late twenties were a difficult time for MacArthur. Louise Cromwell Brooks MacArthur had shed one husband and she would shed two more before the end of her "career." She was a flapper at heart, a party girl, a woman of the twenties whose desire for excitement and sexual gratification went unrequited with her famous military husband. MacArthur, by contrast, was austere, introverted, a bit of a stuffed shirt, who was very ill at ease with that decade. He wanted admiration but was not gregarious by nature; apart from that brief time in France he never had "mates" and he never sought them. To call him socially maladroit would not be an overstatement. While her husband was at the Olympic Games in Amsterdam, Louise saw other men—in Washington, in Baltimore, in New York—and she flaunted her activities. By 1928, the marriage was unsalvageable, and, as he prepared to sail back to the Philippines to begin a much-desired tour of duty, she filed for divorce. He agreed on any terms that would not "compromise my honor." In that era, no divorce could fail to compromise one's honor, and Louise, after a drink or two, was always quite willing to do the compromising.

This was MacArthur's third assignment to the Philippines and, given his domestic situation, probably the most welcome. He was put in command of the Philippine Department. It afforded him the opportunity to cultivate Filipino politicians, particularly his friend Manuel Quezon, and to work with Governor General Henry Stimson, who in 1929 would become President Herbert Hoover's secretary of state. MacArthur did all in his power to get on Stimson's good side, and he probably succeeded. His main duty was to improve the efficiency and morale of the quasi-military force known as the Philippine scouts, not an easy job and not one at which the general had un-qualified success. From the time of Stimson's departure onward, he worked hard to secure appointment as the new U.S. governor general of the islands. MacArthur was always a step ahead of everyone else when thinking of his own career; he liked the Philippines and he did not know what he would do fol-lowing the tour. Even if he became chief of staff of the army, he would be too young to retire. Hence, he began a campaign using Quezon as his go-between to become governor general, going so far as to draft an incredible letter for Quezon to send to Stimson urging the appointment: "I know of no man," Que-zon was supposed to say, "who so thoroughly commands the confidence both of the American people and the Filipinos. His appointment would be a master stroke of statesmanship and diplomacy." Stimson and Hoover had another can-didate in mind and soon named former secretary of war Dwight Davis to the post. MacArthur was deeply disappointed, but he told Quezon, "Great captains ride to victory over minor defeats."[8]

Socially, MacArthur experienced few disappointments during this stay in the islands. He lived in bachelor quarters with four other men who joined him in making the rounds of the boxing matches, vaudeville shows, and Manila night clubs. These four men became his companions or associates rather than friends. More importantly, he sought out and established a torrid relationship with a young vaudevillian and night club entertainer named Is-abel Rosario Cooper, otherwise known as "Dimples." "Dimples," of Filipino and Scots descent, was a sexually experienced woman who, because of her race, MacArthur could patronize and dominate. Indeed, he put her in a "loose woman" category and clearly did not see her as a formidable female like either his mother or his ex-wife. How he "used" Dimples is impossible to say. His letters to her, which he often signed "Your daddy," suggest that, while the relationship may have been sexually intense, it may also have been un-usual. Because of Dimples, he was of two minds when Secretary of War Patrick J. Hurley and President Hoover chose him as chief of staff in 1930. He did not want to leave her, yet he feared taking her to Washington. He could not risk having his mother learn of a Eurasian mistress who was so much younger than he. At the same time, he wanted to become chief of staff, a position that his father desired but could not obtain. His mother carried the day, as she always did. She told him that his father "would be ashamed," he later wrote, "if I showed timidity" about becoming chief of staff.[9]

The appointment as chief of staff did not come his way automatically. Hurley, one of the few figures then in American public life possibly more in-secure than MacArthur, initially had his doubts. How could any man unable to hold his women occupy that important position? MacArthur eventually won Hurley over with flattery. He won Hoover's heart with claptrap about individual initiative and hard work. He took the job, and he arranged for Dimples to follow him to Washington, where he put her up in a hotel near his office. Then he moved his mother with him into the official chief-of-staff residence at Fort Meyer, Virginia.

It was not a good time to head up a military establishment; for a variety of reasons the next five years were not easy ones. By 1930, the Great Depression had begun taking a heavy toll on the nation: farmers, who had not done well since WWI, now lost their land; formerly well-to-do stockbrokers stood in breadlines; unemployment approached 25 percent; banks failed by the thousands. The country had never seen such difficult economic times. Some people starved; thousands suffered from malnourishment. Because the United States produced a surplus of almost everything, this was poverty amid abundance, but poverty ruled the day for most ordinary Americans. Disillusioned with the experience of WWI, which seemed to have solved nothing and enriched the profiteers, Americans became resentful of military expenditure. Despite MacArthur's best efforts, Congress cut his budgets, and year after year he struggled to keep the officer corps intact, to keep the United States from losing even its then-mediocre standing among the world's armies. He protested but to little avail.

The economic crisis brought cries for help from government, and it led to a questioning of orthodox ways of thinking about private enterprise. Though never imminent, revolution seemed a possibility—upheaval that might in some way emulate the experience of Soviet Russia. President Hoover worried about that. So did his secretaries of state and war. So too did General MacArthur. One of the most difficult domestic challenges for the chief of staff and his superiors during these years of the early 1930s, and one that frightened them because of its ostensible revolutionary potential, came in the form of some 22,000 American veterans of WWI, who in 1932 marched on Washington to secure immediate payment of a bonus due them in 1945. The veterans, some with families in tow, set up shantytown "residences" at Anacostia Flats and elsewhere around the city. Ultimately, MacArthur came to see these veterans, most of them needy and desperate but patriots loyal to the United States, as "animated by the essence of revolution" and hence worthy of the harshest treatment.[10]

When the U.S. Senate, strengthened by the threat of a veto from President Hoover, refused to vote the immediate bonus payment, some of the veterans went home on tickets Congress provided. But over ten thousand, however, stayed on to continue their protest. In late July after some violent

Figure 1.2.   MacArthur During a Pause in the Bonus Marchers' Eviction. Reprinted Courtesy of the General Douglas MacArthur Foundation.

incidents, President Hoover ordered Hurley to use the army to disperse the veterans from their makeshift camps. Hurley and MacArthur then exceeded the president's instructions, the latter in particular using over five hundred troops to push the vets across the Anacostia River and torch their shacks. MacArthur was not impressed with Eisenhower's suggestion that it was unseemly for the chief of staff to be commanding these troops himself, and news photos of the action showed the general posing dramatically while doing his solemn "duty." He said he had prevented mob violence, possibly revolution: "that mob down there was a bad looking mob. . . . It is my opinion that had the President not acted today, had he permitted this thing to go on twenty-four hours more, he would have been faced with a grave situation which would have caused a real battle. Had he let it go on another week I believe that the institutions of our Government would have been very severely threatened."[11]

When MacArthur first began worrying about communism is impossible to determine, but the Bonus March probably occasioned his first pronouncements on the subject. Communism, he saw correctly, represented a conspir-acy against humanity that the United States should resist at all costs. Unfor-tunately, he also believed that governmental efforts to ameliorate the effects of the Depression and to achieve the common good put the nation on the slippery slope to collectivism. He saw such activity not only as a threat to freedom but as contrary to religious principle. Pacifism was equally anathema to him because he confused God and country, or at least never distinguished between the two. He worked hard to reelect Hoover in 1932, despite Hoover's Quaker beliefs, because he had developed a close personal relation-ship with the president and because he despised the Democratic alternative, a man who would surely indulge the country's pacifist mood. Franklin D. Roosevelt's victory in the election of 1932 convinced him that his days as chief of staff were numbered. That Roosevelt kept him on until 1935 says a great deal about FDR, and MacArthur.

MacArthur could not accept the New Dealers who took over Washington in 1933. Nor did he display affection for his new commander in chief. The next two years brought a fencing match between the chief of staff and the president, with the latter unwilling to fire the difficult general out of fear of political repercussions (MacArthur had developed a strong following among important Republicans) and the former desperately desirous of preserving his career. Roosevelt feared that MacArthur's connections to powerful Re-publicans would come back to haunt him if he dispatched the general, as much as he wished to take that step. Later, MacArthur privately and often not so privately referred to the president as "Rosenfeld." Each year saw re-duced military spending and to MacArthur, at least, less and less respect for his profession. The economists, the university professors, the public policy specialists, and the lawyers who comprised the New Deal did not like MacArthur personally, nor he them. He was much more comfortable with businessmen.

According to the general, his differences with Roosevelt came to a head in 1933, after which the two men agreed to coexist. Historians should always discount the assertions of a single participant in any dispute, and, given MacArthur's complicated understanding of truth, not to say his massive ego, one should discount his assertions more than most. Moreover, there is no record of the conversation in the Roosevelt papers. In any event, MacArthur said in his memoir written years later that he had marched up to the White House, met the president in the Oval Office, and told him that, unless mili-tary funding was increased, some American soldier at some unspecified future date, as he lay dying on the battlefield, would curse the name "Roosevelt." When the president demanded an apology, MacArthur said he offered to resign. Then they came to an understanding. The conversation, assuming one took place, almost certainly did not go like that; the chief of staff, according to his mistress, "Dimples," wanted to hold his position longer than any of his predecessors, possibly even through a second four-year term, and surely would not have risked it so recklessly.[12]

Not only did MacArthur feel uncomfortable with FDR, his cabinet, and administration subordinates, he also began experiencing problems with Dimples. As an energetic young woman with a sizeable sexual appetite and an intellect to match, she grew restless cooped up in her hotel. She began dating other men, at one point entering law school where she took up with a fellow law student, a young man who would help her achieve final separation from her chief-of-staff lover. In 1934, MacArthur, increasingly hard put to keep her a secret and to look after his ailing mother while taking care of his official duties, sent Dimples a ticket back to Manila—signed from "the humane society." She did not return to Manila, and instead eventually became a "source" for one of the general's major enemies, journalist Drew Pearson.

Pearson was a scurrilous scoundrel, of questionable journalistic talent, but he was a popular scandalmonger in the 1930s whose columns were read daily by millions of Americans. His attacks on the chief of staff, owing in large measure to the general's role in the Bonus March affair, eventually led MacArthur in the spring of 1934 to sue him for the then-incredible sum of $1.7 million. MacArthur claimed Pearson had slandered him with assertions that he had been insubordinate, disloyal toward his superiors, and dictatorial. That Pearson allegedly had been disrespectful of the general's mother became another compelling issue. Pearson, as he always did, went after dirt, some of it supplied by Roosevelt's circle. Then he hit the jackpot; he learned about Dimples from whom he secured a pile of the general's letters. Through an intermediary, he let MacArthur know that he would call Dimples as a witness at the forthcoming legal proceeding. In return for the incriminating letters, many of which referred to Dimples as "My darling baby girl" from "Your daddy," and to prevent Dimples from testifying under oath that he had been verbally disrespectful of superiors, MacArthur agreed to drop the suit. Pearson gave him the letters but kept copies, which he promised not to publish until after the general's death. As part of the deal, MacArthur agreed to pay legal fees of about $15,000, and another $16,000 to Dimples, a total sum equal to well over $200,000 each in early twenty-first-century currency. Where the general could find that much money as a career army officer is an intriguing question. So too is whether FDR or his aides helped Pearson with his "work."[13]

MacArthur's ability to pay his legal bills is only understandable in the context of his next assignment. Roosevelt finessed his concern about the general, whom he considered along with Senator Huey Long of Louisiana as one of the two most dangerous men in America, by sending him to the Philippines.[14] First he extended MacArthur's term as chief of staff indefinitely; then the president encouraged legislation, which Congress passed and he signed, making him U.S. military advisor to the Philippine government—a position in which he could retain his military rank and pay and, in addition, receive generous compensation from the Filipino government. MacArthur, according to the scholarly biographer whose work focuses on his Philippine years, also used his position to participate in a major moneymaking scheme in the islands and take money from the Filipino leadership.[15] Once again, the Philippines proved a haven and salvation for the careerist general. The Philippines would also become the center of his worldview and would precipitate for the first time his involvement in American foreign policy. He and his mother, then dying, arrived in the islands in the fall of 1935.

MacArthur's worldview, and his opinions about American foreign policy, were, like every other issue in which he partook, highly personalized. Stanley Weintraub in his engaging study of MacArthur in Korea relates an amusing story about the general and his wife Jean, whom he married in 1937, as they listened to a radio recording of "The Star Spangled Banner." "Listen, Jeannie," the general is alleged to have said, "they are playing our song."[16] No member of the American military was ever more self-centered or self-absorbed. Had he spent most of his career in Uruguay rather than the Philippines, one must assume that South America would have become the center of his universe and strategically the most important part of the world. As it was, of course, he assigned those qualities to East Asia and the Pacific.

Nor was any member of the American military ever more vain. His vanity was legendary—from his sunglasses, to corncob pipe, to pushdown cap, to his careful positioning of his thinning hair, to his adornment with medals, to his ceaseless posturing. During his encounter with ragtag veterans of the Bonus March, he looked clownish, in his jodhpurs and shiny boots and dress coat, with medals and ribbons abounding. One pose he struck was particularly revealing—he stood with a cup of coffee held aloft between his thumb and forefinger like a wealthy matron at a debutante ball. His critics were aghast, and his "friends" only slightly less put off. Some of his subordinates gently tried to tell him that his posing was unbecoming but he refused to listen; he had earned those medals and had every right to wear them, he said petulantly. One searches in vain for pictures that are unposed: his head held sidewise to affect the perfect profile, his eyes fixed on a distant object to affect profundity of thought. Those were his favorites. And his height; he was terribly anxious to be perceived as tall and lean. He was, in fact, no more than five feet eleven inches tall, shorter than that as he aged, but he insisted that camera angles portray him as taller than those with whom he was photographed. And because he never exercised, he had a sizeable paunch that he worked hard to hide. Adoration sustained him. He received it from his mother. He demanded it from others as well, and, if he failed to get it, he pouted and sulked and complained that his superiors, or the press, or unidentified others were determined to slight him. His vanity may not have been his greatest flaw but it ranked high on the list. So did self-deception, and so did deception of others. He told whoppers unashamedly, knowing that his accounts of himself and of events required suspension of disbelief. He told lies when the truth would have helped him more—his insecurities and their accompanying tactics gaining ascendancy over common sense.

His need for adoration and adulation and his consonant aversion to criticism led him to reject advice that would have helped him avoid mistakes. He surrounded himself with mediocre men, loyal men, sycophants really, who competed with one another for his attention and praised him shamelessly. His marriage to his second wife, Jean Faircloth, a southern belle from Murfreesboro, Tennessee, gave him the emotional reinforcement he needed in his personal life after his mother's death. To her, he was "ma general," who could do no wrong. She never criticized him, kept in the background, let him dominate in every situation, and indulged his ludicrous behavior.

But paranoia was the personal quality most revealing of his worldview. He could not make friends; he wanted admirers rather than friends, so he sustained himself by making enemies—making them in his own mind. Because his perceived opponents, his critics, placed Europe in the first-priority category in the assessment of vital interest, he not only hated them, he hated the entire European continent. Europe became passé as center of the world stage. "They"—meaning Marshall and Eisenhower and FDR and Harry Truman and Dean Acheson and others—with their focus on Europe, were unenlightened and out to get him. This perception can only be understood as part of his paranoia, which one biographer has called "almost certifiable."[17] He was obsessed with Asia and the Pacific and with the Philippines; they were "his," and, because they were "his," they were most important to America's future.

Notes

1. William Manchester, *American Caesar: Douglas MacArthur, 1880–1946* (Boston: Little, Brown, 1978), 3.

2. Carol Petillo, *Douglas MacArthur: The Philippine Years* (Bloomington: Indiana University Press, 1981), 20.

3. Douglas MacArthur, *Reminiscences* (New York: Fawcett World Library and Time Inc., 1965), 32.

4. See D. Clayton James, *The Years of MacArthur, Volume 1, 1880–1941* (Boston: Houghton Mifflin, 1970), 85–109, 553–76.

5. Quoted in James, *The Years of MacArthur*, 96, 99–100.

6. Petillo, *Douglas MacArthur*, 140.

7. Quoted in Manchester, *American Caesar*, 133.

8. Petillo, *Douglas MacArthur*, 148–49.

9. MacArthur, *Reminiscences*, 133.

10. Quoted in Russell D. Buhite, *Patrick J. Hurley and American Foreign Policy* (Ithaca, N.Y.: Cornell University Press, 1973), 53.

11. Buhite, *Patrick J. Hurley and American Foreign Policy*, 53.

12. MacArthur, *Reminiscences*, 101. Also quoted in Manchester, *American Caesar*, 155–56.

13. Petillo, *Douglas MacArthur*, 165–66. Also see James, *The Years of MacArthur*, 412.

14. FDR made the remark to Rexford Tugwell, one of his advisors. Rexford G. Tugwell, *The Democratic Roosevelt: A Biography of Franklin D. Roosevelt* (Garden City, N.J.: Doubleday, 1957), 348–51.

15. Petillo, *Douglas MacArthur*, 208–11. See also Michael Schaller, *Douglas MacArthur: The Far Eastern General* (New York: Oxford University Press, 1989), 38.

16. Story by Shelby Foote quoted in Stanley Weintraub, *MacArthur's War: Korea and the Undoing of an American Hero* (New York: Free Press, 2000), 7.

17. Manchester, *American Caesar*, 4.

CHAPTER TWO

~

The Philippine Years

Douglas MacArthur may have lived a privileged life but he never had a real home. During his youth, his parents moved him from one army post to another, never staying long in any one location. As a young adult, he took assignments as they came, or as they were arranged for him, hither and yon. He never bought a house, never had roots in any particular domicile. The closest he came was in the mid-1920s when he bunked at the estate of first wife Louise Brooks in Baltimore County, Maryland. After President Truman dismissed him in April 1951, until his death in 1964, he lived in a suite on the 37th floor of the Waldorf Towers Hotel in New York. The Philippines provided a haven, a refuge, and, as one biographer has noted, the only place he really felt comfortable.[1] Insofar as he developed a sense of place, the Philippine Islands fulfilled that sense.

In his run for the presidency in 1980, candidate Ronald Reagan blithely announced that during his early years there had been no race problem in the United States. That same innocence obtained until the turn of the twentieth century in reference to the Philippines; to most Americans there were no Philippine Islands. Prior to 1898, few people could have located the archipelago on a map, nor would they have had reason to do so. Philippine reality may have had a long history but not to Americans. Until his father's assignment there, Douglas MacArthur surely shared this ignorance.

Historians and journalists have often mentioned that throughout much of its long history China has been more a civilization than a nation. Until recent years it was certainly not a nation-state in the Western sense of the term. The Philippines, as a conglomeration of over 7,100 islands with a land mass of around three hundred thousand square miles, hardly even qualifies historically as a civilization, let alone as a nation. The archipelago probably became a distinct geographic region over thirty thousand years ago when it separated from the Asian continent. As it developed, it was populated by Negritos, Malay, proto-Malay, and Chinese peoples, most of them living scattered, hunter-gatherer lives. The exception to this unsettled life was the indigenous culture that arose in Luzon, where rice farming became the source of livelihood and where political organization emerged based on land ownership and wealth. Until the arrival of Islam from Indonesia around 1500, outside influence was minimal. It was not until the Spanish came in 1521 that the islands became a factor in the consciousness of the West. There were an estimated five hundred thousand people living in the islands at the time of Spanish discovery.

Ferdinand Magellan, sailing around the world in the service of Spain, was apparently the first European to spot the islands. In March 1521, he landed on Cebu, where a month later a local chief had him killed. Magellan's murder did not prompt the Spanish to give up; over the next forty years they sent a number of missions to the islands, first colonizing Cebu and later Luzon, where they took possession of Manila Bay. The island colony, the only Spanish possession in Asia, eventually received its name in honor of King Philip II, who ruled Spain from the late 1550s until 1598.

Through the 17th and 18th centuries Spain tried unsuccessfully to make the colony profitable. Manila served as an entrepôt for trade between Spanish Mexico and China, but the Spanish empire did not gain significant wealth from the Philippines. Nor did direct trade emerge between the islands and the mother country—except during later stages of the empire. The one area of modest success came in Christianizing the natives. In governing the islands the church and its religious orders, Augustinians, Dominicans, Franciscans, and Jesuits, began playing a decidedly political role. The civil administration looked after administrative issues but the religious leaders, or friars as they were called, gave form and substance to policy. The friars helped Spanish governors implement indirect rule in remote, rural areas of the islands.

Neither Spain nor the indigenous population benefited in any significant way from Spanish rule. From the early 17th century onward, Spain heavily subsidized the colony via Mexico, and Spanish governors perennially worried about the Chinese who came in increasing numbers to participate in the galleon trade. Spain alternated between accommodating the Chinese and suppressing them. In Spanish wars with the Dutch and the British, the

Philippines became vulnerable, the British briefly taking the colony following the Seven Years War. After the loss of its Latin American colonies in the early 19th century, Spain, unable to continue subsidizing the islands, in 1834 opened the colony for international commerce—abaca, sugar, and tobacco becoming the main export commodities. This made the colony vulnerable to foreign influence and to increasing efforts of a *mestizo* class of Chinese, Spanish, and indigenous Philippine descent to assert a nationalist cause.

There were several mestizo uprisings during the 19th century. The Spanish government in the islands, encouraged by the friars, put the rebellions down forcefully, indeed brutally, leading to a strengthening of the nationalist movement by marrying of the cause of the mestizos, or elite, with members of the peasant class. One of the uprisings led by Emilio Aguinaldo terminated with a truce in 1897, in which the Spanish consented to pay the insurrectionists a large sum of money in return for their agreement to disarm and go into exile in Hong Kong. Although Aguinaldo was among the leaders thus exiled, neither he nor his followers planned to remain disarmed or neutralized. At the time of the Spanish-Cuban-American War the United States sought to use these Filipino nationalists to help American forces take control of the islands, and Aguinaldo saw American assistance as a way to defeat the Spanish. Hence, Commodore George Dewey transported Aguinaldo back to the islands, only to be disappointed when the Filipino nationalists began asserting independence of American control. It was the Aguinaldo-led rebellion against the Americans that occasioned Arthur MacArthur's main military activity in the Philippines, and it was his father's assignment that led to Douglas MacArthur's first real knowledge of the islands.

If the Philippines proved more a liability than an asset to the Spanish, who had been there for more than three and a half centuries, it is hard to understand why Americans were interested in claiming the islands. But imperialists in the United States at the turn of the twentieth century were operating on a set of assumptions that seemed logical at the time: it was necessary to project American power around the world to compete with European colonial empires and to do so naval bases were required; it was essential to provide overseas markets and avenues of investment for American business; and it was necessary to take up the white man's burden to impart civilization and modern political institutions to "backward peoples" of other races. Within a few years some key proponents of imperialism, such as Theodore Roosevelt, were questioning the wisdom of the decision to seize Spain's East Asian colony, because the growth of Japanese power made the islands an American "Achilles heel." But the United States had acquired a colony and had to make the most of it.

After 1903 the United States put in place modern educational, judicial, and political systems that it hoped would prepare the roughly 14 million people of the islands for eventual independence. But running a colony was not an easy task for Americans, especially one halfway around the world whose people were 80 percent Catholic, whose population was composed of numerous ethnic groups speaking diverse languages or dialects. Not the least of the problems was addressing an entrenched class system intertwined with family loyalty. The mestizos class controlled the political and economic life of the colonies when the Americans arrived and they continued to do so under American rule. The Chinese also continued to play a crucial role in commerce and finance.

Politics became a national sport for Filipinos during the first half of the 20th century. A party system emerged that American officials believed would lead to competing ideological positions and a healthy democracy. What actually occurred was that the *Nacionalista* party came to dominate Philippine political life, with personal rivalries and pettiness among oligarchs within that party deciding the issues of the day, and responding to American decisions. The major political figures during the period of American control were Manuel Quezon, Manuel Roxas, and Sergio Osmena. Political life, and economic life, depended on the oligarchs working in conjunction with elite families from Manila, whose system of loyalties extended outward to control much of the population. To keep the colony on an even keel, to encourage nationalism but not to let it get out of bounds, to allow American business to prosper, American officials under the governor general–system worked closely with Filipino elites.

Through the years the United States established a mixed record in its colonial venture. It refused to consider equal status for Filipinos and displayed the same racial prejudices as those in effect at home. Americans in the Philippines took Filipino mistresses but seldom wives. Americans did not generally encourage anything more than minimal social intercourse with the islanders by establishing separate schools, churches, and social clubs. The United States dominated Philippine economic life and did not promote anything other than an agricultural economy in the islands, taking Philippine agriculture exports but requiring the importation of manufactured goods. Often the United States seemed to support those Chinese and Japanese living in the Philippines over Filipino businessmen. The United States also blocked the establishment of a Filipino army or navy, which policy left the colony virtually defenseless.

But there was also a positive side. The United States enacted land and corporate laws making it impossible to establish large plantations and cartels in the islands. Compared to other imperial powers, the United States maintained almost no bureaucracy in its colony. It spent far more money on health and education than did the British, French, and Dutch in their Southeast Asian holdings, and it used no insular taxes for the occupying U.S. military force, instead placing the burden on American taxpayers. It imported no coolie labor as in Borneo and Malaya, encouraged no Muslim separatism as in India, and maintained no opium concession. Finally, it should be noted that the United States did not discourage nationalist activity, while the French in Indochina and British in India were imprisoning thousands of Vietnamese and Indians.[2]

MacArthur's final tour in the Philippines coincided with the advent of the commonwealth period for the U.S. colony, a status that came about after several years of political wrangling in both the United States and the islands. Ironically, the impetus toward early independence for the Philippines that occurred in the late 1920s and early 1930s came not from Filipinos but from interest groups in the United States who wished to declare American independence from the Philippines.

Several issues prompted the American move toward independence. The Great Depression, which devastated American agriculture, led American dairy farmers to oppose the importation of coconut oil from the Philippines. And sugar, one of the islands' major exports, competed with sugar, and especially beet sugar, produced in the United States. Therefore, powerful American political figures began to speak out. Senator Harry "Beets" Hawes of Missouri, a leading advocate for sugar beet farmers in his state, became a leading advocate of Philippine independence. But that was only part of the story. Those American banks that had invested heavily in Cuban sugar, the Chase National Bank and the National City Bank of New York in particular, as well as several Boston banks, lobbied hard for independence. Confluence of interests can sometimes make strange bedfellows: in this instance it was midwestern farmers, heirs to the old Populist movement, and eastern banks. But the role of labor was not unimportant, nor was the voice of those who desired independence for racial reasons. Labor worried that Filipino immigrants would work more cheaply than American laborers and thus take away jobs. The sixty thousand or so single Filipinos who migrated to the United States were a concern to those alert to the "browning" of America.

Meanwhile, the Hoover administration developed a position, one with which MacArthur was in substantial agreement. Both Hoover and the general opposed independence without a rather long transition period. Guided largely by the views of Secretary of War Patrick J. Hurley and Secretary of State Henry Stimson, who believed that departure from the islands would send a white-flag signal to an aggressive Japan, President Hoover vetoed the first major piece of independence legislation in January 1933. Both Hurley and Stimson thought the United States should enhance its military strength in the Philippines as a warning to Japan. They also thought the islands unready for independence and worried that unrest and, possibly, revolution would ensue in the wake of the withdrawal of American political tutelage and economic support.[3]

Congress passed the legislation over the president's veto, a bill called the Hare-Hawes-Cutting bill that provided for a ten-year commonwealth period, the imposition of tariffs on Philippine exports to the United States, immigration quotas for Filipinos coming to the United States, the continued presence of U.S. military bases, and the early establishment of a Philippine constitutional government. For those who worried about vulnerability to attack from Japan, and this too was one of the issues for independence proponents, the legislation recommended negotiation of a neutral status for the islands.

Manuel Quezon as president of the Philippine Senate convinced his colleagues in the legislature to kill the bill. No leading Filipino politician who wished to curry favor with his countrymen could afford to oppose independence and Quezon had long been a strong advocate of early independence. Killing the bill reflected a mixture of motives on his part. Partly, Quezon worried that the legislation would be injurious because it phased in quotas and tariffs; he desired continued economic protection. He was also concerned that, while the United States made provision to keep bases in the islands, it made no firm commitment to Philippine defense, and he deemed the envisioned commonwealth period too long. But Quezon's main concern was getting personal credit: during discussion of independence in the U.S. Congress in 1931, his main political opponents, Manuel Roxas and Sergio Osmena, had come to the United States to lobby for the Philippine cause; passage of enabling legislation for which they had lobbied, Quezon reckoned, would unduly elevate their status.

After blocking the Hare-Hawes-Cutting bill, Quezon traveled to the United States in late 1933, ostensibly to get better terms but also to enhance his own image among Filipinos. President Roosevelt convinced him he could get no better terms on tariffs and quotas than those provided in the 1933 legislation but did agree that the United States would not press the issue of army bases. Instead, the United States would request only naval facilities. The subsequent Tydings-McDuffie bill, which essentially replicated the terms of Hare-Hawes-Cutting, passed Congress and received presidential signature in 1934.[4] In July 1934 a constitutional convention opened in Manila, a session in which Quezon exerted massive influence, and the following May a constitution came into effect. In September 1935 Quezon, MacArthur's long-time friend, was elected president.

A year earlier, in the fall of 1934, Quezon had traveled to Washington for a second time in two years, on that occasion with one major concern consuming him: defense of the archipelago. It was his firm belief that the United States as the colonial master was obligated to help provide that defense. He recommended the creation of a military advisory mission on the order of those the United States had sent to Central American countries in the 1920s, and he quickly met with MacArthur to help secure the requisite congressional legislation to that end. MacArthur, who did not want to retire from the U.S. military when his term as chief of staff ended and did not want the demotion in rank that would come from an inferior corps assignment, greeted Quezon's request with great enthusiasm. He hoped to head such a mission, and he not only drafted the legislation Quezon sought but also its cover letter. To the question of whether Filipinos, with American help, could defend themselves MacArthur said: "I don't think the Philippines can defend themselves, I KNOW they can."[5]

President Roosevelt not only supported the military mission, he favored MacArthur's appointment to head it. He wanted the potentially troublesome general out of the country prior to the election of 1936 and saw no better place for him than on the other side of the world. Moreover, sending the ex-chief of staff of the United States army to fill that post might suggest to the Japanese that the United States would not allow its expulsion from East Asia. In the spring of 1935 MacArthur, by virtue of the legislation, FDR's support, and formal agreement with Quezon, became head of the military mission—at a salary of $18,000 and $15,000 in expense money, all in addition to his regular major general's pay. In addition to the generous pay and his title as head of the mission, MacArthur became "Field Marshal" in the Philippine army. The latter title, much coveted and suggested to Quezon by MacArthur, was the object of contempt by the general's aides, among them Major Dwight D. Eisenhower, who could not understand how an officer holding top rank in the U.S. army could possibly desire such an honor from a banana republic.[6]

Head of the U.S. military mission and "Field Marshal" in the Philippines apparently were insufficient titles for the general. He also wanted to become high commissioner to the Philippine commonwealth (successor title for the top U.S. administrator in the islands), a position to which Frank Murphy, then governor general, aspired and a post that would allow for possible future advancement in U.S. industry or politics. Indeed, MacArthur worked hard to undercut Murphy in the months before the general sailed for the islands, telling Quezon, among others, that Murphy, if he stayed on, would work to limit Philippine sovereignty. MacArthur convinced Quezon that the positions of high commissioner and head of the military mission should be combined. In September 1935 Roosevelt seemed ready to do just that but, upon learning that a U.S. statute prohibited military officers from holding such civilian posts, backed away from the idea—much to MacArthur's consternation. Ignoring the general's wishes, he appointed Murphy to the post.

As head of the new military mission, MacArthur's orders called for him to "act as the military adviser of the commonwealth government in the establishment and development of a system of national defense."[7] While MacArthur was maneuvering to head the mission and become high commissioner and while he was still chief of staff, he instructed a committee under the direction of Major Eisenhower and Major James Ord to begin drafting such a defense plan. It reflected MacArthur's ideas both in its grandiosity and its impracticality. A first draft called for an annual expenditure of $25 million, which everyone knew to be egregiously unrealistic. The final proposal envisioned spending $8 million per year for an 11,000-man regular army, an air force of 250 planes, a navy consisting of fifty torpedo boats, and annual training of a 40,000-man citizen conscript force. The plan also called for a Philippine military academy and about 120 training camps in the islands. MacArthur had promised Quezon in 1934 that he would forge the Philippine leader "a weapon that will spell the safety of your nation from brutal aggression until the end of time." Later, he said his plan would uphold "Christian virtues," prevent "rapacious greed," and bring a peace "that will mean continued happiness and freedom for God-worshiping and democratic people."[8]

His rhetoric, as was often the case, reflected a flight of fancy. Drawing upon his father's 1880s assessment of the value of the Far East to the future of Western civilization and on his travels with his parents, he asserted that not only would Asia be center stage for the purveying of influence, it would constitute a vital area for investment and markets. At the center of the center were the Philippine islands. American prosperity and security were dependent on what happened in the East and, even more specifically, in the Philippines.

Few people shared his vision and even fewer his belief that the Philippines were defensible. The war plans division of the chief of staff's office opined that, because the islands were scattered and separated by water, no Philippine army could be concentrated on an enemy and, unless the sea could be effectively controlled by a navy, the islands could be taken piecemeal. There was no prospect of a Filipino navy, except for a few torpedo boats. The war planners also worried that armed Filipino trainees could easily be co-opted by rebellious political leaders in outlying areas. It would be far better, the chief of staff's office believed, to create a force capable of maintaining internal order, or a semblance of it, than to establish a national army. The latter, in any event, could never hope to defend the country against the only immediately projected enemy, the Japanese. MacArthur rejected the war planners' reasoning, responding that any place was defensible if superior forces were assembled.

There were other problems. The Philippine economy, based as it was on agriculture and devoid of the type of industry necessary to supply armaments and munitions, could not support a military establishment. Only large-scale military assistance from the United States would permit creation of a truly armed force. That would be difficult to arrange in the midst of the Depression and at a distance of over eight thousand miles from the U.S. west coast. In addition, as MacArthur knew but hid from public scrutiny, the system of education in the islands had operated terribly unevenly. This meant that many of the recruits were functionally illiterate and trainable only for menial chores, if trainable at all. All this became apparent to MacArthur's chief of staff, Major Eisenhower, and his fellow staff member, Major James Ord, who came to question both MacArthur's intentions and his motives. They pointed out that even near the end of 1936 the Philippines had no bona fide army.

Meanwhile, in August 1936, MacArthur went ahead with his plan to become "Field Marshal" of the Philippine army—a title, noted previously, that originated not with Quezon, as MacArthur wanted everyone to believe, but with MacArthur himself. For the lavish commissioning ceremony, held on August 24, the general decked himself out in the U.S. military's finest mess dress uniform and relished the experience. Eisenhower, who personally turned down an opportunity for a commission in the Philippine force, tried to talk his superior out of accepting the title. He considered the whole affair "rather fantastic," and he thought "it was pompous and ridiculous to be the field marshal of a virtually nonexisting army."[9]

If MacArthur knew of the snickering and the biting sarcasm the ceremony and the "honor" inspired, he never let on. He accepted the honor; then gave a rousing speech to his young Filipino recruits, in which he said the soldier "above all men, is required to perform the highest act of religious teaching—sacrifice. In battle and in the face of danger and death he discloses those divine attributes which his Maker gave when he created man in His own image. . . . The soldier who is called upon to offer and give his life for his country, is the noblest development of mankind."[10] Although not overtly religious or a regular churchgoer, the field marshal seldom refrained from invoking the Deity for dramatic effect, and he regularly conflated military service and religious devotion, but seems never to have questioned his mother's or his wife Jean's Confederate sympathies, as though service and sacrifice were enough in themselves, even in defense of a genuinely evil cause such as slavery.

The general was still trying to please or impress his mother, recently deceased, his father, long deceased, and the new woman in his life. And his personal insecurities would not allow him to forego an honor, or public attention, no matter how absurd. A more charitable interpretation is that he thought the spectacle, and his own performance, would rally young Filipinos to the service of their country.

One can only assume that his mother's death affected him mightily. Seldom far from his side throughout his fifty-five years, she had accompanied him in the fall of 1935. She had grown desperately ill on the trip and died shortly after arrival in the islands of a cerebral thrombosis. His grief was profound, and evidence suggests that for several months he performed his duties only sporadically. It is easy to believe that he continued to worry about her expectations and had a hard time adjusting to the absence of her affirming presence for his accomplishments. He had her body interred in a morgue in Manila for later transfer to the United States and for burial in Arlington National Cemetery alongside his father. He also kept her room in the Manila Hotel sealed, allowing no one to enter until her final burial. The new woman in MacArthur's life was Jean Faircloth, whom he met on board ship and who would take up residence in Manila not long after his arrival there. They were married in 1937. His mother never met her but probably would have approved.

It soon became apparent that the field marshal's surreal certitude about defense of the Philippines contrasted sharply with the ambiguity of the Roosevelt administration's policies toward the islands. In 1935 President Roosevelt had authorized MacArthur's mission as military adviser and expressed warm support for a Philippine army. The general could hardly be blamed for assuming he had the president's backing. Creation of an army, in any event, was not something one could start and stop willy-nilly. By 1936 and 1937, however, Roosevelt and his foreign policy team had begun having second thoughts—and third and fourth thoughts. If a Filipino force emerged, the president's subordinates told him, its behavior might be unpredictable. For instance, if Quezon were no longer in charge and the force fell into the wrong hands, American control of the islands could be jeopardized. The United States had put a mechanism in place for Philippine independence and would eventually leave, but to be driven out ignominiously would be disastrous. There was also concern about Japanese reaction to the force itself. Hurley, Stimson, and MacArthur believed that such a force would lead to greater Japanese restraint. Others had come to the opposite conclusion: a Filipino army, growing in strength, publicized as MacArthur's ego required, might trigger Japanese aggression. That could be damaging for American policy toward Europe and the larger Eurasian land mass. Perhaps a neutralization scheme would offer a way to delay and avoid giving offense and to use the islands to resist a subsequent Japanese offensive.[11]

The problem for American foreign and military officials was that, while no one considered the Philippines a vital American interest, no one thought of them as entirely peripheral either. The United States had assumed a colonial responsibility. It needed to discharge that responsibility. Moreover, the islands might be useful down the road. Still Europe was always the first concern; the threat that a single hostile power, in this instance Nazi Germany, might gain control of the entire European continent was the primary worry. With the Philippines falling between vital and peripheral in the assessment of U.S. interests, no one, not least the president of the United States, knew exactly what to do about them. Ambiguity led to a paralysis of American policy.

Ambiguity did not constrain MacArthur. Trapped by his myopic worldview, which overemphasized Asia, impressed with the dedication of his old friend, Quezon, confident that he could create a defense force, for which he envisioned universal acclaim, enamored of his own status in the islands where he seemed to evoke affection, and pleased with his luxurious home atop the Manila Hotel, he remained determined to succeed. On the final point, MacArthur in the mid and late thirties was the most highly paid military officer in the world. He lived the good life. He seldom arrived at his office before 11:00 a.m.; he took long lunches; he came and went as he pleased; he had a new female companion with whom he was compatible; he had time for reading and reflection and for his western movies, which he and Jean attended assiduously. His library consisted of between seven thousand and eight thousand volumes, much of it inherited from his father, and he spent a great deal of his leisure reading history and biography, especially biographies of Confederate generals. Biographer D. Clayton James says insightfully that his love of western movies may have derived from his sense that these movies reflected the kind of world "he yearned for in real life—fast-moving action, dramatic moments, clearly defined issues, noble heroes, and unmistakably wicked villains."[12]

The general's behavior from 1937 to 1941 did little to bring him credit. Indeed, his actions brought conflict with the president and his cabinet, with his own aides, with the Philippine Department of the Army, and with Que-zon. The trouble with Roosevelt had deep roots, but two issues accounted for the conflict in 1937. MacArthur had supported Alfred Landon for the presi-dency in 1936, in fact was convinced that the Republican candidate would win. A Republican victory could bring happy tidings for the general, for his career, and possibly for his program in the Philippines. MacArthur tried to hide his preferences from the president but word quickly got back to Wash-ington. In addition, Roosevelt received regular advice from his secretary of interior Harold Ickes, who saw the general as a self-serving, political manip-ulator. Former governor general of the Philippines Frank Murphy was also disdainful of MacArthur and did not hide his opinions from the president. More importantly, Roosevelt was also influenced by a State Department rec-ommendation that the United States reconsider the whole Philippine de-fense program.[13]

Aware of the need to hold discussions with FDR, possibly to mend fences, and also to take care of personal business, MacArthur returned to the United States, Quezon in tow, in early 1937. The two travelers found the political climate chilly. Roosevelt was upset with Quezon's frequent demands for early independence and greater economic concessions, and he delayed meeting with the Philippine leader. Nor was the president eager to meet with MacArthur, though he eventually consented to talk with both men. MacArthur's personal affairs included arranging the burial of his mother in Arlington National Cemetery, and getting married. He and Jean Faircloth, who had become constant companions in the Philippines, tied the knot in a civil ceremony in New York on April 30, 1937. Unlike his previous experi-ence this marriage would last. By all appearances, it was reasonably happy, but it would have been difficult to determine, because Ms. Faircloth had been trained from girlhood to subordinate her own interests and require-ments to those of her husband. Her appellations for him are instructive: she never called him "Doug" or "Douglas" or "sweetie" or other terms of endear-ment, but rather "Sir Boss" or "ginral."

Back in the islands in the summer of 1937, MacArthur received a blow to the solar plexus. Acting upon the advice of the aforementioned subordinates and his own dislike of the general, President Roosevelt through Chief of Staff Malin Craig informed MacArthur that as of December 31 that year his tour would end and he would return to the United States for reassignment to a corps command. Roosevelt wanted the general's retirement from the na-tional and international stage. He almost certainly assumed that MacArthur would not accept reassignment and would leave the army. He quickly got MacArthur's retirement, but it did not work out in quite the way the president planned. Upon receiving the news, MacArthur exploded, angrily de-nouncing his Washington enemies and proclaiming that such an assignment would be like Roosevelt returning to the office of assistant secretary of the navy, a position FDR had held in the Wilson administration. Never the model, obedient soldier, MacArthur announced that, because his health was failing, he would retire effective October 11. As events would soon prove, there was nothing wrong with his health.[14]

Meanwhile, the field marshal could do little to further the cause of Philip-pine defense. By mid-1937, the Filipino army remained a fiction, owing to in-adequate training and supply, poor planning, and failure of the United States to provide military support. Part of the reason for the latter was the new mood in Washington, favoring neutralization of the islands. Another factor was the emerging fissure between MacArthur and the Philippine Department of the U.S. army. The Philippine Department had grown weary of the gen-eral's pretensions and his demand for support, especially given the Depres-sion era shortages of men and material. Surely, the Department reasoned, there were better ways to expend critical resources than on a useless defense force and its vainglorious commander.

Most men would have perceived Washington's signals for what they were and found a new line of work. Not MacArthur. He arranged with Quezon to continue as military advisor, at a level of pay similar to what he had been earning—$36,000 (equal to $450,000 in early twenty-first-century dollars), plus expenses, for the rest of his life—a decision that Quezon made by exec-utive fiat. In the new role, the field marshal would report exclusively to the Philippine government, though he was a U.S. major general, on the retired list. The psychic and material perquisites and his comforts in the islands were just too great to forgo. Moreover, his wife was pregnant with their son, due in February 1938.[15]

Always expert at manipulating political and military symbols, the general decided in early 1938 to put on a show of progress in building his new army and thereby to demonstrate his accomplishments as military adviser. He or-dered his subordinates, who remained on the U.S. army active duty list but continued to assist him in his newly defined capacity, to plan a great military parade outside of Manila, an extravaganza so potentially costly that Majors Eisenhower and Ord both protested that it would break the budget. Money badly needed for training and supply would be squandered to no good end. When Quezon heard of the scheme, he became extremely angry and quashed the spectacle. MacArthur, to the absolute fury of his subordinates, denied re-sponsibility and blamed Eisenhower and Ord. Quezon knew better. The two aides never forgave MacArthur, and Eisenhower vowed to leave the islands as soon as possible. Ord died shortly thereafter in a plane crash. Eisenhower left in 1939 and, much to MacArthur's consternation, soon became a close associate of Chief of Staff General George Marshall.[16]

More important for MacArthur, Quezon grew tired of dealing with him, and became disillusioned with the whole idea of a Filipino defense force. Quezon was far more realistic than the general. He saw that American policy did not assign the Philippines a high priority. He could not depend on the United States for defense; Washington was eleven thousand miles away and the Japanese could practically see the Philippines from their colony in Taiwan. So, he made overtures to Japan in 1938 for a possible neutrality agreement. Back in the islands, he cut back on the ROTC program and military training in the schools and called for immediate independence, thinking that these steps might enhance the security of the commonwealth. Increasingly, he came to believe that MacArthur's defense proposals were arrant foolishness. "The Philippines could not be defended," he said in November of 1939, "even if every last Filipino were armed with modern weapons." Quezon then began dealing directly with the head of the Philippine Department of the U.S. Army, General George Grunert, seldom conveying to MacArthur the content of the discussions. To the Philippine president, the field marshal not only seemed personally annoying but professionally irrelevant. In 1940 Quezon asked that Francis Sayre, U.S. High Commissioner, arrange the general's dismissal.[17]

Events of 1939 and 1940, specifically Germany's invasion of Poland and initiation of WWII in Europe, and Japan's pressures on Southeast Asia, raised serious questions about the Philippines and about MacArthur's future. As a way of hanging on in the islands, the general tried in 1939, before Francis Sayre was appointed to the post, to become the new high commissioner. Roosevelt ignored his request and appointed Sayre. In March 1941, when he heard that Sayre would be reassigned, he tried again, writing to his friend in the White House, Stephen Early, the president's secretary, that he was the logical choice for the post. He said he was familiar with the most intimate political, military, and commercial details of East Asia, had the trust and affection of Filipinos, and had the personal acquaintance "of everyone of importance in the Orient." Moreover, he went on, "I believe no American holds the friendship and respect of this part of the world more than myself. . . . I am in robust health." It is possible that his health may have been failing in the fall of 1937 and "robust" in 1941, but the fact is it was failing neither time. He wanted to stay in the Philippines and desperately wanted the top U.S. job there, a position he had now tried to get on four separate occasions. He closed his appeal to Early with shameless obsequiousness to Roosevelt: he must have choked as he told Early that FDR was "our greatest statesman" and "our greatest military strategist."[18]

A military officer needs war in the same sense that a physician needs illness or disease. Without illness, a physician would have no relevance. Without patients a physician may do medical research and work at disease prevention, but may go for long periods receiving little acclaim. Without war, a military officer will receive few promotions, and he or she will seldom be celebrated with high honor for preserving peace, a condition most people would regard as the natural order of things. As MacArthur petitioned the president to become high commissioner, the world careened inexorably toward crisis, a crisis that would cost millions of lives worldwide but salvage the general's career and his reputation.

Between 1937 and 1941, Germany, Japan, and Italy moved to dominate most of the world's resources and much of its land mass. In the summer of 1937, Japan undertook full-scale war in China that within a few years would result in Japanese control of all of China's eastern cities, all of its railroads, outlets of its major rivers, and its mineral producing provinces. Before the war's end, Japan had occupied China with more than a million troops. In Europe, Hitler's acquisition of Czechoslovakia, his annexation of Austria, his attack on Poland and other Eastern European countries, and then his invasion of the Netherlands and France, put Great Britain by the end of 1940 in a precarious position as Germany's only significant enemy. The German invasion and defeat of France and the Netherlands in the spring of 1940 opened up the East Asian colonies of those nations to exploitation, and inextricably linked the European and Asian wars. Japan began making plans for a move to the south, action that became more possible with the German invasion of the Soviet Union in June of 1941, which obviated Japanese concern about its northern flank. About all of this the United States became desperately worried; with none of its consequences was the United States fully prepared to deal.

For a while after his latest attempt to become high commissioner, MacArthur heard nothing about his request; hence he made plans to return to the United States. He had every reason to become frustrated with his assignment: his relationship with Quezon was on the rocks; his creation of a Philippine defense force had foundered; and he seemed to have no support in Washington. But in June and July of 1941 events came to his rescue. In late June in view of the world situation, General Marshall informed him that he would be recalled to active duty and was the logical choice for commander of U.S. army forces in the Far East; and at the end of July, after Japan began moving into southern Indochina, President Roosevelt, through the War Department, created a new Far East command and named MacArthur as its head—the command known in military parlance as USAFE. The Philippine Department of the Army and the air forces in the islands fell under the general's control. Stimson, now secretary of war and Marshall as chief of staff, despite their differences with MacArthur, were most responsible for recommending the general for the assignment. The United States needed someone familiar with East Asia, and the choices were severely limited in that prewar period. Both men knew they were getting a prima donna, a man of ability but a vainglorious self-promoter.[19]

Nearly simultaneous with MacArthur's appointment, Roosevelt froze Japanese assets in the United States and effectively cut off Japanese oil supplies. Between the summer and December of 1941, Japan and the United States, their geopolitical differences highlighted in futile negotiations, slid rapidly toward war.

MacArthur, meanwhile, moved forward optimistically. He began creating a staff, which consisted, among others, of Richard Sutherland as chief of staff, Richard Marshall as deputy chief of staff, Sidney Huff and LeGrande Diller as aides, and Charles Willoughby as head of intelligence—most of the group comprised of men who had served him as military advisers. He put Lewis Brereton in charge of his air force. His new command changed everything. The people and leadership of the Philippines, he said, had renewed hope in the future of the islands. He had strong support from Quezon, and labor leaders "pledged" him "their personal allegiance." Reaction throughout China, the Netherlands East Indies, and Malaya he recalled "was one of complete jubilation." Tokyo "was dumfounded and depressed." He boasted that his Philippine army, numbering nearly 200,000 men could defend the entire archipelago. He would "crush" the Japanese on the beaches.[20]

Though convincing to some of the general's visitors, most of this talk was little more than political blather. In 1940 the Philippine army had fewer than 500 officers, fewer than 4,000 enlisted men; and the reserve, 133,000 strong, on which MacArthur pinned his hopes, was largely a fiction. It was little better in the late summer of 1941. It was a paper force. Its troops had received inadequate training; it had inferior, sometimes nonexistent equipment and almost no coordination; it could not possibly carry on communication among the various places at which the Japanese were expected to invade.

If the optimism seemed strangely Pollyannaish, the military deficiencies in the Philippines were not entirely or even largely MacArthur's fault. The United States paid little heed to its moral obligation to defend the islands. First priority in 1941, as throughout the war, was Europe. What this meant in practice was the development in Washington of a new army and navy military plan, termed Rainbow 5, which called for defense of only Manila and Subic bays. When MacArthur learned of this limited plan in October, he flew into a rage, calling the scheme "appeasement" and once again insisting that he could defend the entire archipelago. Somehow he convinced Marshall, Stimson, and Roosevelt to alter the war plan and commit additional American supplies to that end. Most of those supplies had not arrived when Japan attacked Pearl Harbor. The one weapon that might have made a difference in defense of the islands, the new B-17 bomber, because of some production and delivery delays, but largely owing to basing problems, did not help much. There were as many as thirty-five of these bombers in the Philippines on December 7 and a great many of them remained concentrated in a nondefensible position on Clark Field on Luzon. Nor with his focus on ground forces did MacArthur pay sufficient attention to use of this new weapon or, for that matter, use of the navy, to hit the Japanese.

Though American policymakers had done little for China in the period since 1931, that country became an issue in negotiations between the United States and Japan in late 1941. The major American concern was Southeast Asia with its rich raw materials on which the industrial nations of the West were dependent; and it was Japan's move to the south that prompted Washington's intransigent, get-tough approach. But it was impossible to withdraw China from the mix of issues. President Roosevelt was ultimately convinced by his advisers and by Prime Minister Winston Churchill of Great Britain not to compromise with Japan over China, not to help the Japanese solve their "China problem" in the interest of a larger peace, because such a deal could be seen as a sellout of Chiang Kai-shek. Any arrangement of that sort would ostensibly only free up Japanese forces for use elsewhere in the Pacific; there was utility in having them tied down in China and the Chinese could become a significant factor in the war itself. Given the American unwillingness to compromise the China issue and the American economic sanctions, which could hurt badly, the Japanese military planners made a decision to strike a blow at the American Pacific fleet. The result was the attack at Pearl Harbor on December 7, 1941.

In the aftermath of the Pearl Harbor disaster, Admiral Husband Kimmel and General Walter Short, commanders, respectively, of U.S. naval and army forces in Hawaii, suffered court martials and disgrace for their failure to take adequate security precautions. How General MacArthur avoided a similar fate is one of the mysteries of the early WWII era. Word of the Pearl Harbor attack reached MacArthur at about 3:30 a.m. on December 8 via a Signal Corps enlisted man who passed the word to Richard Sutherland, who in turn conveyed the information to MacArthur in a phone call. At

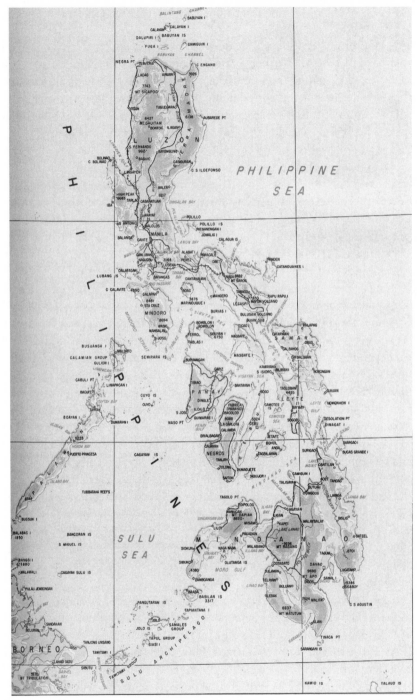

Figure 2.1. The Philippine Islands. Reprinted Courtesy of the General Douglas MacArthur Foundation.

3:40 a.m. the general received another call from Brigadier General Leonard Gerow, head of the army's war plans division, confirming the Hawaii disaster and stating that the Japanese also could be expected to attack the Philippines. According to MacArthur's own dramatic account, after Gerow's call he asked wife Jean to bring him his Bible, which he read for awhile before going to his office.[21]

MacArthur then proceeded to fritter away nine precious hours. General Brereton requested permission to use his B-17s to attack Japanese targets on Formosa (Taiwan) without knowing what targets existed there. MacArthur denied the request, though he did sanction reconnaissance flights. In the interim, General Henry "Hap" Arnold in Washington notified Brereton that to avoid a repeat of the destruction suffered at Pearl Harbor he must disburse his planes, must get them away from Clark Field. Brereton continued to press for permission to attack the Japanese colony of Formosa. When MacArthur finally approved, it was too late; the Japanese struck and most of the B-17s and fighter aircraft were destroyed on the ground.[22]

Why had it taken a general who had insisted he could make the Philippines invulnerable so long to act? Why had he permitted a virtual duplication of the Hawaii fiasco? The explanation most charitable to MacArthur is that he believed, for some reason—perhaps Quezon's prior negotiations with the Japanese—that the islands would remain neutral and a U.S. strike at Formosa would undermine that neutrality. Or he might have believed his own propaganda and assumed that the Japanese feared the Philippine military force. Or, as seems most plausible, he simply succumbed to indecision caused by an overload of information and responsibility, not the first military commander to freeze in such a situation, nor the last.

The Japanese soon began their invasion of the islands. MacArthur neither destroyed them on the beaches nor threw them back into the ocean, as he had promised. He executed a skillful retreat into Bataan Peninsula and Corregidor Island, thus following the requirements of War Plan Orange, which he had for so long disdained. When he declared Manila an open city on December 24, he removed his wife and three-year-old son Arthur with him to Corregidor. He also moved supplies from forward areas to Bataan and Corregidor and after the Japanese began their offensive on Bataan moved many of those same supplies to Corregidor. Although many Filipinos agreed to collaborate with the Japanese, President Quezon joined MacArthur on the "sanctuary" in Manila Bay. From his dugout on Corregidor the general frequently emerged to expose himself to apparent danger but only once in three months did he visit his troops on Bataan. For this failure he earned the contempt of his troops and the sardonic sobriquet, "Dugout Doug."

In one of the supreme ironies of WWII, MacArthur then became a great national hero in the United States. Hungry for some sign of success in the Pacific war, anxious to avenge Pearl Harbor, and encouraged by an administration in Washington desirous of maintaining morale, the American people, fed by a compliant press, began to celebrate MacArthur's defense of Corregidor as a victory. Against all odds and outnumbered by a wide margin, according to twisted conventional wisdom, the American general and his Philippine and U.S. forces were defying the Japanese invader. While it is true that American troops held out far longer in the U.S. colony than did either the British or the Dutch in their Southeast Asian possessions, MacArthur's behavior was hardly heroic. Indeed, during the three months of his semicaptivity in Manila Bay he and his staff sent over 140 press reports to American newspapers, a great many of them composed by MacArthur himself, describing mythic battles. To the American people the general was made to appear as a veritable knight slaying his opponents single-handedly, as he seldom mentioned his troops as he filled the press reports with personal pronouns. Eisenhower captured the "heroic" MacArthur in his diary: "Poor Wainwright! (General Jonathan) he did the fighting in the Philippines, another got such glory as the public could find in the operation."[23]

MacArthur and Quezon repaired their differences and began a new relationship cemented by money. On January 3, 1942, the Philippine president offered the U.S. general $500,000, which MacArthur quietly accepted. At the same time Quezon gave MacArthur's aides sums ranging from $25,000 up to $75,000. The enormity of the payment to MacArthur is striking, leading the biographer who uncovered the deal to speculate on the reasons for Quezon's generosity. She says it derived from Filipino culture in which relationships were often affirmed or reaffirmed through gifts that contributed to the psychological bond between individuals or families. Others may be excused for thinking it was a bribe to guarantee the general's best efforts at preventing an abandonment of the islands to their fate. Whatever Quezon's motives, MacArthur's acceptance of the gratuity was clearly illegal, given the prohibition of such transactions by military rules. MacArthur was on active duty at the time of the gift and had been since July of 1941.[24]

To employ a metaphor used in China by General Joseph Stilwell, MacArthur and Quezon had the feeling that policymakers in Washington had put them on a raft and set them adrift at sea. Both men came quickly to believe that few resources would come their way, and the general persistently blamed General Marshall, Eisenhower, and Stimson for that failure. In fact, through January and February he complained bitterly to his superiors about the lack of supplies and of relief for his troops. Eisenhower termed him a "baby" and wondered why he had failed to protect his planes or make a better showing on the beach. Stimson believed MacArthur was not only pestering him for more support, but also "harassing" him. There was little, in fact, that Washington could do; the Japanese noose on the Philippines had been drawn too tight. For that turn of events, Quezon and MacArthur, despite their own deficiencies, had every right to be frustrated.

This frustration led MacArthur into serious indiscretions. At one point he praised Josef Stalin's leadership in the war against the Germans and, ignorant of the Japanese-Soviet neutrality pact of April 1941, proposed to Washington that the United States bring the Soviet Union into the war in East Asia to save U.S. interests. The general received no serious reprimand for his foray into diplomatic policy. But his continuing insistence on naval support to bring supplies to the Philippines, when such action was impossible to implement, became extremely annoying to his superiors. When in February Quezon proposed immediate independence and thereafter a separate peace with the Japanese MacArthur crossed the boundary into unacceptable behavior by appearing to endorse the idea. Marshall and Stimson were furious. Coming as it did only two months after the treacherous Japanese attack on Pearl Harbor, the Philippine president's proposal was outrageous, as was the general's implicit endorsement. At Marshall's direction, Eisenhower drafted an order to MacArthur directing him to fight to the last. Chastened, the general responded that he would remain with his garrison, as would his family.[25]

MacArthur had no intention of staying with his garrison, as he knew that President Roosevelt had prepared plans to evacuate Quezon, Francis Sayre, MacArthur's family, and the general himself from Corregidor. Nor was his acceptance of the huge gratuity from Quezon consistent with an intention to suffer the fate of his garrison. Roosevelt intended to move MacArthur to Australia where the general would assume a new command. He would wait until the president gave the order so as not to besmirch his reputation, by appearing to flee; then he would depart. This was important to his image back home where the anti-Roosevelt press led by William Randolph Hearst, Roy Howard, and Henry Luce continued to build him up.[26] Roosevelt gave the order near the end of February; MacArthur waited for a proper moment, announced dramatically on March 11 that he would leave, and departed the island on March 15. After two days of excruciating sea sickness aboard small PT boats, MacArthur, his family, and the rest of his party reached Mindinao; and two days later flew on to an air strip near Darwin on a B-17 bomber, the latter part of the trip as difficult for the general as the first, owing to airsickness. A flight from near Darwin to Alice Springs on board a DC-3 was less uncomfortable but difficult nonetheless. As throughout history, natural elements were a great leveler, imposing their own brand of humility. The "hero" of Corregidor seemed anything but heroic as he retched pathetically both on the patrol boat and the B-17 bomber. Deeply relieved to have survived those conveyances, he made the final leg of the trip to Melbourne by train. Safe in Australia, he basked in undeserved glory as the American military commander who had fought the Japanese and daringly escaped from them.

Notes

1. Carol Petillo, *Douglas MacArthur: The Philippine Years* (Bloomington: Indiana University Press, 1981), 153.

2. Petillo, *Douglas MacArthur*, 39–42. Also see Michael Schaller, *Douglas MacArthur: The Far Eastern General* (New York: Oxford University Press, 1989), 21–24.

3. Russell D. Buhite, *Patrick J. Hurley and American Foreign Policy* (Ithaca, N.Y.: Cornell University Press, 1973), 64–65. Also see Theodore Friend, *Between Two Empires: The Ordeal of the Philippians, 1929–1946* (New Haven, Conn.: Yale University Press, 1965), 1–9.

4. The bill bore the name of Senator Millard Tydings of Maryland and Representative John McDuffie of Alabama.

5. Douglas MacArthur, *Reminiscences* (New York: Fawcett World Library and Time Inc., 1965), 102; D. Clayton James, *The Years of MacArthur, Volume 1, 1880–1941* (Boston: Houghton Mifflin, 1970), 480–88.

6. Robert Ferrell, ed. *The Eisenhower Diaries* (New York: Norton, 1981), 14–15; Schaller, *Douglas MacArthur*, 34–35.

7. Quoted in James, *The Years of MacArthur*, 484–85.

8. Quoted in Schaller, *Douglas MacArthur*, 33.

9. Ferrell, *The Eisenhower Diaries*, 21; James, *The Years of MacArthur*, 506.

10. Quoted in William Manchester, *American Caesar: Douglas MacArthur, 1880–1946* (Boston: Little, Brown, 1978), 172.

11. James, *The Years of MacArthur*, 535–42, 550; Petillo, *Douglas MacArthur*, 181–82.

12. James, *The Years of MacArthur*, 559.

13. Schaller, *Douglas MacArthur*, 36–37.

14. Schaller, *Douglas MacArthur*, 38.

15. James, *The Years of MacArthur*, 524–25.

16. Schaller, *Douglas MacArthur*, 39. Dwight Eisenhower, *At Ease* (Garden City, N.Y.: Doubleday, 1967), 225–28.

17. James, *The Years of MacArthur*, 337–38.

18. Schaller, *Douglas MacArthur*, 42.

19. James, *The Years of MacArthur*, 585–92.

20. Schaller, *Douglas MacArthur*, 48–49.

21. MacArthur, *Reminiscences*, 117; Manchester, *American Caesar*, 205–18.
22. MacArthur, *Reminiscences*, 117; Manchester, *American Caesar*, 205–18.
23. Schaller, *Douglas MacArthur*, 61–65, 66; Ferrell, *The Eisenhower Diaries*, 52.
24. Petillo, pp. 208–13.
25. Schaller, *Douglas MacArthur*, 60–61.
26. Schaller, *Douglas MacArthur*, 60–61.

CHAPTER THREE

~

"I Shall Return"

As General MacArthur, his family, and his staff waited at Cagayan on Mindinao for a B-17 to transport them to Australia, the general penned a message to Quezon that was illustrative of his self-perception and his intentions for the prosecution of the war in the Pacific: "The United States is moving its forces into the southern Pacific area in which is destined to be a great offensive against Japan. The troops are being concentrated in Australia which will be used as a base for the offensive drive to the Philippines. President Roosevelt has designated me to command this offensive and has directed me to proceed to Australia for that purpose. . . . I was naturally loath to leave Corregidor but the Washington authorities insisted, implying that if I did not personally assume command the effort could not be made." Then he protested a bit too much: "As a matter of fact, I had no choice in the matter, being peremptorily ordered by President Roosevelt himself. I understand the forces are rapidly being accumulated and hope that the drive can be undertaken before the Bataan-Corregidor situation reaches a climax."[1] MacArthur knew that Quezon would shortly join him in Australia and would confront journalists waiting to pass the Philippine president's thoughts—and his own—along to the American people.

When the general reached the Adelaide, Australia train station on the last leg of his trip to Melbourne, he made a statement to reporters that seems outrageous now and seemed equally outrageous then. It certainly seemed offensive to those still on Bataan as well as to those whom he would command in the future given his obvious play for publicity in both Australia and the

47

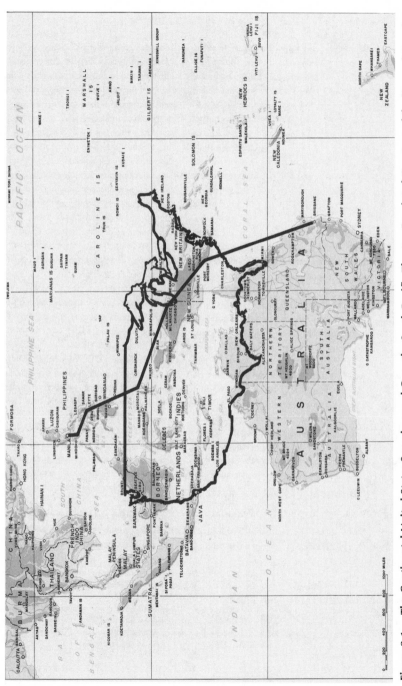

Figure 3.1. The Continental United States Superimposed Over the South Pacific Theater. Reprinted Courtesy of the General Douglas MacArthur Foundation.

United States: "The President of the United States ordered me to break through the Japanese lines . . . for the purpose, as I understand it, of organizing the American offensive against Japan, a primary object of which is the relief of the Philippines. I came through and I SHALL RETURN."[2] Greater pomposity would be hard to imagine, as would greater damage to the morale of subordinates and those young men who would fight the battles—so *he* could return.

What MacArthur found in Australia and what was soon confirmed about war strategy altered his initial forecast. As he journeyed from Alice Springs southward to Adelaide, he began contemplating possible offensive plans for retaking the Philippines. When the train stopped at a small station just north of Adelaide, his deputy chief of staff came aboard to inform him that the total number of troops available in all of Australia was barely thirty thousand, with few of them ready for combat; and the number of airplanes, all antiquated, totaled no more than one hundred. He also learned that the Europe-first approach to fighting the war could mean a long wait for supply convoys to reach the southwest Pacific. Not only was an offense against the Philippines impossible, he also quickly came to fear, as did the Australians, that the Japanese would invade the continent and take over a critical portion of the north. Conditions seemed so desperate that Australian officials began contemplating a plan to defend only the southeast coast of the country in accord with the "Brisbane Line."

The situation was bad, but not that bad. He could look forward to the comforts of Melbourne, which seemed plush compared to the caves of Corregidor; he had his family with him, and, though seemingly deprived of support, he assumed a command that would ultimately receive a large share of the American war supply shipped outside the western hemisphere. He could also look forward, with eager anticipation, to receipt of the highest honor accorded an American serviceman.

In January and February Congress, influenced by the press releases on the general's "battles" against the Japanese, had begun to consider awarding MacArthur the Medal of Honor. General Marshall thought the president should preempt such an award by granting it himself and asked his staff members for their thoughts. Stimson was supportive. Eisenhower averred that no general should receive the award because no general was ever close enough to the fighting front to deserve the honor. President Roosevelt agreed with Marshall, thinking the award would generate positive public opinion in the United States. At the end of January, Marshall asked MacArthur's chief of staff, Richard Sutherland, to provide paperwork, including necessary documents recording the general's specific acts of bravery, for final processing of the award. Sutherland did so, upon consulting with MacArthur on the proper wording of a glowing, hagiographic letter about the latter's exploits. When, after the escape from Corregidor, the Japanese and the Germans turned their propaganda on MacArthur, calling him a "deserter" and a "coward," and as the men left behind on Bataan expressed their own bitterness, the president gave final approval for the citation. MacArthur received the medal after his arrival in Australia, but he knew it was coming. And he had a hand in crafting the encomiums to himself.[3]

Nothing could have given the general greater pleasure, and his hero status in the United States was enhanced. Newborn babies were named after him, streets across the country bore his name, and the press, especially the anti-Roosevelt newspaper chains, lionized him as the only true "warrior" in the American military. They urged that Roosevelt put him in command of all U.S. troops, not just those in the Pacific. Eventually they urged that he become a candidate for the presidency in 1944.

Meanwhile, American and Filipino troops in the Philippines struggled on. MacArthur created four commands in the islands as he was leaving, all under his control and intended to assist in his return. He also ordered that the men fight to the last. As it turned out, fighting to the last did not mean fighting much longer. On April 9, the bedraggled, malnourished, disease-ridden troops on Bataan surrendered, and on May 6 General Wainwright gave up Corregidor, under the injunction that, unless he did so, the Japanese would slaughter every last man on the island. The men who surrendered suffered unspeakable horror over the next three years, a fate Wainwright shared. Following the war, he too won a Medal of Honor at Marshall's insistence, but over the stubborn resistance of the ungenerous, always jealous, MacArthur.[4]

Not long after the general's arrival in Australia, the British and American Combined Chiefs of Staff agreed upon a division of responsibility for fighting the global war. The United States received primary authority in the Pacific. Despite MacArthur's wishes for a single command, the War Department and the president set up a divided American authority. Navy personnel would not accept MacArthur's control because they had little confidence in him, and naval officials also argued persuasively that, because so much of the war would be fought at sea, a naval officer was needed for much of the command. Hence, Admiral Chester Nimitz was placed in charge of the Pacific Ocean Area and MacArthur was made commander of the Southwest Pacific Area (SWPA). MacArthur, who dwarfed Nimitz in seniority, chafed under this arrangement.

Although his orders directed him to stop the Japanese advance and prepare for offensive action as he saw an opportunity, it would be months before

MacArthur could make much of a contribution to the war. In fact, into September he remained largely inactive. His plan to reconquer the Philippines depended on the logical step of first taking New Guinea, from whose northwestern coast U.S. and Australian troops could embark for the islands.

Several factors complicated implementing that strategy. Military planners in Washington determined that the Japanese advance south and east toward control of the entire Pacific had to be stopped first. Moreover, the quickest and easiest route to Japan lay not through the Philippines but along a course through the central Pacific where the United States would punish the Japanese navy and seize key, strategic islands. During the first two years of the war, U.S. policymakers also sought to strengthen China's ability to resist the Japanese and, in the process, to make China the spot for launching an eventual invasion of Japan. Although China required significant American resources, Germany remained the Allies' first priority. That priority meant bolstering the Soviet Union and invading the European continent. In the short run, because of British opposition to a "premature" second front on the coast of France, it meant defeating German forces in North Africa.

The U.S. campaign in the central Pacific led, in June 1942, to a great victory in the battle of Midway Island, in which the U.S. navy sank four Japanese aircraft carriers and crippled the Japanese fleet for the remainder of the war. The previous month U.S. naval forces had defeated the Japanese in the battle of the Coral Sea, and in July the navy and the marine forces attacked the Japanese on Guadalcanal in a bloody encounter that went on far longer than military planners anticipated.

Much of this activity offended, even angered, MacArthur who referred to the Joint Chiefs of Staff as "bunglers." He saw the invasion of North Africa as a military sideshow, useless in the grand scheme of the war and designed by Eisenhower and Marshall to deny him an opportunity to begin an offensive against Japan. He railed against Roosevelt, Marshall, and Eisenhower as conspirators out to deny him publicity. He saw no need to hasten an invasion of the European continent, and he was contemptuous of the strategy that called for defeating Germany before Japan. Horrible as they might seem, the Nazis, in MacArthur's opinion, reflected a long history of civilization. They would mellow or moderate, and the United States could deal with Germany, even a fascist Germany. Let the Soviets and the Germans fight it out. If the Germans won an early victory the United States could accommodate that result, at least temporarily. On the other hand, he deemed the Japanese beyond the pale, bestial in their behavior and hopelessly barbaric. He urged divesting the European, Atlantic, North African, and Russian fronts of American supply and concentrating everything on defeating Japan. Continued support for the Soviet Union should occur only if Stalin agreed to join the Asian/ Pacific war. Possible German defeat of the United Kingdom did not seem to bother the SWPA commander, nor did Hitler's control of a good portion of the Eurasian land mass. MacArthur gave slight consideration to prewar German-Japanese linkages or to the U.S. policy that led to American entry into the conflict. How much he knew of the latter is an open question.[5]

After American success at Guadalcanal and in the naval battles of 1942 in the central Pacific, MacArthur received approval to undertake an offensive in New Guinea. He considered it high time. His opinion had long been that seizing New Guinea and then returning to the Philippines would do two things: it would satisfy the U.S. moral obligation to its colonial possession; the United States could not simply abandon the archipelago to its own defenses when times got tough. And retaking the islands would cut Japan's lifeline to the resource-rich Southeast Asian region. Of course, capturing New Guinea and returning to the Philippines would enhance the general's personal prestige. In late summer the SWPA commander authorized the establishment of a base of operations at Port Moresby on the southwest coast of New Guinea and then in mid-November an offensive against the town of Buna on the southeast coast. The latter was heavily defended by a Japanese force of over sixteen thousand men. It was necessary to take Buna in order to begin a drive along the eastern and northern New Guinea coast, whose northernmost point was only a short distance from the southern Philippines. The first effort failed but a subsequent offensive led by General Robert Eichelberger succeeded in January 1943. MacArthur had directed that Eichelberger take Buna or not come back alive. He also promised Eichelberger that if he achieved victory in the battle that promised to be extremely difficult and costly he would receive decoration and highly favorable publicity in the United States. MacArthur subsequently waited at least a week before mentioning Eichelberger's name in connection with the battle, thereby taking personal credit for the victory. When Eichelberger received favorable press from journalists who knew the truth, the SWPA commander threatened to bust him to colonel and "send him home."[6]

Stealing any publicity from MacArthur was, in Eichelberger's opinion, like driving "a dagger through his heart."[7] In his original orders MacArthur had been authorized to control all communiqués concerning forces under his command. No officer during WWII took this authority more seriously, and the "MacArthur communiqué" became an object of derisive, even scornful, humor among GIs, over the following two and one-half years. It is often noted that truth is an early casualty of war because confusion and miscommunication prevent accurate portrayal of events. Truth was the first casualty of the MacArthur propaganda machine because the general's regard for facts was always subordinate to his desire for self-promotion. Under the direction of the head of his censorship apparatus, his press officer, Colonel LeGrande Diller, lies and outrageous lies flowed from the SWPA. No information came through that did not serve several themes important to the commander: that he was personally leading every offensive; that his forces were winning every battle, decisively, killing more Japanese at far less cost in American lives than was true on any other front; that he was being denied the support he needed; and that the quickest way to win the war against Japan was to concentrate U.S. forces on retaking the Philippines. Both during and after the war MacArthur often noted that he and General George Patton were the only real "fighting" generals of WWII and that most others were simply "worthies" who sat at desks like Washington bureaucrats "managing" conflict in their theaters. This fit with his self-perception/deception, with the ethos of the cowboy hero of his beloved "B" grade western movies, and with the myths generated by his communiqués. It was also as untrue as the other aforementioned themes.[8]

Some of MacArthur's battles were very costly, as the campaign in Papua, New Guinea amply demonstrated. Over one-fourth of Allied forces were either killed or wounded. When he succeeded in battle at little cost it was often because he enjoyed vast superiority over the enemy for two reasons: he was well-supplied with men and material, and the enemy often chose to fight ferociously to defend Pacific islands that it knew represented a more important strategic route to the home islands, but elected to defend more lightly some of the assets under attack by SWPA forces.[9] For much of the early part of the war MacArthur did not leave Australia, and, as was later the case in the Korean War, he often limited his visits at the front to photo opportunities or to put on a show of personal bravery. His other theme, that the U.S. defeat of Japan would come sooner at less cost and on higher moral ground through the Philippines, is debatable. Officials in Washington, including General Marshall, were certainly justified in thinking that the earliest possible defeat of Japan, most likely through the central Pacific offensive, could also lead to the earliest possible liberation of the Philippines.

Unfortunately facts mattered less than the beliefs of the American people. They were enthralled by the news from the SWPA. They saw MacArthur as winning the war single-handedly. They practically deified the "hero" of Corregidor. Reinforcing all this was a move by the general's political friends in the United States, who were emboldened by Republican successes in the 1942 congressional elections, to promote his candidacy for president on the Republican ticket in 1944. The effect of the general's image at home and of

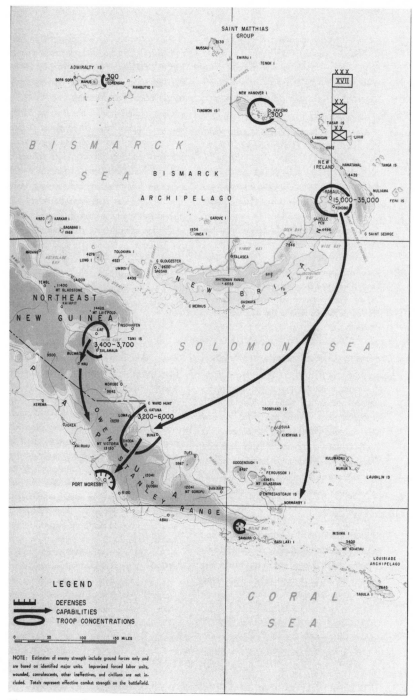

Figure 3.2.   The Japanese Strongpoint of Rabaul and Eastern New Guinea.
Reprinted Courtesy of the General Douglas MacArthur Foundation.

President Roosevelt's concern about his possible Republican challenger on the decision to recapture the Philippines was a critical question in wartime strategy.[10]

The SWPA commander's military achievements of 1943 and early 1944 lent credibility to his claim for support in waging a Philippine campaign. After the defeat of the Japanese force at Buna, MacArthur began preparing airfields for an assault on New Britain, considered a prime target not only in the SWPA commander's mind but also in the minds of Japanese war planners. New Britain under Japanese control could threaten the U.S. move along the eastern coast of New Guinea. Both sides particularly valued the large Japanese base at Rabaul on the eastern end of New Britain. MacArthur was determined to take the base and the Japanese were equally determined to hold it. Accordingly, Japan undertook military action designed to control bases at the New Guinea port towns of Lae and Salamaua, both lying not far to the north of Buna. When the Japanese sent a force of three thousand men to secure an airfield near Salamaua, MacArthur had a brigade of Australians waiting to rout them. When the Japanese sent a large naval contingent from Rabaul toward Lae, SWPA bombers sank numerous Japanese vessels and scored a significant allied victory. MacArthur, who had become enamored of land-based aircraft in waging warfare, hailed the victory as "decisive," held a press conference, and sent along another of his communiqués boasting of his accomplishment and claiming that control of the seas was no longer of the utmost importance. His way of war was superior, he strongly implied, to that of the navy. Whether it was or not, his successes, even if somewhat overblown, were genuine.

Working closely with Admiral William Halsey, with whom he was on good terms and who was now under his command, MacArthur undertook several additional offensive actions in late 1943 designed to facilitate the capture of Rabaul. His troops took Salamaua and Lae and several small islands northeast of Papua; marines under Halsey captured New Georgia. American bombers began pounding the Japanese Eighteenth Army at Wewak along the central eastern coast of New Guinea. All these activities were impressive, but officials in Washington and the combined military staffs thought of them as merely supportive to the main effort through the central Pacific; and no one was anxious to have MacArthur take on the Japanese at Rabaul, where they had about one hundred thousand troops and well-fortified airfields.

If 1943 was a time of significant Allied military accomplishment, it was also a year of important wartime conferences. At these summit meetings the Allied heads of state (Stalin attended only the conference at Teheran) made critical decisions on political and military issues: Casablanca in January; Washington in May; Quebec in August; Cairo in November; and Teheran from November 28 to December 1. Among the most important of these decisions was the demand for the unconditional surrender of Germany, Italy, and Japan and the postwar Soviet role in eastern and central Europe. Essential to MacArthur's operations were the military planners' commitment to an invasion of Italy and then in the spring of 1944 an assault on the coast of France, while simultaneously continuing the offensive against Japan primarily through the central Pacific. The latter activity would include seizing key Pacific islands, perhaps to include the Japanese colony of Formosa, a naval blockade of the Japanese home islands, bombing of Japan either from the islands or China, or both, and an invasion of Japan. The Joint Chiefs of Staff and the U.S. Navy on several occasions strongly recommended making the SWPA theater subordinate to the central Pacific command or Pacific Ocean Area (POA).

Needless to say, MacArthur took this latter recommendation personally and fought strenuously against it. He not only wanted greater support for his operations in New Guinea, but also lobbied for a single command under his direction and an absolute commitment to liberating the Philippines. In a tactical sense, he wanted authorization to attack the major Japanese base at Rabaul. These were the major issues in the SWPA commander's mind at the time of the August 1943 Quebec conference. When the Joint Chiefs of Staff (JCS) ruled out an offensive against Rabaul in favor of bombing the base into insignificance, he railed at the decision. The JCS proved right and the general later claimed credit for what proved a wise choice. He used his political clout to combat the combining of his operations with those of Admiral Nimitz and bypassing the Philippines.

MacArthur's career is filled with unbecoming attempts at self-promotion but his "run" at the presidency in 1943 and 1944 ranks near the top or bottom of the list. At one point he informed General Eichelberger that he would like to be president "to beat that S.O.B. Roosevelt." In April 1943, he met with Robert Wood, a conservative Republican and head of Sears Roebuck who was visiting in Australia, to discuss strategy for getting the nomination. Wood was helping fund and working with Senator Arthur Vandenberg of Michigan and a number of anti-New Deal newspaper publishers in a shadowy effort to promote the general's candidacy. Nearly simultaneously, MacArthur had his chief of staff Richard Sutherland and head of his air force, General George Kenney, meet with Senator Vanderberg and Congresswoman Clare Boothe Luce to weigh the prospects, leaving little doubt not only of his interest but his willingness to initiate behind-the-scenes activity. He also authorized his friend, journalist Frazier Hunt, to begin a campaign biography, highlighting all his strengths but none of his weaknesses. In the summer of 1943 he sent his intelligence chief General Charles Willoughby to Washington to work on strategy with Vandenberg, Wood, and others to promote a "draft" MacArthur movement. Meanwhile, he carried on a lively correspondence with Republican Congressman Albert Miller of Nebraska, in which he made clear that he opposed the New Deal, President Roosevelt, and the left-leaning crowd around the president, and would like very much to replace him. There can simply be no doubt, despite the general's contentions to the contrary, that he wanted the Republican nomination and was seeking it—if he could do so without resigning from the army or risking his ego.[11]

That the efforts of his Republican friends in the United States, most of them either isolationists, Asia-firsters, or opponents of British and Soviet imperialism, or all three, failed attests to the strength of the candidacy of Governor Thomas Dewey of New York and to the efficiency of the regular Republican organizational moves on Dewey's behalf. At the Republican convention in the summer of 1944, MacArthur received the vote of only one delegate. Hence, the boom for the general ended with barely a whimper. As events transpired, the significance of the MacArthur maneuvering resided in what it conveyed about the general's ambitions and how it affected President Roosevelt and his handling of his prima donna general.

Roosevelt considered MacArthur a charlatan, but he had seen such individuals succeed in American politics before, and he had long considered the general a potential political threat because of his florid oratory and demagogic skills. Moreover, FDR had spent considerable time and energy building the hero myth about MacArthur as a way of evoking public support for the war. He could not in 1944 risk alienating the general, nor did he wish to force MacArthur's retirement and make him a martyr. In addition to those considerations, he had to take into account MacArthur's military accomplishments, which by then included the seizing of the Japanese-held island of Los Negros in the Bismarck Sea and Hollandia, along the northeast coast of New Guinea.

In early July 1944, Chief of Staff George Marshall, who had been deliberately snubbed by the SWPA commander on a visit to Australia, ordered MacArthur to prepare for a trip to Hawaii for a meeting with "Mr. Big." MacArthur knew immediately that the reference was to the president, but that did not mitigate his annoyance at being summoned to what he considered correctly a blatantly political conference. Roosevelt boarded the heavy cruiser *Baltimore* in San Diego on July 21 for the trip to Oahu, in what was to be an expensive and time-consuming junket (six destroyers and a fleet of aircraft protected the cruiser on the five-day voyage) while MacArthur flew for twenty-six hours in a B-17 bomber to get there. Roosevelt, running for an unprecedented fourth term, wanted to be photographed with the popular general. He also wished to meet personally with his naval and military commanders, to have them hash out in front of him military strategy involving the Philippines, other Pacific islands, including Formosa, and the final thrust toward Japan. The president, though in serious decline, suffering from advanced arteriosclerosis and heart failure, put great stock in his abilities to size up situations and deal with individuals, whom he confronted face-to-face. Confusion was the order of the day in Washington on how to proceed in the Pacific; the president would settle the matter once and for all—or so he hoped, while also advancing his reelection campaign.

Roosevelt made the most of the meeting. He listened to his officers as they made their respective cases. MacArthur, more eloquent than Nimitz, stressed the importance of retaking the Philippines by first seizing Mindinao, then Leyte, and then Luzon. His emphasis was as much on the ethical and moral and virtuous as the military rationale. The "Oriental" mind, which he thought he understood better than any other American official, would accept no reneging on the American promise "to return." He was sure he could take the islands, a jumping-off spot for the final assault on Japan, relatively quickly and at comparatively low cost. Nimitz argued the case for bypassing at least the northern part of the Philippines and taking Formosa. In the end, the president accepted MacArthur's argument. And in the end, so the general claimed, it came down to a promise of support from Roosevelt in return for his commitment not to participate in anti-Roosevelt politics and provide good military news for FDR in the fall of 1944. MacArthur's assertions cannot be documented, but Roosevelt gave the go-ahead, finally, in October for an offensive in the former American colony.

The conference, which lasted from July 26 through the 28th, went amicably enough, or so it seemed, and MacArthur and Nimitz seemed to put aside differences in a professional airing of their views. MacArthur's opinion of Roosevelt did not improve, however; nor did the president's view of his troublesome general. Roosevelt was mightily annoyed at the general's frequent attempts to upstage him, including MacArthur's grand, and deliberately late, arrival in a fancy limousine at their first meeting. Despite his allegations of a "deal," MacArthur could not put aside his profound contempt for the commander in chief.[12]

After the war, while supreme commander in Japan, MacArthur revealed his thoughts about the Hawaii meeting to Faubion Bowers, his military secretary. Referring to the late president as "Rosenfeld," the general said, "There I was fighting Roosevelt's ("Rosenfeld's") war for him and he wanted to meet me. For what? I didn't want to meet him. Well, I made him cross over to Hawaii. That was as far as I was going to leave my work. He's rolled down the gangway, holds out his hand, forces me to come to him, and says, 'Douglas.' How could he use my first name? I didn't know him. And now we're even worse off with that Jew in the White House" (Truman).[13] Roosevelt, accustomed to the familiar with subordinates and those whom he wished to influence, called MacArthur "Douglas" throughout the meetings and social occasions, apparently displaying inadequate deference to his self-important, hypersensitive, military commander. MacArthur's crude anti-Semitism aside, he found plenty in FDR's persona and policies to dislike, and he believed that the president's victory in the election of 1944 reflected a rejection of American ideals and further support for "regimentation" of U.S. society.

Meanwhile, MacArthur benefited from a military circumstance that allowed him to advance his timetable for an attack on the Philippines. The Joint Chiefs gave approval to begin his Philippine offensive, but, owing to the observations of a downed and rescued flier in Admiral Halsey's command, it was discovered that the Japanese had fortified Leyte, a major island in the south central part of the Philippines, far more lightly than expected. Halsey forwarded this information to the JCS, and they recommended that MacArthur go directly to Leyte, rather than waste time, effort, and lives in taking Mindinao. This decision was reinforced by the Japanese seizure of Chinese airfields, thereby forestalling an attack on Formosa or the immediate use of bases there for an assault on Japan. The SWPA commander jumped at the chance and toward the end of October began his campaign on Leyte.

Leyte Gulf is known as the site of the greatest naval battle in world history. Over 280 American and Japanese ships engaged in a struggle between October 23 and 26, 1944 that resulted in a disastrous defeat for Japan. It was no sure thing for the United States—accident and poor Japanese timing and mistakes played a part in the U.S. victory. So, too, did U.S. naval power and the men who commanded it. Prior to this enormous sea engagement, nearly 200,000 men under General MacArthur, with air cover and the assistance of naval artillery under Admiral Halsey, went ashore near the town of Tacloban on the northeast side of Leyte. Their assault on the island was no cakewalk. Japanese troops put up fierce resistance, and when those troops on hand felt the strain their leaders brought in reinforcements from Luzon. Nearly as important to the slowing of the American offensive was the weather. Torrential downpours pounded the troops with nearly three feet of rain in the first month of military activity, making it impossible to construct airfields and hard to carry on the battle. During the initial phase of the invasion, indeed during the first day, MacArthur waded ashore (he was furious at the landing craft commander and the beachmaster for this turn of events) in water up to his knees, ruining the crease in his khakis. When he realized later that photographs of his wading had made a highly favorable impression among his countrymen, he staged the event in subsequent landings. In any event, he went ashore, flouting danger, to announce, "I have returned."[14]

The Leyte campaign was bloody and costly for both sides, and it lasted far longer than the SWPA commander expected. MacArthur announced just after Christmas in 1944 that it was all over but for the "mopping up." But the mopping up cost the Japanese over 27,000 killed and thousands of American casualties. Altogether Leyte resulted in the deaths of 65,000 of Japan's best troops and the destruction of a good part of its fleet. In fact, Japanese officials after the war conceded that the loss of Leyte led directly to the loss of all of the Philippines. MacArthur was on his way to Manila.

Getting to and capturing Manila was no easy proposition. The SWPA commander jumped into the surf at Lingayen Gulf in Luzon about a hundred miles north of Manila on January 10, as head of a huge army of 280,000 men, thus providing another dramatic photo opportunity for American journalists. MacArthur had a proclivity for dramatic announcements, which meant that he often proclaimed victory and reaped the international attention, then allowed his subordinates to complete the so-called mopping up operations. In the first communiqué from Luzon his press officer announced, "General MacArthur is in personal command at the front and landed with his assault troops." The facts were quite different: he went ashore for military theater, then retreated to his ship, the light cruiser *Boise*, for several days before moving to the island to direct operations. As he had done in New Guinea and on Leyte, the general also informed the American people prematurely on February 5 of his success in conquering Manila long before he had actually defeated Japanese forces there. Speculation existed at the time that he timed his announcement to call attention to himself during the Yalta Conference where other issues and other figures were receiving the bulk of world publicity. At any rate, the battle of Manila lasted nearly another month, as over 1,000 Americans, 16,000 Japanese, and more than 100,000 Filipinos perished. Damage to the city left much of the urban area little more than a burned-out wasteland. The Japanese troops, the great bulk of them, had taken to the mountains, but General Tomoyuki Yamashita allowed over 20,000 of them to stay in Manila. These troops turned their wrath on the local population so that many Filipinos not killed in the horrific battle lost their lives to the brutal Japanese invader. Altogether, excluding subsequent

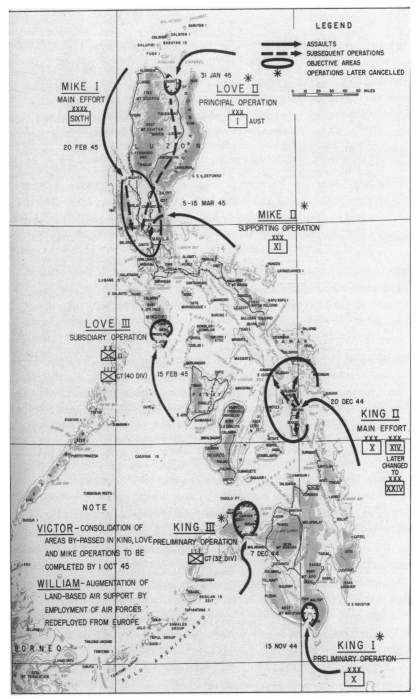

Figure 3.3. MacArthur's Return to the Philippines November 1944–February 1945. Reprinted Courtesy of the General Douglas MacArthur Foundation.

operations on other smaller islands, the battle for Luzon cost nearly 50,000 U.S. casualties and 200,000 Japanese deaths and hundreds of thousands of Filipinos injured or killed. These totals either rivaled or exceeded the cost in lives expended in the central Pacific theater.[15]

The debate continues as to the wisdom of the Philippine campaign, but on one issue there can be no debate. After the capture of Luzon, MacArthur pursued the Japanese on a number of smaller Philippine islands, most of them lacking any strategic value, without the prior consent of the Joint Chiefs of Staff. For largely personal reasons he wished to be seen as liberator of all of the Philippines and would not be deterred. These operations killed over 20,000 Japanese troops and resulted in the loss of nearly a thousand Americans. Not until July 5, 1945 did the general proclaim all of the Philippine islands liberated.

What MacArthur found in the islands was not a source of comfort to him or to officials in Washington. In the summer of 1945 the Philippines possessed roughly 18,000,000 inhabitants, plus the remnants of the Japanese army, which at its peak strength had numbered approximately 400,000. Most of the latter had either been killed, committed suicide, or withdrawn when MacArthur declared the archipelago liberated. Among the Filipinos, there were generally three classes of people: collaborators, guerrillas and resistance fighters, and much of the indigenous population that remained indifferent, their lives little changed by the Japanese occupation. The guerrillas fell into two categories: the so-called Huks or members of the Hukbalahap faction, under Luis Taruc's leadership, who were mainly Marxist in orientation, and the more moderate or mainstream resistance. Both of these groups had had clandestine contact with MacArthur and his staff, while the general remained stuck in Australia and during his military campaigns from New Guinea northward. The collaborationists and the Huks were to pose problems for the SWPA commander. Equally troubling was the economic condition of the islands. Manila, as noted, had been devastated by the battle there, but so too had other parts of the archipelago. Restoring order economically and politically and determining the island's postwar relationship with the United States would be vexing issues.

MacArthur chose to deal with the Huks in a peremptory manner, declaring their leadership radical and hence unreliable in rebuilding the islands. The collaborators the general came to believe, despite his wartime warnings to the contrary, would be useful to the United States. Many of them had cooperated with the Japanese out of fear for their lives and those of their loved ones. Some had been opportunists. Some were truly favorable to the Japanese. Whatever the case, many saw a chance to advance their careers, as was apparently the case with the prewar Filipino leader, the charismatic and pro-MacArthur, Manuel Roxas. Roxas was the Philippine equivalent of the fabled French statesman Charles Maurice de Talleyrand who was able to bend with the wind, able to work with authority wherever he found it. When the SWPA commander pardoned Roxas, he undermined his ability to treat other collaborators more harshly. But apart from that prejudicial action, the general understood correctly that this was the group of Filipinos who had the competence to run the government and the economy.

MacArthur's old patron, associate, friend, and president of the Philippines, Manuel Quezon, who had fled the islands soon after the general's departure, had died of tuberculosis at a sanatorium in Saranac Lake, New York in August 1944. His successor, Vice President Sergio Osmena, was a man of modest ability and even more modest social skills and, more importantly, a man who had often opposed MacArthur. President Roosevelt just before his death had met with Osmena and found him personally unimpressive, declaring to associates that MacArthur should run things in the islands when they were freed from Japanese occupation. President Harry Truman, new to the office in June and July of 1945 and confronted with more pressing issues, did not take an active interest in the Philippines. Unrestrained, MacArthur forced Osmena to make unpopular decisions, while the general promoted Roxas and the old social, political, and economic elites. When MacArthur left for Japan on August 30, the islands remained in a chaotic state, their relationship with the United States unclear, their economy in tatters, and their political status undecided. MacArthur did not return until the following July 4, for the ceremony marking Philippine independence and, thereafter, not until he had been long retired and living in New York.

Having "returned," MacArthur's opinion of the future of colonial empire, not only in the Philippines but also that of European colonies, became relevant to his subsequent tenure in Japan and in the formulation of his postwar worldview. Correctly understanding that radical solutions to the end of colonialism, that is to say communist solutions, would only impose new forms of tyranny, the general strongly favored the Philippine example for independence in the colonial world. Many of MacArthur's contemporaries shared his assumptions on this issue, and an evolutionary approach to independence for the colonies of European nations informed the judgments of U.S. policymakers during the Cold War years.

During WWII, President Roosevelt found himself at odds with Prime Minister Churchill over British imperialism. Churchill announced that only over his dead body would British colonies be designated for possible independence. The British had not started the war, he often proclaimed, and he saw no reason for their sacrifice at the end of it. MacArthur's and FDR's views were clear. MacArthur feared that the war could become a struggle for the re-assertion of empire, particularly the British empire. He also held to his belief, formed much earlier in his life, that there was no reason that educated elites in the colonies could not provide the leadership necessary for self-governance. Roosevelt agreed, but the requirements of the wartime alliance, not to say his own personality, made it hard for him to challenge Churchill on this point. MacArthur did not show a similar hesitancy, especially in conveying his opin-ions to his political allies back home in the United States. It had long been a conviction of many in the Republican Party that a major reason for the Europe-first strategy in fighting the war, as opposed to defeating Japan first, was to save the European colonial possessions; the general, for reasons of personal convic-tion and political expediency, reinforced this theory.

Opponents of President Roosevelt's foreign and military policies also ar-gued that he did far too little to contain Soviet expansion in either Europe or Asia—and was thereby serving the interests of British imperialism and So-viet Communism. The Yalta agreements provided the ostensible evidence of Roosevelt's failings. Postwar Republican political catechism held that Roo-sevelt had participated in a "sellout" of American interests to Stalin, that the president had abandoned both Eastern Europe and Nationalist China. In the postwar era MacArthur clearly lied about his contemporary thoughts on these accords, most especially on the Far Eastern parts of the agreements, as he joined in advancing these charges. There is plenty to criticize in the Yalta agreements, but the general's opposition was undercut by his own pro-nouncements in 1945.

In late February MacArthur told General George Lincoln, one of General Marshall's aides, that "we should make every effort to get Russia into the Japanese war before we go into Japan." Only a few days later he told Secre-tary of the Navy James Forrestal that American strength would have to be re-served for the invasion of Japan and "this could not be done without the as-surance that the Japanese would be heavily engaged by the Russians in Manchuria." Just prior to learning of the dropping of the atomic bomb on Hi-roshima MacArthur told a group of war correspondents that "Russian partic-ipation in the war [is] welcome."[16]

As anyone studying MacArthur's worldview quickly discovers, he was, in fact, deeply ambivalent about the Soviet Union; did not understand the British or their interests; and was profoundly confused and often contradic-tory about international politics. He personalized everything and, as his best scholarly biographer has noted, "MacArthur's traits included a desperate need to save face, even if it involved lying."

Although he was right about colonial empire and would achieve some dramatic successes in Tokyo, his weltanschauung did not become more sophisticated during his assignment in Japan.

Notes

1. James K. Eyre, Jr., *The Roosevelt-MacArthur Conflict* (Chambersburg, Pa.: Craft Press, 1950), 90–91. Also quoted in William Manchester, *American Caesar: Douglas MacArthur, 1880–1946* (Boston: Little, Brown, 1978), 264.

2. D. Clayton James, *The Years of MacArthur, Volume 2, 1941–1945* (Boston: Houghton Mifflin, 1975), 108–9.

3. James, *The Years of MacArthur, Volume 2*, 111; Manchester, *American Caesar*, 275–76.

4. James, *The Years of MacArthur, Volume 2*, 150–51.

5. See Michael Schaller, *Douglas MacArthur: The Far Eastern General* (New York: Oxford University Press, 1989), 69–74, for a perceptive assessment of these issues.

6. Jay Luvaas, ed., *Dear Miss Em* (Westport, Conn.: Greenwood, 1972), 6–65. Also see Schaller, *Douglas MacArthur*, 71.

7. Luvaas, *Dear Miss Em*, 6–65; Schaller, *Douglas MacArthur*, 71.

8. James, *The Years of MacArthur, Volume 2*, 164–67. Schaller, *Douglas MacArthur*, 72, 73.

9. James, *The Years of MacArthur, Volume 2*, 279–80.

10. James, *The Years of MacArthur, Volume 2*, 134–40.

11. James, *The Years of MacArthur, Volume 2*, 248–52; Schaller, *Douglas MacArthur*, 78–84. Schaller correctly places greater emphasis on MacArthur's interest in the presidency and his maneuvering to get it than many other scholars, including James.

12. Schaller, *Douglas MacArthur*, 85–87; Douglas MacArthur, *Reminiscences* (New York: Fawcett World Library and Time Inc., 1965), 196–99; James, *The Years of MacArthur, Volume 2*, 529–35.

13. Faubion Bowers, "The Late General MacArthur, Warts and All," *Esquire* 67 (January, 1967): 168.

14. James, *The Years of MacArthur, Volume 2*, 554–57.

15. Schaller, *Douglas MacArthur*, 96–98.

16. Russell D. Buhite, *Decisions at Yalta: An Appraisal of Summit Diplomacy* (Wilmington, Del.: Scholarly Resources, 1986); Schaller, *Douglas MacArthur*, 91–92.

CHAPTER FOUR

~

Viceroy in Japan

By mid-August of 1945, Japan had reaped the whirlwind of Pearl Harbor. Its far-flung empire was gone. Its home islands had suffered extensive destruction. Its cities had been rendered uninhabitable, with buildings in rubble and once teeming marketplaces and productive factories now little but barren landscape. Its communication and transportation systems, modern by prewar Asian standards, were no longer functional. An estimated two million homes had been obliterated. Nearly 700,000 civilians had been killed by American bombs. Food production could accommodate only a fraction of the population. Over one million troops had died in action. Seven million more, about to be repatriated, had nothing to come home to. Japan, in sum, experienced near total defeat. As supreme commander and ultimately American viceroy, MacArthur faced a formidable challenge.

While the general concentrated on ending his Philippine campaign, there was much about U.S. policy toward Japan that he did not know. Officials in Washington carried on complicated discussions through the summer of 1945 about a number of critical issues: whether once the atomic bomb were known to work, the United States should continue to plan for an invasion of Japan; whether or not to retain the emperor; whether to still urge Soviet participation in the Asian war or unilaterally revise the Yalta accords; what to do about a possible Soviet zone of occupation. None of this came to MacArthur's attention. On the matter of dropping the atomic bombs, MacArthur did not receive notification until sometime near the end of July, even though other American commanders, including

Eisenhower, already knew. MacArthur rightfully found this fact deeply troubling.

Despite President Harry S. Truman's distrust of MacArthur's self-serving behavior and the president's questioning of the general's WWII performance, he saw no alternative but to appoint MacArthur as supreme commander in charge of the surrender of Japanese forces in East and Southeast Asia and the occupation in Japan. Truman understood that Roosevelt's pandering to MacArthur for domestic political and morale reasons had made the general such a hero in the United States that his hands were tied. Information about the appointment was also late in coming to the general; he did not learn of it formally until August 10. When he did learn of the assignment, MacArthur was ecstatic; he foresaw an opportunity to put into practice his self-proclaimed understanding of the "oriental mind," a chance to join in determining the future of Japan.

MacArthur's longtime associate and sycophant General Courtney Whitney always maintained that the newly appointed supreme commander dictated his occupation policy for Japan on the plane carrying him to Atsugi (a Japanese military base located fifteen miles west of Yokohama) on July 30—devising it as he paced along the aisle. According to Whitney, MacArthur laid out his plan for a demilitarized, democratic, peace-loving country, displaying in the process the mind of philosopher-king. The general reinforced this version in his reminiscences. It is mostly nonsense. Beginning two years before the end of the war, the State-War-Navy-Coordinating Committee (SWNCC), totally unknown to MacArthur, had begun developing policy toward Japan. The extended document containing this policy was handed to the general on August 29 as his plane stopped in Okinawa on the way to Atsugi. MacArthur's enumeration to Whitney of the points of "his plan" was nothing more than a summary of the SWNCC document. MacArthur's vaunted policies, despite public perception over the years to the contrary, reflected very closely those approved in Washington by the SWNCC, the Joint Chiefs of Staff, and President Truman.

The four-part document spelled out American policy, not MacArthur's policy. Part one specified that Japan would have a new government conforming as closely as possible to democratic self-rule, but would not be subjected to any system imposed by the United States or the Allied powers that lacked Japanese support. The government, however, would have to become responsible and peaceful. Part two indicated how the supreme commander would relate to the Japanese government, how he would exercise his authority through that government and its agencies, and how he would work with the emperor. In part three, the document spelled out how Japan would be demilitarized and demobilized, purged of its old military leadership and its supranationalist ethos. This section among other things also required freedom of worship (of questionable value in an essentially secular society but included nonetheless) and tolerance of racial differences and other practices that accorded with the ideals (though certainly not the practices) of the United States and other democracies. Part four prescribed economic democracy in its various facets: rights for labor, breakup of the giant industrial and banking combines, and opportunities for small farmers and especially for women. MacArthur's preeminent scholarly biographer has written perceptively: "The fifteen reforms for which MacArthur claimed authorship, then, were incorporated, either directly or by implication, in the four key documents, all drafted by SWNCC."[1]

The sequence of events relating to MacArthur's arrival in Japan and his acceptance of Japanese surrender are both important and interesting. After learning of the emperor's announcement on August 15 that Japan would put down its arms, the general took a number of critical steps. He demanded that a contingent of sixteen Japanese officials come to the Philippines to discuss surrender documents and arrangements; this group was to be escorted first to Okinawa then on to Manila in American planes. The Japanese planes taking the contingent to Okinawa, MacArthur insisted, must be painted white and adorned with green crosses. From Okinawa, the group rode on in American C54s to its destination in Manila where the general, holding himself aloof in the manner of a new Japanese emperor, did not meet the delegation but let his staff officers conduct the discussions. On August 28, in haste to get to Japan before the navy or the marines, he sent an American airborne force of 150 men under the command of Colonel Charles Tench to Atsugi. MacArthur insisted they had to land at Atsugi—even though he could not be sure what reception they would receive. This uncertainty resulted from the Atsugi airfield having served as the training site for Kamikaze pilots, surely the most fanatical troops among many thousands of Japanese who had fought fanatically. Also hundreds of thousands of armed Japanese of one description or another were in the vicinity.

Tench's arrival, though tense and scary for him and his men, went off without serious incident. The Japanese were curiously compliant and welcoming. Next to arrive was General Robert Eichelberger who was to make final preparations for MacArthur's dramatic entry.

On August 30, shortly after 2:00 p.m., the general's plane, a C-54 which MacArthur had named "Bataan," landed at the airstrip at Atsugi. The general made a display of being unarmed and unadorned. It was an effective symbol, and it was an act of bravery, given the existence of young, hypernationalistic

Figure 4.1.   MacArthur Lands at Atsugi, Japan August 30th 1945. Reprinted Courtesy of the General Douglas MacArthur Foundation.

Japanese youths roaming about, anxious to prevent surrender under any circumstances and quite willing to kill not only foreigners but their own countrymen to avoid capitulation. MacArthur was determined to arrive before the admirals and the marines and to demonstrate to the Japanese, a gesture considered foolhardy by his aides and many military men around the world, that he was fearless and in command of Japan's future.

One of Eichelberger's tasks was to secure the area around the New Grand Hotel in Yokohama for MacArthur's check-in later that afternoon. He did so with a 500-man force of American troops. He also secured automobiles for the fifteen-mile trip eastward from Atsugi to Yokohama—a trip that even today seems longer than fifteen miles. MacArthur traveled in an American car, a Lincoln. The rest of the American group rode in an assortment of Japanese vehicles, some powered poorly by charcoal. Along the route at least thirty thousand Japanese troops stood at parade rest with their backs turned to the general's caravan, averting their eyes as a sign of submission and to guard against possible attack by renegade soldiers. What the general and his retinue found in Yokohama was a city at least 80 percent destroyed by American fire bombing the previous May, with a well-appointed hotel standing strangely undamaged in its midst. MacArthur was shown to the nicest suite of rooms, whereupon he took a nap prior to dinner. That evening he enjoyed a meal during which he refused a request by General Whitney that a Japanese official taste his steak for poison before eating it. He believed that word would spread widely of his act of trust and conciliation. The next evening he met General Jonathan Wainwright, frightfully thin and haggard owing to years of prison abuse at the hands of his Japanese captors, who had made his way over the previous four days from captivity in Manchuria to Yokohama. The result was an emotional reunion with a man whom many in Washington wished had been removed from Corregidor to Australia instead of MacArthur. Though he had not always been so generous to Wainwright, MacArthur greeted him warmly and authorized his participation in the formal surrender proceedings of September 2 on board the battleship *Missouri* in Tokyo Bay.

Those ceremonies provided the stage for additional MacArthur theatrics. For a fabulist who saw himself as the hero in every one of his imaginary productions, the events of the morning of September 2 provided a realistic setting more dramatic for the general than anything he could have conjured up in his fertile brain. Japanese officers were brought aboard to sign the surrender documents at precisely the right moment. MacArthur made his entrance on cue, then gave a speech that in cadence and in phrasing suggested heavy influence of Lincoln's Gettysburg Address: "we are gathered here," "it would be inappropriate to discuss here," "sacred purposes we are about to serve," "a better world shall emerge." Japanese officials signed the documents, then members of the American delegation did so, and, as befitted his role, MacArthur sat down at the table, the last to sign. Having signed with an assortment of pens to be preserved for posterity, he stood up and said: "These proceedings are now closed." A contingent of American fighter planes, in a predetermined gesture, roared over the *Missouri*, after which MacArthur stepped to the microphone and delivered a speech to the American people. It was a fitting ending to a cruel war; it was an eloquent speech; and it was all wonderful theater.

A popular, best-selling biographer has written that the Japanese brought out the best in MacArthur and MacArthur brought out the best in the Japanese.[2] Surely, it would be more accurate to say that the assignment in Japan brought out both the best and the worst in MacArthur; and the Japanese, who came to admire the general, made a conscious decision to transform their culture in accord with new realities. They had suffered a devastating loss in the war, and they needed to rebuild and adjust their behavior to both American demands and international norms.

Characterizing prewar and wartime Japan in a few short sentences is not an easy task. Mostly Japan constituted a fascist, totalitarian nation-state, reflecting the qualities of a tradition-directed society. Historically, the Japanese combined emperor worship with folk ritual in a culture rife with myth and superstition. Only in the late nineteenth century, for instance, did peasants begin to recognize that locomotives were not dragons or that the sound of wind blowing through telephone or electrical wires was not an ominous other-worldly sign. In some ways the industrialization and modernization that followed the 1860s made things worse: they led to pollution, the spread of horrific diseases, child labor, extra burdens for women, who were nonparticipants in public life, and growing militarism. As the twentieth century progressed, ordinary people had no civil rights, no civil liberties, nothing resembling democracy, despite the existence of a Diet formed on the German model. Truth was defined by the state, and the purpose of conversation was more to convey politeness than information. In the economic realm, the giant industrial and banking combines controlled nearly every area; food production came from sharecropping; industrial production came from oligopoly. Religion was a form of nationalism wedded to fealty to the emperor.[3]

Within weeks of assuming his position MacArthur began personalizing the occupation: every idea, every plan, every initiative, every decision came from the general, and he made certain that all the publicity focused on him. Why did officials in Washington tolerate this? Partly it was because of MacArthur's imperious personality; partly his seniority; partly his "heroic" exploits during WWII; partly because President Truman and his advisors were afraid of the political fallout if they sought to diminish his status; and largely because the general was at least moderately effective in carrying out the American program. At the instance of the Chinese, Soviets, and British, Allied officials set up two agencies to oversee the occupation, neither much of a hindrance to MacArthur's arbitrary ways. The Far Eastern Commission, a body of eleven members that sat in Washington, was virtually powerless. A smaller body, the Allied Council for Japan, convened in Tokyo as an oversight group, but the general treated its members with contempt, always arguing that to let them have any power would be to encourage Soviet-inspired communist activity in Japan. There were tactical differences to be sure and there were flare-ups over policy, but the American occupation proceeded fairly smoothly with a minimum of Allied, that is, Soviet, interference. This was hardly insignificant during these early Cold War years when the United States found itself locked in struggle with the U.S.S.R. elsewhere.

Despite his personal behavior, or perhaps in great measure because of it, the Japanese came to venerate MacArthur, who, depending on how one chooses to define his role, became the country's preeminent Shogun or sub-stitute emperor. Very few Japanese ever met, talked, or consulted with him. He was ever contemptuous of Japanese society and culture, seeing the nation and its people as immature in the evolution of nation-states. He did not travel about the country and only left Japan twice during the years of his res-idence in Tokyo prior to the Korean War. He made trips to Seoul and to Manila.

His daily routine was remarkably consistent. At his residence in the American embassy compound he rose early, had his breakfast, and read pa-pers and military history and whatever else suited his fancy until about 10:30, when he entered his car for the short trip to his office. His office, the head-quarters of the occupation, was in the Dai Ichi insurance company building, which provided adequate space for him and his staff. Even at his office he was often "too busy" to see those who needed to consult him on policy matters, though he usually made himself available to any worthy from Washington who could further his purposes. In early afternoon he returned to his resi-dence for lunch and a nap. He then returned to work where he remained into the evening, which caused considerable consternation among his staff, who arrived at 8:00 a.m. and often could not leave until he retired at 8:00 p.m. Extraordinarily aloof, he did not entertain, except for an occasional lunch with someone important to him. When he left the office all the traffic lights en route to his residence were turned off so his car could make the trip unim-peded. The great man had truly superb perquisites, though his lifestyle could not have exceeded what he experienced in the Philippines before the war.[4]

The apparatus of occupation included about 3,200 people. Most of these were grouped into twelve sections that served as a shadow government guid-ing the Japanese toward reform in a variety of areas. Meanwhile, in a sensi-ble U.S. policy decision, the existing Japanese governmental structure was kept in place as a vehicle for carrying out day-to-day operations. Among the most significant of the American sections was the Governmental Section, presided over by Courtney Whitney, which looked after restructuring the po-litical system, including remaking the Japanese constitution and many of the nation's laws. Incredibly, Whitney listened to his advisors and quibbled little with those New Deal reformers sent to guide his efforts. The results in this area were overwhelmingly salutary. Presiding over the economic restructur-ing of the country was General William Marquat whom MacArthur had known in the Philippines. In the early period of the occupation his main du-ties involved economic relief and recovery, but he too served the American

Figure 4.2. MacArthur and Hirohito, Japan 1945. Reprinted Courtesy of the General Douglas MacArthur Foundation.

effort well by heeding advice from Washington. This was an especially good thing because as an antiaircraft officer he knew very little about economic matters. In charge of intelligence was General Charles Willoughby, who along with Whitney was one of MacArthur's closest and most loyal aides. Willoughby, German born and extremely conservative, came about as close to accepting fascist ideology, without actually doing so, as possible. He forged strong ties with many figures in the old Japanese secret police and army and helped provide useful information to the general on many issues. He was in a sense General MacArthur's J. Edgar Hoover.[5]

In perhaps the most dramatic move among many in the early period of the occupation, the Governmental Section drafted and in 1946 presented to the Japanese a new constitution. To gain early acceptance, MacArthur indicated he would put the document to a vote of the people unless the Diet and the current cabinet quickly endorsed it. Neither of these bodies liked the constitution but accepting it seemed preferable to invoking popular sovereignty. The constitution brought several lasting reforms: it forbade the establishment of military power or its use in war; it guaranteed women the right to vote and other legal rights; it enhanced the power of the Diet; it extended voting rights beyond anything previously imagined; it moved some political power from Tokyo to the provinces; and, very importantly, it eliminated the concept of the emperor's divinity. The latter was reinforced when the emperor himself publicly denied such status.

The constitution conformed with a directive issued in only the second month of the occupation that in some ways resembled the American Bill of Rights. This order guaranteed the right of free speech and assembly. But it also provided for the release of all political prisoners and authorized the legalization of political parties, including interestingly, given MacArthur's predilections, the Communist party. Within the next year the Supreme Commander of the Allied Powers (SCAP) ordered a purge of militarists, supernationalists, right-wing businessmen, and bureaucrats from positions of power. Not all of these figures remained out of power and some came back within a few short years. But the move was both symbolically and practically important, and it was fairly popular with a broad swath of the Japanese people. In addition, SCAP dramatically reformed the public education system, thereby minimizing, though not eliminating, inculcation of nationalism. This was a decisive step in the democratization of the country, as was SCAP's orders allowing for the formation of labor unions, which thenceforth grew exponentially. At the end of WWII there were about seven hundred union members in the country; within two years there were over six million. But probably no step was more useful in promoting stabilization and democratization, or more controversial, than land reform. Under the leadership of Colonel Charles Kades, an ardent follower of New Deal precepts, SCAP pushed through the Diet a measure that broke up the large feudal landholdings. This step had MacArthur's strong backing because he believed, correctly, that it would invest the peasants in the Japanese economy, give them more purchasing power, allow for greater food production, and head off rural radicalism of the type that had taken hold in China.

Meanwhile, one of MacArthur's most visible early assignments as SCAP was to punish Japanese leaders responsible for carrying out the war in Asia and the Pacific. Some of the most notorious offenders were Japanese troops and officers who had operated in China and Southeast Asia. Responsibility for punishing these Japanese militarists fell mainly to the Chinese and British, who, together with the local populations in Southeast Asia, imprisoned and executed thousands of their former tormentors. MacArthur had charge of the Philippines; and it was in Manila that two of the most famous war crime prosecutions took place: the trials of General Tomoyuki Yamashita and General Masoharu Homma.

MacArthur's arrogance, together with his contempt for the normal processes of jurisprudence, quickly came to the fore. He appointed a commission of five generals to try Yamashita, a proceeding that began on October 29, 1945. He then permitted the use of evidence similar to that often submitted in front of hanging judges on the American frontier: second- and third-hand reports, hearsay, uncorroborated newspaper articles, and most anything that would strengthen the prosecution's case. He gave the defense insufficient time to prepare its case and, when the commissioners at one point agreed to an extension, overruled them. The main charge against Yamashita was that he had permitted men under his command to sack Manila in early 1945 and to kill both soldiers and civilians by the tens of thousands. The tribunal refused to accept the defense argument that Yamashita himself had fled to the hills, had not authorized the atrocities (which he had not), and that many of the most deplorable acts had been committed by forces under another Japanese commander. On December 7, the court handed down a verdict of guilty and decreed that Yamashita be stripped of his rank and his uniform and be hanged—a punishment most humiliating for a military hero. MacArthur not only pushed for a hasty decision, he refused to reconsider the verdict despite a petition from over 80,000 of Yamashita's countrymen. As MacArthur's defenders were quick to point out, the tribunal's verdict was ultimately upheld by the U.S. Supreme Court and President Truman. Yamashita was executed near Manila on February 23, 1946. It is hard to escape the conclusion that this was an act of vengeance, inconsistent with

MacArthur's attitude toward the Emperor Hirohito or others charged with war crimes.[6]

General Homma's case went just as rapidly. Homma had defeated MacArthur at Bataan, and he was charged with responsibility for the atrocities that occurred in the battle for control of the Philippines as well as for those of the Bataan death march, in which over two thousand prisoners died. He was equally responsible, the prosecution contended, for the subsequent deaths of about 28,000 prisoners. His defense claimed that Homma's men acted without his authority. The defense got nowhere with that argument, and MacArthur also upheld the guilty verdict in this case. The tribunal sentenced Homma to death by firing squad, a judgment that the U.S. Army carried out on April 3, 1946. MacArthur's critics tended to agree with H. L. Mencken that MacArthur was only too anxious to dispatch the Japanese general who had defeated him so ignominiously in the Philippines. Even though the U.S. Supreme Court refused to hear the case, two justices issued a strongly dissenting opinion—as they had done after the Yamashita conviction—that fairness had given way to haste. Fairness and proper procedures aside, Americans in 1945–1946 believed that Homma and Yamashita, like other Japanese who had participated in the aggression of the preceding fifteen years, got what was coming to them. Their executions were popular in the United States.

Trials in Tokyo condemned seven other Japanese. Over 1,100 Japanese, including Prime Minister Hideki Tojo, were tried as war criminals before a tribunal consisting of eleven judges chosen by MacArthur. One hundred and seventy-four of these individuals, of whom Tojo and his fellow prime minister Koki Hirota were foremost, received the death penalty. Only seven, Tojo and Hirota among them, were executed. In the Tokyo circumstances, MacArthur proved more generous than toward Homma and Yamashita, simply purging from position of authority many of those individuals responsible for Japanese military activities.[7]

If the general possessed a decent understanding of labor, land, and education reform and how such reforms might affect Japanese culture, there were some areas in which he appeared only marginally knowledgeable. It is possible that MacArthur, as primarily a nineteenth-century man isolated by his sheltered military experiences from the real world, did not understand monopoly capitalism and its features. It is likely that he was influenced to some degree by the populism and progressivism that swept the United States during his formative years and developed sympathy for the needs and interests of common folk. But he held conflicted views of what to do about the giant Japanese industrial combines known as the Zaibatsu, in part, it seems, because his wealthy corporate friends in the United States looked unfavorably on aggressive antimonopoly activity by the occupation and because he simply did not understand fully how monopoly had worked in Japan.

The initial postsurrender directive to MacArthur required that he move to dissolve the giant industrial and banking organizations owned by a handful of families. Toward that end, in the fall of 1945 the general accepted a plan put forward by the Yasuda family that contained gaping loopholes. Under the scheme the Yasudas and other families could effectively retain control of their vast enterprises. Later MacArthur received word from Washington that he must force the Japanese government to create an agency to reorganize Japanese business. Still later, MacArthur had the Japanese government place a ban on securities trading by Zaibatsu companies and impose a heavy tax on the companies. He also forbade the government from honoring war contracts and wartime plant expansion, thereby hitting the combines fairly hard. Knowing, though never admitting, what he did not know, the general then asked Washington for help on the monopoly issue.

In January 1946, an eight-member commission put together by the State and War Departments traveled to Japan to study the Zaibatsu. Under the direction of Professor Corwin Edwards of Northwestern University, an expert on cartels, this commission developed a report that was not only critical of the Yasuda plan but of MacArthur himself. It noted that MacArthur "had not really prepared anything but a superficial juggling of the Japanese economic setup." The report went on to recommend a complete breakup of the Zaibatsu to further free trade and competition. Predictably, MacArthur criticized the Edwards report as too sweeping, as promoting too much bureaucracy, and, if carried out fully, as too restrictive for the Japanese economy. The general's objections aside, the report became the basis of SWNCC policy later in 1946.[8]

A measure of MacArthur's uncertainty in dealing with the Zaibatsu was the criticism he received and his responses to that criticism. In implementing American policy through the remainder of 1946 and in 1947, the general ordered the breakup of numerous trade associations and then in January 1947 he issued a purge order that divested well over two thousand corporate leaders, chairmen, presidents, and managers of their positions. Later, he ordered the breakup of the Mitsui and Mitsubishi combines. The antimonopoly action prompted an attack by the Tokyo bureau chief of *Newsweek* magazine that the purge was going too far. The editor's objections probably reflected the opinions of corporate bigwigs in the United States. But, as previously noted, MacArthur was ambivalent about these reforms. He realized that the purges and other actions did little to injure the Japanese economy, and he was not committed to opposing monopoly. As his intelligence chief noted: "The general was never really sold on going after Japanese big businessmen. As for the stepped-up attack in 1947, he may have been too busy with other things and gave his antitrust people too much leeway."[9]

Whatever MacArthur's motivation or intention, there is no question that after 1947 the United States began seriously to scale back its anti-Zaibatsu policy. In 1948 policymakers in Washington put together a body called the Deconcentration Review Board, which went to Japan in May and quickly began reversing the 1947 rules on the breakup of Japanese industry, including redefining what constituted unfair trade practices. Over the next year, many of the industrial combines resumed their activity, and many of the former leaders of the family businesses were depurged. By 1949–1950, the old business practices had largely returned, though it is true that industry in Japan had been reorganized on a broader and fairer basis than prior to the war. That aside, there was little justification for MacArthur's pronouncement in a speech commemorating the fourth anniversary of Japan's surrender that he had achieved the democratization of Japanese economic life with his reform of monopolistic industry. Such a pronouncement neither accorded with what had occurred nor with the general's predilections. As he had done previously in his career, particularly in the Philippines and during WWII, MacArthur magically disposed of troubling details.

The fact is that American policy on the Japanese economy reflected a significant change in the U.S. approach to world affairs from 1946 onward. Mightily concerned about potential Soviet expansion in Eastern Europe and Germany, U.S. officials began conceptualizing and then putting in place the containment strategy. U.S. charge d'affaires in the Soviet Union, George Kennan, warned of Russian motivation in his famous Long Telegram of February 1946. This was followed by Winston Churchill's Iron Curtain speech in March at Westminster College in Fulton, Missouri, which was in turn followed by the decision in May of that year to terminate reparations to the Soviet Union from the British and American zones of occupation in Germany. Then in September, the Clark Clifford report, drafted by his assistant George Elsey, calling for a more active American policy to thwart the Soviet Union, became part of Truman administration thinking. The next year, 1947, saw the implementation of the containment policy in the Truman Doctrine and Marshall Plan to stabilize Western Europe and the eastern Mediterranean. With the advent of the Cold War, it seemed necessary to rebuild the western sector of Germany, to make it over on the Western Allied model—a move that led to the Berlin Blockade and crisis of 1948–1949, in which the Soviet Union and the Western powers came close to war. It seemed logical, moreover, to begin a stabilization process in Japan. Increasingly, the latter appeared less like the old enemy and more like a possible partner in the struggle against the Soviet Union. More than that, by 1948 and 1949 the impending victory of communism in China portended the need for stability in Asia that a strong, economically viable Japan could provide.

Stability accorded with MacArthur's military mind and his innate uneasiness with disorder. He found little to dislike in the conservative political movement that dominated Japanese politics in the early occupation period. In April 1946 in the first election held in the country after the war the Liberals and Progressives—both titles misnomers because of their conservative orientation—achieved a majority in the Diet, while the communists and other liberal groups looked on from the outside. Over the first year after elections, Yoshida Shigeru, though initially deemed lazy by MacArthur, led a cabinet of conservative ministers in a government that on most issues had the general's approval.

In June 1947, a socialist coalition took power but did not last long and by the next spring had been replaced by a coalition led again by Shigeru and known as the Democratic-Liberal Party. By whatever name, moderate liberal or conservative coalitions held power in Japan for most of the last half of the twentieth century. Part of MacArthur's legacy, but with concurrence of Washington officials, was thus a conservative trend in Japan. A politics of the Left seemed risky during the Cold War. Whether such politics would have permitted Japan's rebuilding with a greater degree of fairness is debatable.

MacArthur always portrayed himself as the friend of Japanese labor, a portrayal in which there was some, but not the whole, truth. His position reflected considerable ambivalence. As the labor reforms of the early occupation took effect, unions formed and workers assumed they could bargain collectively with employers. In 1946 and 1947, however, reform ideals clashed with the realities of the economy. Throughout this period the economy struggled, leaving people with barely enough to get by. The country experienced hyperinflation (nearly 1,000 percent at one point), serious unemployment, food shortages, and inadequate wages. Unions conducted mass demonstrations, walkouts, and strikes in 1946, and in early 1947 planned a general strike. Although at first rhetorically favorable to labor, MacArthur increasingly attacked the demonstrations as radically motivated by either socialists or communists and as a danger to the country. Fearing Soviet influence, he banned the general strike. For one accustomed to the authoritarian approach of the military, any mass movement proved threatening. As he did with the Bonus Marchers in Washington, he perceived unions as motivated by the essence of revolution and hence a menace.

An outstanding scholarly biographer of MacArthur has argued that, "At various times between 1945 and 1950 MacArthur advocated both preserving and dissolving industrial combines, protecting and suppressing organized labor, banning and building permanent American military bases in Japan, cooperating with and excluding the Soviets from a peace treaty, and ignoring and hiding behind the Allied consulting organs created in 1945." He goes on to say that the general never really understood or cared much about key events of the period: important issues of Soviet-American discord and communist accession to power in China. What MacArthur was most concerned about was positioning himself to look good in the United States, partly to feed his ego and in large measure for political reasons connected to the presidential election of 1948.[10] This author may well be right. There is no doubt that the general had political ambitions and hoped for the Republican nomination for president in 1948. But it is also true that U.S. foreign policy from 1947 onward would have forced any supreme commander in Japan, no matter how incidental his ego or uninterested in politics, to undergo contortions. Moreover, MacArthur, for all his pretensions to greatness, did not have the necessary knowledge or ability to chart an entirely consistent course.

As noted, by the end of 1947, key officials in Washington—General and then Secretary of State Marshall, Undersecretary of State Dean Acheson, Secretary of the Navy and then first Defense Secretary James Forrestal, Head of the Policy Planning Staff George Kennan, as well as President Truman—had concluded that containment of the Soviet Union required the rebuilding of Japan. This meant encouraging Japan to seek raw materials in Southeast Asia and markets throughout Asia; it also meant an end to those New Deal reform measures, including the dissolution of the Zaibatsu, that MacArthur, often reluctantly, had put in place in the country. In one of the great ironies of the period, the general received bitter criticism in 1945 and 1946 in the liberal and moderate American press for not moving fast enough or strenuously enough to punish Japan, but in 1947 and after he evoked criticism for enacting reforms that ostensibly smacked of socialism and gave encouragement to the communists. Meanwhile, MacArthur made things more difficult for himself by refusing to brook what he considered Washington's interference with his prerogatives. Someone, usually one of his old "enemies," most especially Marshall, Eisenhower, or the old "navy crowd," was always out to get him, to make him look bad.

Totally apart from his conviction that he had done good work as SCAP, MacArthur concluded that 1947 and 1948 afforded him an opportune time to declare the occupation a great success and urge the conclusion of a peace treaty with Japan. He would meet the new initiatives from Washington by declaring victory. Such a course would also give him momentum toward the presidential election of 1948.

The general actually had begun to position himself politically not long after assuming the assignment in Japan. Acting on the advice of his friend and benefactor, Robert Wood, President of Sears Roebuck, MacArthur quickly entered into the civilian policy debate in Washington over the size of the American military. Originally U.S. officials believed that a 6.8 million-man force would be necessary to conclude the war in the Pacific. When use of the atomic bombs shortened the war, there were strong pressures in the United States, both among the public and in Congress, to demobilize and bring the men home as soon as possible. But American policymakers worried about taking precipitous action because of the obligations that the occupation of Japan and Germany would impose on the military, and they worried that an overly rapid demobilization would leave the United States in a weakened position relative to the Soviet Union. They worried too that the rapid release of troops would have an unsettling effect on the American economy. It seemed, therefore, that continued conscription might be necessary for the foreseeable future.

Wood warned MacArthur that Washington officials would shift the blame to him for continued conscription and hence hurt his chances in 1948 unless he made it clear that the occupation could get by with a minimum number of forces. The general should strike a preemptive blow against his "adversaries" in Washington. On September 17, 1945, barely settled in Tokyo, MacArthur announced that, because the occupation was going so smoothly, he would need only 200,000 troops rather than the 500,000 troops originally envisioned. MacArthur demonstrated how disingenuous this announcement was by giving other estimates over time that ranged up to a million forces needed. The announcement hit the State and War Departments like a ton of bricks and in particular infuriated Dean Acheson, soon to become undersecretary of state, and President Truman. Had Truman not been so fearful of the general's celebrity status in the United States and his political clout within Republican circles, he would have sacked him then and there. In retrospect, it all seems like a tempest in a teapot. But, in the context of the time, when the size of the military was a critical issue in foreign policy, it struck officials as an unwarranted intrusion into civilian responsibility. To the historian, MacArthur's actions bespeak his political intentions.

By 1947 the major issue between Washington and MacArthur had become the performance of the Japanese economy and the need to delay a peace treaty until economic stability had been achieved. American officials in Washington wanted to build Japan up as an economic bulwark against the Soviet Union, believing increasingly that the occupation must continue until that was achieved. MacArthur on the other hand believed, or so he said, that economic stability could come only with the end of the occupation. What the general wanted was a spectacular peace conference, out of which would emerge a treaty that he thought would meet the approval of the American people and his nomination to the Republican Party for the presidency.

It was during 1947 that MacArthur pushed the deconcentration of the Zaibatsu most vigorously. He argued to the consternation of most of his superiors that he was undercutting socialism, that in fact the interlocking enterprises of the large families comprised a kind of private socialism. He may have been right in that argument; it was a form of national socialism. But George Kennan and Secretary of the Army Kenneth Royall, among others, insisted that the United States had to change course or the Japanese economy would fail. MacArthur obstinately pushed for breakup while Washington, acting on new world realities, insisted the issue was no longer monopoly but order and productivity.

The general sometimes seemed blissfully oblivious to world events. He tended to look upon the Marshall Plan, the Truman Doctrine, and moves to stabilize Europe as a continuation of the wrongheaded approach of the WWII Europe-firsters. Because his world was Asia, it was the most important. But even there he showed little sophistication. Toward the civil war raging in China his solution was all-out aid to Chiang Kai-shek. He thought the Korean peninsula deserved a laissez-faire approach to allow the Koreans to purge themselves of their destructive tendencies. And, at one point, he suggested a treaty with the Soviet Union to neutralize Japan. Here his and Kennan's views converged to a certain degree. Kennan thought the United States and the Soviets could agree to a trade-off: a noncommunist Korea in return for a neutralized Japan. Increasingly, however, MacArthur began aligning himself with his Republican friends in the United States. The mantra of these friends, especially many Midwesterners, was that stopping communism in Asia should take precedence over the effort in Europe.

MacArthur hoped that his political rivals in 1948 would cancel one another out, opening the way for his candidacy in which he could effectively use his successes in Japan and popularity at home to gain the nomination. He referred to Thomas Dewey, the Republican nominee in 1944, and Senator Robert Taft of Ohio, a prominent contender, as "shopworn," as old faces within the party. He thought of Harold Stassen of Minnesota as a lightweight, a joke, and not a serious contender, a view eventually shared by many within the United States. His main worry was his old aide and now nemesis, Eisenhower. He disparaged Eisenhower as a "Swedish Jew," a man of little talent, a general guilty of indiscretion in his private life while in England (meaning, presumably, his relationship with his driver Kay Sommersby), a person of excess ambition, and a "good-time Charley" who would sell out the interests of the country for his own purposes. On the other hand, he had to take his old aide seriously, and he talked at one point of a deal with Eisenhower: he would announce for the Republican nomination in 1948, assuming he would win; but he would serve only one term and let Eisenhower have his shot in 1952.

MacArthur and his supporters believed he could bridge the gap that existed within the Republican Party between the isolationists, represented by the Taft wing, and the internationalists represented by Eisenhower, Dewey, and others. It was also MacArthur's belief that his reform program in Japan, including what can only be termed intermittent attacks on the Zaibatsu, would appeal to liberals in the United States. The general's massive ego worked for him and against him: for him, in the sense that it led him to believe he could become a viable candidate and, more importantly, a successful president; against him, because he would not return to the United States to allow his fellow citizens to scrutinize him and his ideas. To those supporters such as Robert Wood, who encouraged him to come home and launch a campaign, he always issued a flat "no." He worried about the criticism and he worried about failure, and he did not want to abandon the certainty of his military position. What he wanted was acclamation, adoration, and applause; then he would return and run a campaign.

As events unfolded the general's apprehensions were correct: despite a coordinated effort between a staff member in Tokyo and supporters in the States, his showing proved pathetic, his following anemic. In response to urgent entreaties from his backers in the States, MacArthur, though not yet agreeing to come home, in early March finally declared himself a candidate. He expected as a native son to do well in the Wisconsin primary, but he finished a distant second to Harold Stassen. He then did even more poorly in Nebraska. In an unopposed race in Illinois, he won. But at the Republican convention in June he picked up only eight delegates, all of whom soon switched to Dewey. The results were devastating; they reflected his dimming status and, equally important, the superficial nature of his celebrity status. Despite fulsome praise from the Hearst, Gannett, and McCormick newspapers—Hearst ran regular pictures of the general on his front pages—the public no longer appeared interested in his act.[11]

MacArthur's act, although still fairly popular among the Japanese, played particularly poorly among American policymakers. They now told him what to do and often in no uncertain terms. They were determined to move forward with Japanese recovery. What this meant in practice was reversal of many of the earlier occupation reforms toward labor and monopoly, aggressive action in favor of a buildup of industry, and the development of a vigorous export economy. MacArthur often protested, but after Truman's victory in November he had no choice but to get on board.

Among the general's most influential and intellectual critics was George Kennan as head of the State Department's Policy Planning Staff. The victim of MacArthur's imperious and deliberately rude behavior during a visit to Tokyo, Kennan in 1948 told his friend and State Department colleague Walton Butterworth that the general's entourage resembled the court of Catherine II of Russia in its final days—or perhaps, more accurately, "the final stages of the regime of Belisarius in Italy." The "cackling" wives of the general's subordinates seemed to think the war had been fought so they could live in luxury. Kennan lost no time in pushing through the policy establishment a clear plan for economic rehabilitation.[12]

Meanwhile, MacArthur continued to emphasize his contribution to the spiritual regeneration of Japan along Christian lines. Although the general issued an edict in December 1945 requiring the separation of church and state, he believed that the occupation would go more smoothly and Japan could be made over into a Western-style state only if it adopted Christianity. It is interesting and a bit ironic that MacArthur would take this position. An Episcopalian by denomination, he never went to church, nor did he count among his few friends any military chaplains. His knowledge of Christianity came from some Bible study and the principles of the faith that he tended to equate with Americanism, and he seldom separated the two things.

Fearing criticism, he was always highly selective about those Americans he allowed into Japan, but never failed to permit the entry of missionaries. Indeed, he sent messages to churches in the United States urging that they send missionaries to the country, and at one point he asked that the faithful back home send ten million Bibles. He also had critical references about Christianity excised from textbooks. His Christianization campaign was complicated and involved both ideological and practical considerations. He informed Secretary of the Navy James Forrestal in 1946 that what Asia needed was a commitment to Christianity to counter godless Marxism/Leninism; and he made similar comments to George Kennan, a man not easily duped or impressed. When he spoke about filling Japan's spiritual vacuum, and he did so frequently, he meant that it was necessary to provide the population something to hold onto, given the de-emphasis on Shintoism.

But it seems equally clear that to MacArthur the basis of the American way of life, its greatness, of which he saw himself as the advance agent, was the marrying of democracy and Christianity. "True democracy," he once told a religious editor, "can exist only on a spiritual foundation. It will endure when it rests firmly on the Christian conception of the individual and society." Ignoring the influence of the Enlightenment on the American founders but foreshadowing a force that in the late twentieth and early twenty-first century would be known as the "religious right," he believed that neither Japan nor any other nation could become democratic without Christianity. At one point he spoke of how China, Japan, and the Philippines all had Christian leaders (they lost power quickly in a development that the general never addressed). Once, he also gave a speech in which he stated that owing to American efforts—meaning of course his own—Japan then had 2,000,000 Christians and that number was rapidly growing. The 2,000,000 figure, it is interesting to note, came from his Civil Information and Education Section. As its members were preparing information for the general, they concluded that prior to WWII Japan had about 200,000 Christians and that afterwards had far fewer. But they decided that MacArthur would not be satisfied with 200,000, so they added three zeroes to the number. To the general it was henceforth two million.[13]

Ignorant of the indifference, or hostility, to the Christian faith among most Asians, MacArthur deluded himself into the belief that his "missionary" activities would change the course of world history for a thousand years. (Such grandiose time sweeps were a common rhetorical device for the general, and often most impressive to the casual listener.) He would have been sorely disappointed to learn—apparently no one chose to tell him of the phenomenon—that thousands of Japanese males loved the Bibles he imported largely because the paper came in handy to roll cigarettes. By 1951, when MacArthur was sacked, Japan had roughly the same Christian population it had had in 1941: there were over 45 million Buddhists, 17 million Shintoists, and millions more who belonged to various sects, but only roughly one-half of one percent of those who professed a religion called themselves Christians. For a man who considered himself, along with the pope, as a leading proponent of Christianity, this figure would have been difficult to accept.[14]

MacArthur's ultimate failure to convert the Japanese to the dominant Western religion does not mean that the SCAP did not achieve many successes in the social and cultural areas of the occupation. The SCAP Public Health and Welfare Section, with General Crawford Sams in the lead role, performed near-miracles during the first five years of the occupation via programs that MacArthur either knew of or directly sanctioned. Among the most important of these efforts was to improve water, sanitation, and sewage systems; provide nutrition for children through free lunch programs; rebuild hospitals, veterinary clinics, nursing schools, and other parts of the public health infrastructure destroyed by the American bombing and by years of neglect during Japan's overseas military adventures.

Disease control was a particularly important part of the American contribution to the rebuilding of Japan. Sams and his subordinates rushed to deal with an epidemic of typhus in Osaka, and to vaccinate thousands of Japanese as smallpox threatened to rage out of control. In 1946 cholera, brought back to the home islands from China, became a problem that needed attention and received a relatively quick remedy. Over the years Japan had developed one of the highest incidences of tuberculosis in the world but through the application of antibiotics from the United States the disease, if not totally eradicated, was controlled. Much of the disease prevention and control of contagion was made possible with new medicines, particularly antibiotics and DDT, the latter used to dust large segments of the population that may have later developed cancer from this extremely carcinogenic chemical. At any rate, it proved successful in dealing with the immediate problem.

Control of venereal disease raised issues of social contact and what came to be called "fraternization." The incidence of VD among both American occupying troops and returning Japanese reached nearly 30 percent shortly after the war, prompting the need to both limit sexual contact or transmission and to administer antibiotics. SCAP set up clinics to dispense condoms to U.S. soldiers as a first step. MacArthur outlawed licensed prostitution, believing that the licensing itself did little good to control disease. He was encouraged to end the streetwalking form of prostitution but did little toward that end. Indeed, Americans interested in whoring suffered little inconvenience from SCAP intervention. Owing to the new medicines and condom use, however, venereal disease was reduced among American troops to about 13 percent by the end of the occupation, and substantially curtailed among Japanese as well.

Fraternization was a tricky matter. MacArthur believed the nonfraternization order from the War Department ill-advised and did little to implement it. He thought that Americans visiting in Japanese homes and places of business not only made his job easier but also that social interaction between peoples would be good for Japanese-American relations in future years. Though he could demonstrate signs of bigotry, he did not curtail interracial dating or marriage. He deserves credit for an enlightened approach on this issue.

His promotion of a new status for women in Japanese society was also enlightened. He took no stand on birth control, which had become an issue because SCAP disease prevention and health measures and Japanese social custom had led to a significant increase in population. But the general did take a highly positive stand on women's rights. From 1945 to 1950, the population went from about 70 to 83 million, threatening to strain the country's natural resources. This was only one issue affecting women. Equal rights in marriage, access to divorce, ending of arranged marriages, voting rights, and participation in public affairs and in the workplace were all new in Japan. And they were written into the civil code. There is debate about how much MacArthur contributed to this agenda and how much came from the Japanese themselves, but there can be no doubt that the general abetted the efforts. "In the history of Japanese women," MacArthur biographer D. Clayton James has written, "the occupation period is a watershed and . . . the progress . . . would not have been as rapid or substantial without the intervention of SCAP."[15]

Although MacArthur had been humbled by the political events of 1948 and chose thereafter to follow the administration's more conservative course, he still had battles to fight. The House Appropriations Committee threatened to reduce funding for the occupation, a move that the general saw as potentially injurious to the well-being of the Japanese people and to the relief program in particular. This angered him. What bothered him most, however, was the threat, originating in the State Department and in the Department of the Army, to give the occupation over to civilian authorities. With the establishment of the Federal Republic of Germany in 1949 and the assignment of an American ambassador to that newly sovereign nation, it seemed appropriate to develop a similar arrangement for Japan. This would have ended the military phase of the occupation and turned direction over to an American ambassador reporting to the State Department. MacArthur was furious at the thought, probably seeing in the effort a reprise of his father's difficulties with William Howard Taft in the Philippines. He vowed to thwart any attempt to force his resignation.

Army Chief of Staff General Omar Bradley defended the new arrangement as logical in a message to SCAP. Since MacArthur and the State Department were in substantial agreement on the need for a peace treaty with Japan, Bradley suggested, it made sense that military responsibility be withdrawn. Eventually the idea was dropped in September 1949, probably because of intense rivalry in Washington between Secretary of State Dean

Acheson, an old foe of the general's, and Secretary of Defense, Louis Johnson, a MacArthur supporter. Johnson, who at this point disliked the prospect of relinquishing Defense Department control over Japan and a bitter rival of Acheson, won the round with Truman's backing. He prevailed because of larger geopolitical developments in Asia, specifically the imminent Communist victory in China, anxieties over development on the Korean peninsula, and the belief that MacArthur could be helpful in concluding the eventual peace treaty.

The general also battled the press. Some of the press criticism that MacArthur received in 1948 and 1949 was fair and some not. He objected most strenuously to suggestions he was following a radical program in Japan by implementing a socialist economy that seemed to follow a pseudo-Soviet model. His response was always self-congratulatory: he had succeeded in putting in place most of the key parts of the occupation in the first two years, carried out the critical social and cultural reforms, and put Japan on a democratic and Christian course. He only received a directive to revive the economy, he said disingenuously, late in the game. That he failed to understand how to do so or that the policies he implemented were strategically timed to help him secure the Republican nomination for the presidency never appeared in his explanations.

MacArthur was certainly not the first public figure to have trouble with the press, nor the last. But his effort to control his SCAP's image was legendary. He employed tight censorship of publications, radio reports, and films that adopted even a slightly negative tone. For example, his regime did not allow the showing of the movie *Citizen Kane* and banned John Steinbeck's *Grapes of Wrath*. He had several journalists expelled and refused to allow reporters from some publications to reenter the country. He harassed others, or had his lackeys do so. Much of this censorship, especially during the first two and a half years, was aimed at protecting himself, and at preserving his hero status in the United States. Later he claimed to be controlling the communist threat within Japan.

By the end of 1949 it had become apparent to most policymakers that a peace treaty with Japan was necessary and that only the timing was at issue. The State Department, despite its Policy Planning Staff's earlier remonstrance against a treaty, now believed that Japan could achieve economic progress only with the conclusion of a treaty and that drawing Japan closer to the United States psychologically and strategically by ending the occupation was essential. Defense Department officials demurred, while contending that only continuing the occupation would work to advance American interests. The differences, while acrimonious, were mainly tactical and focused on which approach would serve best to meet the Soviet threat. As the year 1950 progressed, and with it the conclusion of the Sino-Soviet alliance and beginning of the Korean War, the question answered itself. After lengthy negotiations to establish the groundwork, the United States held a conference in San Francisco, attended by fifty-two nations, out of which came a treaty with Japan on September 4, 1951. The treaty officially ended the occupation. The Korean War, meanwhile, led to President Truman's termination of MacArthur's career.

Despite his use of his command for political advantage and Washington's initiation of most of the key reforms in Japan, MacArthur's performance overall merits praise. He ran an efficient and generally effective administration of the occupation. He played on the Japanese penchant for heroes, on their situational ethics that allowed submission to a new authority figure, and on their desire for fairness. He also made a strong personal commitment to the American reform program, central features of which were demilitarization and democratization. If he sometimes seemed like a New Dealer, it was because he did not disagree with those parts of the New Deal that owed inspiration to the progressive era. Beyond all that, in what might have been his greatest contribution, he helped prevent the spread of communism and consequent Soviet influence in the country.

Notes

1. D. Clayton James, *The Years of MacArthur, Volume 3, 1945–1964* (Boston: Houghton Mifflin, 1985),14; D. Clayton James, *The Years of MacArthur, Volume 2, 1941–1945* (Boston: Houghton Mifflin, 1975), 74–75; Michael Schaller, *Douglas MacArthur: The Far Eastern General* (New York: Oxford University Press, 1989), 106–19.

2. William Manchester, *American Caesar: Douglas MacArthur, 1880–1946* (Boston: Little, Brown, 1978), 462.

3. See Manchester, *American Caesar*, 461–62.

4. Manchester, *American Caesar*, 476–77. See Faubion Bowers, "The Late General MacArthur, Warts and All," *Esquire* 67 (January, 1967): 91, 95.

5. James, *The Years of MacArthur, Volume 3*, 45–46, 53–54. Schaller, *Douglas MacArthur*, 121–22.

6. James, *The Years of MacArthur, Volume 3*, 93–97.

7. James, *The Years of MacArthur, Volume 3*, 98–108. Manchester, *American Caesar*, 483–88.

8. Quoted in James, *The Years of MacArthur, Volume 3*, 168.

9. James, *The Years of MacArthur, Volume 3*, 173.

10. Schaller, *Douglas MacArthur*, 134.

11. See Schaller, *Douglas MacArthur*, 135–59, for an insightful account of MacArthur's political maneuverings.

12. Schaller, *Douglas MacArthur*, 151.

13. James, *The Years of MacArthur, Volume 3*, 287–95; Schaller, *Douglas MacArthur*, 127–28. Schaller based his account of the two million figure on Faubian Bowers's comments in the Columbia University Oral History Project.

14. James, *The Years of MacArthur, Volume 3*, 487–95 and, for James's comments on the use of Bible paper to roll cigarettes, 290.

15. James, *The Years of MacArthur, Volume 3*, 283.

CHAPTER FIVE

~

Korea: Background to War

An accident of history put Soviet and American armies on the Korean peninsula in late summer 1945. That historical development, occasioned by conclusion of the Japanese war, eventually became a tragedy for the United States, the Soviet Union, China, and, most importantly, Korea. General MacArthur's record in American policy toward Korea is mixed: not as sterling as he and his defenders wanted posterity to believe but not as horrible as his harshest critics have charged.

It was never MacArthur's intention to assume much responsibility for Korea, nor did it seem as WWII came to its end even within the remotest possibility that the United States would become militarily entangled in an area considered nonvital to American security. The major postwar American objective was to promote a free, independent, and democratic Korea in accord with the Atlantic Charter and the Cairo Declaration, which required independence for Japan's colonies. The United States had no interest in controlling Korea or in securing a long-term military occupation of the peninsula. Apart from seeing Korea become free, independent, and democratic for its own sake, the United States hoped to prevent Korea's becoming a base for a threat to Japan or a troublesome irritant in American relations with the Soviet Union and China.

If Korea was a peripheral area for the United States, it was anything but for the Soviet Union. The peninsula is seven thousand miles from the United States, but contiguous to the Soviet Union. The Soviets' optimum objective was control of the whole country. Korea was a vital strategic area for the Soviet Union just as it had been for Imperial Russia, which in the early part of the twentieth century had engaged in intense rivalry with Japan over the territory. And Japanese control of the peninsula had contributed significantly to Russia's defeat in the Russo-Japanese War of 1904–1905, a fact not lost on Soviet officials. Control of Korea would safeguard Soviet concessions in Manchuria, influence events in China, and neutralize resurgent Japanese power. Short of domination of the entire country, Soviet leader Josef Stalin certainly hoped to control a large segment of it and might have accepted, if need be, domination north of a latitudinal line such as that suggested by the czar in 1895: division of the peninsula at the 38th parallel. He surely must have seen the American proposal of that dividing line for accepting Japanese surrender as a U.S. attempt at Realpolitik, when it was nothing of the sort.

Stalin's minimum objective was influence through the Korean Communist Party, whose actions the Soviets had long directed. This party, which never had a huge membership, received extensive Soviet and Chinese communist support during WWII. One segment of the Korean party was based at Yenan in communist-controlled China, and another alternately in Manchuria and on Soviet territory near Vladivostok. When the war ended Stalin expected that these Korean communists, though not fully in agreement in their visions for their country, would go home, capitalize on nationalist fervor in their homeland, expunge Japanese influence, and establish a Korea friendly to the Soviet Union. Soviet naval officers reported to an American OSS operative that postwar Korea would be independent in the same sense that Poland would be independent: "We have 100,000 Koreans in Central Asia ready to go back."[1]

During the spring and summer of 1945, there was one important limitation on Soviet objectives: the Soviets did not know when and if they would get to Korea. They certainly did not know if they would arrive in the peninsula before the United States, because they were unsure how or exactly when the war with Japan would end. The United States might occupy both Japan and Korea before the Soviets entered the Asian war.

Important variables also influenced American policy. The United States could not know if and when its armies would land in Korea. As events transpired, the Soviets arrived first. The Soviets entered the war with Japan on August 8, hastening to fulfill obligations undertaken at the Yalta Conference. Following their main offensive against Japanese troops in Manchuria, the Soviets moved into Korea on August 12. At a conference in the War Department on the night of August 10, American military officials, including Brigadier General George Lincoln and Colonels Charles Bonesteel and Dean

Rusk, concerned about Soviet worldwide aspirations and fearful that the Soviet Union would quickly occupy all of Korea, proposed that Korea be divided at the thirty-eighth parallel for acceptance of Japanese surrender. This
proposal survived the vetting of other offices and President Truman sent it
on to Stalin on August 15. To anyone questioning the role of accident and
inadvertence in history, this decision should offer an important lesson: Rusk
and his colleagues knew nothing of the czar's 1895 proposal of a partition of
Korea! Although Soviet troops could have occupied the entire peninsula, as
Rusk and his colleagues had feared, Stalin accepted the offer and American
forces arrived on September 8.[2]

General MacArthur made serious mistakes in Korea, not least among
them the appointment of Lt. General John R. Hodge to head the American
occupation forces there. Korea was within MacArthur's purview because as
supreme commander he was in charge of taking Japanese surrender in areas
for which the United States had responsibility. MacArthur, who assumed his
duties in Japan would consume him, did not want to deal with Korea; hence,
as the record demonstrates, he gave the peninsula as little attention as he
could manage. His appointment of Hodge for this assignment was a disaster.
A combat officer, most recently stationed in Okinawa, he may have had
fewer diplomatic skills, if that were possible, than either Generals George
Patton or Joseph Stilwell. He had no idea how to deal with Koreans with
whom he came in contact; in fact he knew little about Korea and cared even
less. MacArthur appointed him because from Okinawa he could get to the
Korean peninsula more quickly than any other American commander.
Among his first decisions was to compare Koreans to the Japanese and use
Japanese troops to maintain order for more than two months.[3] MacArthur
gave him no help. Indeed, MacArthur's September 7 decree severely exacerbated problems between Koreans and American occupiers in the south.

MacArthur's proclamation of American military control south of the 38th
parallel, a mistake nearly as serious as the appointment of Hodge, manifested
monumental insensitivity: "I hereby establish military control over Korea
south of 38 degrees north latitude and the inhabitants thereof. . . . All powers of government . . . will be for the present exercised under my authority.
All persons will obey promptly all my orders. . . . Acts of resistance . . . will
be punished severely. You will pursue your normal occupations, except as I
shall otherwise order. For all purposes during the military control, English
will be the official language. . . . Further proclamations, ordinances, regula-
tions, notices, directives and enactments will be issued by me . . . and will
specify what is required of you."[4] Koreans might have been excused for thinking they were inhabitants of a defeated enemy state.

As MacArthur's insensitivity demonstrates, American officials found themselves completely unprepared for the conditions they encountered in Korea. First and foremost, a spirited nationalism informed opinion in the country that the Japanese had colonized since 1910. Neither Hodge nor MacArthur had any idea how to respond. Second, they found fierce factionalism among both communist and noncommunist political groups of Koreans. In addition, the effort of Korean communists to unify the country under control of the Soviet-backed regime north of the 38th parallel proved maddeningly difficult to counter. To maintain order and protect their property, the Japanese, prior to the Americans' arrival, had granted authority to a quasigovernmental body in the south, referred to as the Preparatory Committee. This body soon came under the sway of the communists, who in September declared the People's Republic of Korea, which claimed control over the whole country. Hodge knew nothing about the origins of this committee or the People's Republic's self-proclaimed authority. Neither did U.S. officials in Washington, most of whom were equally unprepared for a Korean occupation. Washington officials charged with Korean matters included General John Hilldring, who became assistant secretary of state for occupied areas but had no special expertise on Korea; John Carter Vincent, director of the Office of Far Eastern Affairs, who was a China specialist at that time consumed by the China problem; and Joseph Grew, a Japan expert and prewar ambassador to that country. The State Department sent political advisers but they were of little help in the early days of the occupation.[5]

Since Hodge's directive prevented his acceptance of any presumptive government of Korea, he rejected the claims of the People's Republic, just as he did with the pretensions of another Korean group, the Korean Provisional Government. The latter was a noncommunist, conservative pretender to power that had spent the war years in Chungking, China, and returned to its homeland in November 1945. In the meantime, Syngman Rhee, a previous head of this Provisional Government and its representative in Washington during the war, had also returned to Korea, flown in on an American plane. Rhee, an elderly Korean nationalist and an expatriate, had earned a Ph.D. at Princeton University and had spent over thirty-five years in the United States. He was married to an Austrian Roman Catholic, who would become an object of derision and scorn to many Koreans. Yet Rhee himself was fairly popular in Korea and quickly became a leading figure in the Provisional Government.

During the fall of 1945, the American policy in Korea reflected a preoccupation with a trusteeship arrangement for Korea. During the early years of the war, trusteeship had surfaced as a way of dealing with Korea after the presumed defeat of the Japanese. At the Yalta Conference in February 1945

President Roosevelt had recommended that the United States, the British, the Soviets, and the Chinese serve as advisers or trustees to the new Korea that would emerge at war's end. These powers would help bring unity, a stable government, and, Roosevelt hoped, democracy to the peninsula. The Allied foreign ministers, meeting in Moscow in December 1945, confirmed the commitment to trusteeship. But trusteeship proved elusive. Koreans in the American zone of occupation soon became impatient with their occupiers and began insisting on a greater role in their own governance. As Americans attempted to establish stability in the South in the furtherance of trusteeship for the whole country, the Soviets were setting up a pro-Soviet regime north of the 38th parallel. This situation led one of the American political advisers in the country, William Langdon, to inform his superiors in Washington: "I am unable to fit trusteeship to actual conditions here or be persuaded of its suitability from moral and practical standpoints." American policy was too predicated, Langdon believed, on advising the Koreans and on cooperation with the Russians. The envisioned five-year trusteeship would cause intense resentment. Koreans should be allowed, he thought, to work out their own problems in the South and if possible, in the North.[6]

MacArthur in December 1945 agreed with Langdon's assessment. Continued insistence on trusteeship, he thought, might cause a revolt in Korea. What the United States needed to do was enter into an agreement with the Russians removing the 38th parallel as a barrier, make a public statement abandoning trusteeship, promise extensive Japanese reparations to the Koreans, and, most importantly, reiterate the Allied commitment to early independence. To continue drifting, as the general put it, created an extremely explosive situation in the South and did nothing positive toward solving the "problem" of Russian control in the North. Making matters worse was the fact that the two segments of Korea were interdependent economically and the United States had to subsidize the South to keep it afloat; something had to be done quickly or the United States occupation would fall into "a political-economic abyss." MacArthur urged serious consideration of a mutual agreement with the Russians "to withdraw forces from Korea simultaneously and leave Korea to its own devices and an inevitable internal upheaval for its self purification."[7]

The foreign ministers' meeting in Moscow in December 1945 resulted in an agreement that proved much easier to make than to implement. It called for a joint Soviet-American commission that would set up a provisional government for all of Korea after consultation with the most interested parties. The trusteeship would oversee the government for a period of five years. After an initial period of support for the trusteeship idea, the Soviets turned away from it. They did so for the same reasons that American Foreign Service officers had predicted. It was an unpopular idea with Koreans and the Communist Party began to lose strength throughout the country. With violent demonstrations occurring throughout the peninsula, the United States began suggesting in 1946 that, if the Joint Commission resulted in an early provisional government, trusteeship might not be necessary.[8]

What followed over the next two years would have made MacArthur's comments in December highly prophetic and his prescription wise had the latter been pursued. Through the spring of 1946 neither the United States nor the Soviet Union could agree to let the Joint Commission do its work. The United States, given its perception of an aggressive and expansionist Soviet regime with global aspirations, rejected the establishment of a government that resulted in communist domination. The Soviets in turn blocked the creation of a government that did not guarantee communist ascendancy.

In June 1946 the State Department developed a policy paper, accepted by both the War and Navy Departments and eventually implemented, that it hoped would break the impasse. The paper reiterated American objectives to create an independent, democratic Korea based on a sound economic system. Independence was important both for the Koreans themselves, and because an independent Korea would promote stability in East Asia. Conversely, Japanese or Russian domination of the country would threaten Manchuria and thus challenge the cornerstone of postwar American Asian policy—a strong, stable, noncommunist China. Korea, in other words, was increasingly tied to the China question in the minds of American policymakers. Korea also had to be viewed in the context of Soviet-American relations, which meant that an understanding over the peninsula could go a long way toward eliminating a potential flash point in the emerging Cold War. American officials did not see much latitude for maneuver. They decided that the only way to proceed was to develop some leverage with the Soviets and at the same time reduce the nationalist animosity in the South. This meant involving Koreans more directly in the administration of the South and providing greater amounts of American financial aid.[9]

Meanwhile, MacArthur seemed delighted to let the State Department wrestle with the Korean issue, stating within earshot of his secretary, Faubion Bowers, that he wanted no part of the Korean mess. Into 1946, Hodge made plea after plea to the Supreme Commander for help with Korean problems, only to be put off with polite replies that MacArthur was too busy with the occupation of Japan or did not know the situation in Korea sufficiently to offer advice. That the general had never in the past let a lack of knowledge constrain him from dogmatic assertion confirms his comments to Bowers.

Hodge visited in Tokyo on four separate occasions but never secured much direction from MacArthur—usually eliciting only the Supreme Commander's expansion of confidence in his work and admonishment to do what he thought best. When Hodge issued an appeal in the summer of 1946 for a quick transfer from the Korean cauldron, MacArthur refused, insisting that all he needed was a forty-day rest in the United States. Nor did MacArthur deign to visit Korea. Prior to the beginning of the Korean War, he traveled to the peninsula only once, for the inaugural ceremony of Syngman Rhee as president of the United Nations-sponsored government of Korea in August 1948. During the trip, he spent no time addressing political or military issues in the country.[10]

As a way of promoting the new American policy and evoking support from politically conscious Koreans, including both Left and Right, U.S. officials directed General Hodge to authorize the establishment of an interim legislative assembly in South Korea on August 24, 1946. The assembly, which began functioning on December 12, consisted of ninety members, forty-five of whom were appointed by the American military. Although the United States hoped that "moderates" would dominate in the assembly, forty of the elected seats went to rightists. The U.S. military tried to appoint some "moderates," but with only limited success. The Communists, as was expected, boycotted the assembly, which did not satisfy the nationalist impulse in the South, but was at least a measured step toward involving Koreans more directly in running their own affairs.

The new line of American policy prompted two developments in the fall of 1946, both of which brought the Korean situation into sharper focus. The Soviets urged resumption of the Joint Commission's activities toward creating a unified government, thus suggesting to American policymakers that the new leverage was working. At the same time, General Hodge passed along to Washington reports that the Soviets were preparing the North Koreans for an invasion of the South as a way to trigger mutual withdrawal of Soviet and American troops. John Carter Vincent of the State Department's Far Eastern Affairs office considered withdrawal premature and dangerous if done prior to creation of a fully functioning government for all of Korea. Interestingly General Hilldring, assistant secretary of state for occupied areas, foreshadowed what would soon become the military position: "If the Russians would come forward tomorrow," he told Vincent, "with a proposition for both of us to pull our troops out of Korea, we would decide, and very properly in my opinion, to haul our freight."[11]

By early 1947, the United States faced serious questions about Korea. Russian actions in Europe and the Mediterranean were moving U.S. officials to more muscular containment at the same time Congress tightened defense spending. Therefore, U.S. policymakers had to assess objectives and the means to achieve them, worldwide. No one in policy circles considered Korea a vital interest of the United States, and the army in particular was anxious to withdraw from that country. Nationalist verbal sniping at the United States occupation in the South reinforced the impulse to get out. But American officials hesitated to leave in the face of these pressures, and some feared withdrawal because that action could send the wrong message to the Soviets as well as to America's existing and potential Cold War allies.

General MacArthur, manifesting a degree of prescience if not wisdom, recommended a solution. Anticipating future U.S. policy, the Supreme Commander urged in January 1947 that American officials turn the Korean question over to the United Nations, while at the same time making a strong appeal to the Russians for a unification agreement. MacArthur's recommendation was very much in accord with his own developing strategic vision about U.S. interests in East Asia: he believed that the United States should be concerned primarily with defending a strategic perimeter off the coast of the Asian continent that included Japan, the Ryuku Islands, the Philippines, and the Aleutians, but excluded Korea. This was essentially the same defensive line that Secretary of State Dean Acheson enunciated in his famous, or infamous, National Press Club speech of January 12, 1950.[12]

MacArthur's Asian worldview and the concerns of the military about the nonstrategic value of Korea did not generate enthusiasm among key policymakers in Washington, particularly General Marshall, who had just returned from a year-long mission to China and had become secretary of state. Given the civil war in China, which the Communists would likely win, Marshall was concerned about Korea as another territory that could soon be lost to the Soviets. A noncommunist Korea could be valuable to the United States in the emerging Cold War standoff. He and Secretary of War Robert Patterson organized a panel to do a quick, intensive study of the Korean question. The panel concluded that drift and American occupation in the South were having deleterious effects in the peninsula. But the United States could not withdraw because it had made a commitment to establish an independent, unified Korea, and because to leave would cause a loss of American prestige in the test of strength with the Soviet Union. American credibility was at stake whether or not the peninsula had strategic value. The best course of action, the panel suggested, was to build up the South economically and bring more Koreans into the political process while continuing to negotiate with the Soviets. General Hodge and most civilian officials dealing with Korea agreed with the panel's recommendations. Secretary Patterson did not. Early withdrawal, he thought, was the only course that accorded with Korea's strategic value. MacArthur's views, depending on when he expressed them, both agreed and disagreed with Patterson's. Patterson ultimately acquiesced in the proposals because Acheson and Vincent convinced him that they offered the best means of eventually reducing American commitments.[13]

The new American approach worked in that it impelled the Soviets to renew negotiation toward unification, but they were not yet ready to accept unification of the peninsula on terms other than their own. The Joint Commission resumed its work but its achievements were no greater than before. The Soviets insisted on the disqualification of nearly all noncommunist groups from political activity.

In the meantime, Syngman Rhee and other so-called Rightists proved an embarrassment for the United States. They refused to cooperate with the commission, anticipating that if its efforts failed they could move more swiftly to create a separate government in the South. This caused consternation among American officials, who, while generally supportive of the conservatives and Rhee, were also distrustful. Rhee was a particular concern. One official portrayed him as "a vain man who loved flattery" and who "would sell his soul to be the chief of State of a united Korea, or even over South Korea if there is no united Korea." Another suggested that "Rhee was not mentally well-balanced," was "totally self-seeking," "a nuisance," and "a destructive force." Hodge in the summer of 1947 thought of throwing Rhee in jail, an inclination reflecting Hodge's temperament as much as Rhee's.[14]

By the end of 1947 American officials concluded that the best way out of the Korean mess was to take the matter to the United Nations. The plan was to create a separate South Korea through the device of UN auspices, a move that would bolster containment, satisfy world public opinion, preserve American credibility, and facilitate the removal of most American troops. Whether or not to guarantee the survival of an independent South Korea was the key question. George Kennan bluntly expressed his views on that matter to Walton Butterworth, director of the Office of Far Eastern affairs: "From the discussions we (meaning the Policy Planning Staff of the State Department) have had with members of the armed services on this question, we do not get the impression that Korea is militarily essential to us. If this is correct, we feel that our policy should be to cut our losses and get out of there as gracefully but promptly as possible."[15]

It was clear by early 1948 that two basic lines of thought were emerging among American policymakers. One held that, while it was not a particularly pleasant prospect for the United States, Soviet domination of the Korean peninsula probably could not be prevented and should not be resisted. Korea was simply not a good place for the United States to fight, nor a good place to contain the Soviet empire. It was too far from home, too inhospitable geographically, and contiguous to the Soviet Union. The second assessment deemed containment a seamless doctrine and, if the United States were to remain credible as a guarantor, it had to be prepared to take action in regions not always strategically vital—especially if the United States and the Soviet Union had already faced off in those areas.

In view of the contending lines of thought, the UN solution seemed not only a sensible resolution but also imperative for both international and intragovernmental reasons. Given its domination of the UN General Assembly in the late 1940s, the United States correctly saw the United Nations as an arm of American diplomacy and a vehicle for implementing U.S. Korean policy. The plan, in brief, was for the United Nations to create a commission that would send teams to Korea to hold elections throughout the country preparatory to the establishment of a UN-sponsored unified, national government. Since U.S. officials were aware from the start that the Soviets and the North Koreans would not permit UN teams to oversee elections in the North, two things were necessary: make certain the UN commission supervising the operation in Korea was answerable to the United States, and certify that the UN commission would go ahead with elections in the South even if indeed the Soviets blocked elections in the North. The UN General Assembly adopted the U.S. plan in January 1948 when it sent a commission to Korea to supervise elections. When denied access to the North, the commission sanctioned separate elections in the South.

The Soviets responded by working hard to prevent elections, both North and South. They orchestrated demonstrations, strikes, and propaganda against the UN efforts. Despite Soviet opposition, the elections took place in the South as scheduled on May 10, 1948, with Rhee's party receiving the overwhelming majority of the votes. Rhee, then seventy-three years old, became president of South Korea on August 15. In September the Soviets established the People's Republic of North Korea, which was immediately recognized by other communist countries and portrayed by the Soviet Union as the legitimate government of all of Korea. The Soviets also began withdrawing their troops and by December 1948 announced the removal of all of their forces. This announcement contained an element of deception, however, as the Soviets left a sizable body of advisers within the country and armed the North's forces much more heavily than the United States would do in the South.

Rhee's inauguration provided the occasion for General MacArthur's first visit to Korea. When the general, his wife, and his aides, including Whitney and Huff, arrived at Kimpo airfield on the morning of August 15, a large delegation of Koreans, led by Rhee himself, met and welcomed them. Hodge was there as well, though he would soon be on his way out of the country, much to his relief following prolonged conflict with Rhee. MacArthur responded enthusiastically to his hosts. He told Rhee, "I'm glad to see you. Indeed I wouldn't have missed this for the world." Later, at the inauguration ceremony in Seoul he told the newly elected president, privately, but within easy hearing of numerous newspaper correspondents, "If Korea should ever be attacked by the Communists, I will defend it as I would California." In his speech the supreme commander reinforced Rhee's own belligerent rhetoric about unifying the peninsula with force, if necessary. MacArthur said he was proud to stand on Korean soil "to see liberty reborn, the cause of right and justice prevail." Yet, he continued, he was saddened by one of the great tragedies of contemporary history, the artificial border across the peninsula. "This barrier," he said, "must and shall be torn down. Nothing shall prevent the ultimate unity of your people as freemen of a free nation." The general's words were not ambiguous: the United States would both guarantee the existence of South Korea and work assiduously to unify the country.[16]

When four days later Rhee flew to Tokyo for further consultation with MacArthur, the general again crossed the line into policymaking. He told the press after meeting Rhee that he would protect South Korea "as I would protect the United States."[17] MacArthur's motivation is hard to fathom, but it may have been related to his poor showing at the Republican convention held only two months earlier. Smarting from that ignominious defeat, he may well have been indicating that he would have been a far better choice than Thomas Dewey, that he would stand up to what he and many of his countrymen considered monolithic communism.

Whatever MacArthur's motivation, he had entered a policy area he should have avoided. There was serious debate within U.S. policy circles about guaranteeing the viability of Rhee's government, a debate into which no military officer had any business publicly intruding. The National Security Council (NSC) opposed abandoning the South Korean government because to do so would encourage Soviet-backed North Koreans to unify the country and make it part of the Soviet power system. A unified communist Korea would endanger Japan and China, and undercut the U.S. desire to write a peace treaty with Japan. The economic stability of Japan and American ability to leave Japan depended on Japan's economic relationships in the region, which in turn could be jeopardized if all of Korea were communist. More importantly, to abandon a government set up under UN auspices would weaken the world body. On the other hand, the NSC did not want to portray possible Soviet aggression in Korea as a casus belli. The solution was to strengthen South Korea, at least to some degree, and train its military. Most of the U.S. State Department came to agree with this assessment. The military favored getting out; the State Department, with the exception of Secretary Acheson, favored staying in for credibility's sake, and for the peninsula's "considerable" strategic value. In his 1948 pronouncements, MacArthur did not exactly endorse the State Department line, but he came close.

However well reasoned the State Department view may have been, Secretary Acheson did not believe it justified overturning the judgment of the national military establishment, and, from early 1949 until June 25, 1950, the line of thought that excluded Korea from America's defense perimeter remained ascendant. Consequently, when the UN General Assembly passed a resolution on December 12, 1948, calling upon the United States and the Soviet Union to withdraw troops from Korea as soon as was "practicable," U.S. officials made no attempt to use America's enormous influence to alter the decision.[18]

Accordingly, the army, which had begun a phased withdrawal in September, 1948, pulled out virtually all remaining U.S. forces in June 1949 despite State Department reservations. Furthermore, despite the considerable debate about guaranteeing the viability of South Korea's government, the United States did little to prepare the South for its own defense. Until June 1950, the United States had given the South Koreans approximately $17 million worth of weapons. These consisted of about 60 cannons, 140 antitank guns, 27 armored cars, and 10 training planes, but no tanks or heavy artillery. Altogether, American assistance helped arm a constabulary of fewer than 80,000 men, a military establishment recognized as inferior to that of North Korea. At the same time Acheson put pressure on the Rhee government to end the rampant inflation in the country and follow through with scheduled elections in the spring of 1950. In effect, Acheson informed Rhee that unless his government conformed to certain principles it would forfeit American support, a cogent reminder that the United States might at any time terminate the relationship.

MacArthur expressed his views on Korea twice during 1949, on both occasions contradicting what he had said privately to Rhee and publicly after Rhee's visit to Tokyo. Although he would later excoriate Acheson for his remarks in January 1950 to the National Press Club, MacArthur said effectively the same thing in March 1949. The American defense line in the Pacific included the Philippines, Okinawa, Japan, and the Aleutians; it did not include Taiwan, China, or Korea. In September, he told a group of congressmen that the United States should not be overly concerned about Korea. There was no need to give Rhee heavy weapons; there would be no Soviet-sponsored invasion of the South and little possibility the South would be overrun by the North. Privately, he may have believed the United States should back Rhee, who often spoke in bellicose terms about unifying the peninsula, or he may have believed that some of the time, because the struggle in Korea was part of the battle for freedom and universal ideals. Privately he may have thought of Korea as a critical area for the United States—in ways civilian officials in the United States had come to see it—and as essential to the credibility of containment. But there is simply little hard evidence that he really wished to do battle for Korea in the period prior to June 1950.[19]

When Secretary of State Acheson articulated the official definition of the defense perimeter in January 1950, Stalin probably assumed the definition governed American policy and would permit a relatively inexpensive North Korean unification of the country. One of the most distinguished scholars of American policy in Korea has noted, in any event, that Acheson, and ultimately President Truman, deserved blame for failing to signal Stalin that he should not back an invasion of the South. Of one thing there can be no doubt. The North under the leadership of Kim Il Sung could not and did not attack the South without Stalin's permission and support. The evolution of Soviet support for military action, we now know from Soviet documents, went back at least to March 1949. The Korean War, as one important scholar has argued, may have been a civil conflict, but only in part.[20]

In March 1949 Kim visited Moscow and implored Stalin to allow him to attack the South. He argued that the Rhee government would invade the North when it felt strong enough to do so, but that at the moment the North was stronger and could achieve its goal quickly. Moreover, Kim said, his forces could expect support from indigenous guerrillas willing to rise up against the reactionaries of the South. To all of this, Stalin expressed a firm negative, owing to his concern that the United States might yet respond with force and out of fear that Kim did not have sufficient force to achieve his goal. Stalin also knew of the North's economic weakness since the regime depended for its very existence on Soviet aid.

Kim did not give up. In mid-August he met with the Soviet ambassador to North Korea and again urged Stalin's support for an invasion of the South. He argued that, since American troops had withdrawn, there was no worry from that quarter, and that the 38th parallel had less meaning because of the mutual withdrawal of U.S. and Soviet troops. Moreover, Rhee's government had rejected calls for peaceful unification, meaning, according to Kim, that before too long South Korean forces would invade the North. Indeed, they were already attacking Kim's troops along the 38th parallel. Stalin again re-jected the request. He worried that the United States might return, but, most importantly, he failed to see the large superiority of force that Kim claimed to possess.

After Acheson's speech Stalin began to come around to Kim's position. Several factors accounted for this change of heart. The communist victory in China's civil war not only led to another major communist success in the world, it also contributed to a huge diminution of American prestige, because the United States had backed the losing Nationalist forces under Chiang Kai-shek. The United States now seemed more vulnerable in Asia than ever before. Beyond that, the Soviets had signed a treaty of alliance with the Peo-ple's Republic of China in February 1950 that would likely give the Ameri-cans pause as they contemplated any aggressive activity in Asia. Then, too, the Soviets had achieved a successful test of an atomic bomb the previous August, a development that gave them greater international standing among their communist satellite states and with the United States and its allies. Stalin was feeling good about the Soviet position in the world, and he clearly took into account Acheson's statement on January 12 that excluded Korea from the U.S. defense perimeter.[21]

Stalin also responded to the unilateral move to conclude a peace treaty with Japan. John Foster Dulles, who played a leading role in the negotiations to arrange the treaty and subsequently served as secretary of state under Pres-ident Eisenhower, always believed the Korean conflict was at least in part a Stalinist riposte to the American effort toward Japan. And it takes no great perspicacity to believe that the presence of Secretary of Defense Louis John-son, the Joint Chiefs of Staff, and Dulles in Japan at the same time during the spring of 1950 signaled an American rebuilding and remilitarization of Japan, and thus influenced the timing of the Soviet/North Korean action.[22]

Kim received Stalin's positive decision during another visit to Moscow in April 1950. To reinforce his request, this time Kim stressed that the North Koreans must be allowed to emulate their brethren in China. It made little sense to see the Chinese revolution succeed and not permit Communists to unify Korea, an argument to which Stalin was receptive assuming the Chi-nese would also go along with Kim's plan to attack the South. In May Kim stopped in Beijing where he received Mao's unenthusiastic approval. The Chinese leader was much more concerned about taking Taiwan than he was about Korean unification, but he went along. At this point Stalin confi-dently provided material to mobilize North Korean forces for battle while se-curing Kim's agreement to portray the start of the conflict as a defensive struggle occasioned by a South Korean invasion of the North. The latter was the more plausible because of Syngman Rhee's ongoing bellicosity. On June 25, Kim sent his troops across the 38th parallel.[23]

What Stalin did not know, or did not, in retrospect, seem adequately aware of, was the line of thought contending with the view expressed in Acheson's National Press Club speech. This line of thought had slipped below the surface in American policy circles but it was not far below the surface. It only took aggressive action by the Soviets to bring it into ascendancy. Several things account for this development. One was the continuing attack on the Truman administration by Senator Joseph McCarthy of Wisconsin that Truman and his advisers were not tough enough on the Soviet Union, and that both the Truman and Roosevelt administrations had harbored and protected Communists. Another was the growing belief that the administration had done too little to prevent the fall of China to the Communists, meaning to many that it was allowing a red tide to sweep over both Europe and Asia. Still another was the considered opinion of many leading policymakers that Korea had value—strategically, psychologically, to the viability of containment, and as a symbol of the value of the United Nations.

What MacArthur truly believed into June of 1950 is hard to determine, but it was probably something close to what he had expressed in March of the previous year—something similar to Acheson's January 1950 pronouncement. After all, that was the essential military opinion. He claimed later that he had for some time held a more positive view of Korea's importance. Although he never asserted it, that may be partly true, as he was coming closer and closer to a hard line on communism in all of Asia after the fall of the Kuomintang in China. He came to see Chiang Kai-shek highly favorably, as did his Republican friends in the United States, and, as the occupation of Japan was coming to an end, he expressed a desire to become adviser to and commander of Chiang's military. He clearly included Taiwan within the U.S. defense perimeter.

By the beginning of 1950 Taiwan was a complicated case for policymakers and military officials in Washington, as well as for MacArthur. President Truman, averse to pouring more American money down what he considered the rat hole of Nationalist China, on January 5, 1950, specifically stated that he opposed military support for Chiang's forces, then ensconced in Taiwan, whence they had fled from the mainland in the fall of 1949. Acheson on January 12, 1950, omitted Taiwan from the U.S. defense perimeter, though it is by no means clear that the United States would have abjured involvement in the face of a Chinese communist military offensive to seize the island. Both emerging strategic concerns and political pressures from the American Right probably would have led to

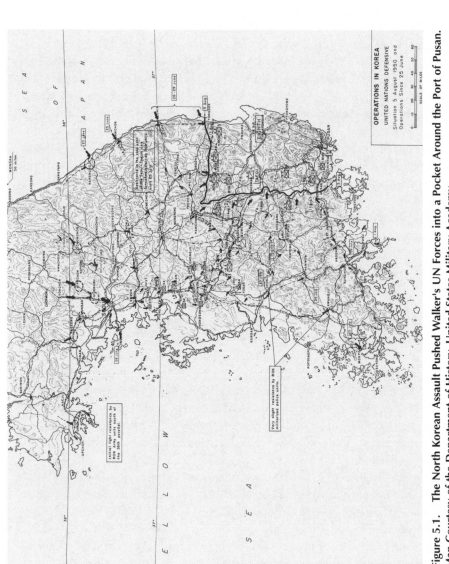

Figure 5.1. The North Korean Assault Pushed Walker's UN Forces into a Pocket Around the Port of Pusan. Map Courtesy of the Department of History, United States Military Academy.

U.S. attempts to secure the island's defense. In the spring of 1950, the Joint Chiefs of Staff began recommending support for what remained of Chiang's military, and they urged that MacArthur either go himself or send a mission to Taiwan to determine the generalissimo's military requirements. By the end of May 1950, MacArthur pronounced Taiwan "an unsinkable aircraft carrier," which could be used by the Soviets to accomplish an aggressive strategy in East Asia. "The strategic interests of the United States," he told Secretary of Defense Louis Johnson, "will be in serious jeopardy if Formosa (the Portuguese name for Taiwan) is allowed to be dominated by a power hostile to the United States."[24] Interestingly, MacArthur, even as his views on Taiwan evolved, still did not include Korea as an area essential to U.S. interests as of early June 1950.

In any event, after the final pullout of American troops from Korea in June 1949, MacArthur no longer had authority over the peninsula. That responsibility fell to the State Department, for which the general was ever grateful. If he could not have command and control, he wanted nothing to do with the sticky issue of Korea.

Once American officials concluded that Soviet-North Korean aggression rendered inaction impossible, which they did immediately after the invasion, they decided on June 26 to aid South Korea with air and naval forces. This decision received the support of both the civilian and military sectors of the policy establishment. Then, when it became apparent that naval and air units alone could not save South Korea, American officials on June 30 agreed to commit two divisions of ground forces, thus undertaking what major strategists had long opposed: a land war on the continent of Asia. From June 1950 until July 1953, the United States fought a major war over territory that until June 25 had been officially considered tangential. MacArthur now had a last chance at glory.

Notes

1. OSS Memorandum to President Truman, June 25, 1945, OSS Memoranda, Harry S. Truman Library, Independence, Mo. For an assessment of Soviet and American objectives, see Russell D. Buhite, *Soviet-American Relations in Asia, 1945–1954* (Norman: University of Oklahoma Press, 1981), 139–41.

2. Buhite, *Soviet-American Relations in Asia,* 144.

3. Buhite, *Soviet-American Relations in Asia,* 144–45.

4. Quoted in D. Clayton James, *The Years of MacArthur, Volume 3, 1945–1964* (Boston: Houghton Mifflin, 1985), 391.

5. Buhite, *Soviet-American Relations in Asia,* 144–45.

6. Langdon to the Secretary of State, Nov. 20, 1945, Department of State, *Foreign Relations of the United States 1945*, vol. 6, 1130–31 (hereafter cited as *FRUS*).

7. *FRUS*, 1147–48.

8. Buhite, *Soviet-American Relations in Asia*, 148–49.

9. *FRUS*, *1946*, vol. 8, 697–98.

10. James, *The Years of MacArthur, Volume 3*, 392–93.

11. *FRUS*, *1946*, vol. 8, 764–65. Quoted in Buhite, *Soviet-American Relations in Asia*, 153.

12. Buhite, *Soviet-American Relations in Asia*, 154. See also *FRUS*, *1947*, vol. 6, 601–3.

13. Buhite, *Soviet-American Relations in Asia*, 154–56.

14. *FRUS*, *1947*, vol. 6, 703–4, 646, 746.

15. *FRUS*, *1947*, vol. 6, 814. Buhite, *Soviet-American Relations in Asia*, 158–59.

16. Quoted in James, *The Years of MacArthur, Volume 3*, 395.

17. James, *The Years of MacArthur, Volume 3*, 395.

18. Buhite, *Soviet-American Relations in Asia*, 160–68.

19. James, *The Years of MacArthur, Volume 3*, 399–402.

20. See William Stueck, *Rethinking the Korean War: A New Diplomatic and Strategic History* (Princeton, N.J.: Princeton University Press, 2002), 79–81. Also see William Stueck, *The Korean War: An International History* (Princeton, N.J.: Princeton University Press, 1995), 3–30.

21. See Stueck, *Rethinking the Korean War*, 69–77.

22. Buhite, *Soviet-American Relations in Asia*, 136.

23. Stueck, *The Korean War*, 35–37. Stueck, *Rethinking the Korean War*, 73–75. Much of the recent thinking on the beginning of war in Korea, including Stueck's, comes from Kathryn Weathersby, "Soviet Aims in Korea and the Origin of the Korean War, 1945–1950: New Evidence from Russian Archives," working paper no. 8, Cold War International History Project, Woodrow Wilson International Center for Scholars, 1993; and Weathersby, "Korea, 1949–1950: To Attack or Not to Attack? Stalin, Kim Il Sung and the Prelude to War," working paper no. 8, Cold War International History Project, Woodrow Wilson International Center for Scholars, Spring 1995.

24. *FRUS*, *1950*, vol. 6, 161–65. Also quoted in James, *The Years of MacArthur, Volume 3*, 408–10.

~

CHAPTER SIX

Hubris Unbounded

A fundamental obligation of the historian is to retrieve and order the past. That task is made difficult by chaos in the human condition, by confusion in the recording of events, by contradictions over time in what individuals do and say and think, or by an overload of information that may often be as intellectually debilitating as insufficient data.

A cursory examination of intelligence indicates similar difficulty. Information available about Japanese capability and intentions in the months prior to Pearl Harbor would suggest—as it has to many—culpability on the part of President Roosevelt and his advisors. At the very least it suggests (wrongly, in the view of the most careful scholars) that, if American officials did not anticipate the events of December 7, 1941, they might have done so. That the administration of President George W. Bush had plenty of information providing warning of terrorist attacks prior to the World Trade Center Towers' destruction on September 11, 2001, now seems beyond dispute. But for Bush's people, as for Roosevelt's, sifting through a welter of incomplete or conflicting data, gaps in that information, and misinterpretation of the facts, resulted in an obvious policy failure. A policy failure in this sense may be interpreted as consisting of an inability to take what becomes known, or seems to be known, and anticipating what might happen. Such a failure occurred at the start of the Korean War. General MacArthur shared in that failure just as he shared in several flawed military and foreign policy decisions during that conflict.

In the months and weeks prior to June 25, 1950, intelligence reports from a variety of sources said both that a North Korean attack was imminent and that such an attack was unlikely. When the Joint Chiefs of Staff visited with General MacArthur in January and February, they came away with the opinion that there was no crisis on the Korean horizon, but that, even if there were, the government of the South could handle it. At the same time, Central Intelligence Agency (CIA) agents reported that North Koreans were undertaking a military buildup just north of the 38th parallel preparatory to an invasion, the date of which they did not predict. Secretary of State Dean Acheson later conceded that a possible invasion had been considered or predicted for some time but without an assessment of just when it would occur. Army intelligence, meanwhile, did not think an invasion would occur any time soon. When John Foster Dulles, then a State Department advisor working on the peace treaty with Japan, visited Korea in mid-June 1950, he discounted the possibility of an attack. MacArthur's intelligence officer, General Charles Willoughby, did predict an imminent invasion, but also submitted reports contradicting that prediction; moreover, his abrasive manner and habitual rudeness tended to make his reports unwelcome in Washington.[1]

At roughly 3:00 p.m. Washington time on Saturday, June 24, North Korea, with logistical backing from the Soviet Union and assurance of support from the People's Republic of China (PRC), initiated the Korean War. (It was 4:00 a.m. Sunday, June 25, on the Korean peninsula.) The American ambassador to South Korea, John Muccio, did not report the attack until 9:30 p.m. Washington time. In other words, the North Koreans were six and one-half hours into the invasion, advancing rapidly toward Seoul, before top officials of the U.S. government received official word. Secretary of State Acheson was on his farm in Maryland. President Truman was visiting with his family in Independence, Missouri. When the secretary of state informed Truman that Saturday night, the president immediately decided to return to Washington the next afternoon (Sunday, the 25th), and he urged Acheson to go forward with a proposal that the United States call a meeting of the UN Security Council, also on that Sunday afternoon.

General MacArthur's report to Washington was even slower than Muccio's, coming in fourteen hours after the attack. His response to the invasion itself, however, came much more quickly: He gave orders on Sunday the 25th, Tokyo time, that U.S. ships, under cover of air support, provide munitions to South Korean forces. That the general issued this order prior to receiving authorization from his Pentagon superiors demonstrates two important points: He was behaving in typical MacArthur fashion, arrogantly assuming that he knew better and sooner than officials in Washington what to do; and he had indeed come around to thinking that Korea was of value.

In other words, the overt military act by the communist side in Korea may have brought to the forefront of his consciousness a long-gestating concern that writing Korea off strategically, leaving it outside the defense perimeter, had been a mistake—an error in which he had shared but about which he was coming to have second, and third, thoughts.[2]

Meanwhile, with the Soviet Union absent from the Security Council the United Nations met on Sunday afternoon, June 25, to address the Korean problem. The Soviets' absence represented a continuation of their boycotting of the Security Council to protest Nationalist China's presence there rather than a delegate from the Communist People's Republic. Often explained as Soviet indifference to the North Korean invasion or lack of Stalin's foreknowledge of it, the absence is probably better explained in terms of bureaucratic inertia or events getting ahead of anticipated Western responses. In any event, the UN meeting at Lake Success, New York (the site of such sessions prior to the completion of the new facilities in the city) produced a resolution demanding that North Korea halt its attack and withdraw back across the 38th parallel.

When President Truman reached Washington on the evening of June 25, he found that his subordinates had taken several important steps, many of them orchestrated by Secretary of State Acheson. Military and State Department officials conveyed to MacArthur a preview of their later recommendations to Truman that the United States should attempt at least limited military support for South Korea. At the meeting with Truman at 8:00 p.m. at Blair House, where President Truman was living during renovations of the White House, Acheson worked diligently to keep the focus on Korea rather than on Taiwan, which some of his colleagues considered far more important strategically than the Korean peninsula and which Chinese communist forces seemed on the verge of seizing. Truman agreed to authorize MacArthur to provide military supplies to the South Koreans and to use air and sea power to blunt the North Korean offensive. The general was to protect the area around Seoul until American dependents could be evacuated. Reflecting his disgust with MacArthur's ambitions and his knowledge of the general's behavior over the years, Truman refused at that initial Blair House meeting to appoint MacArthur to the commander-in-chief assignment in Korea.[3]

MacArthur's rosy belief in the South Koreans' ability to defend themselves soon gave way to abject pessimism, and by June 26 he reported that the South would surely fall without a major American intervention. His pessimism was soon reflected in decisions made at another Blair House meeting on June 27 in which Truman and his advisors agreed that American air forces could attack any and all North Korean military targets south of the 38th parallel, and that the United States would move the 7th Fleet into the Taiwan Strait. The decision on the placement of the fleet, announced publicly the next day, while portrayed as a neutralizing act designed as much to prevent Nationalist aggression against the mainland as to stop a PRC attack on Taiwan, was clearly aimed at Communist China. It also embodied MacArthur's and Washington's growing belief that Taiwan was not only strategically valuable in its own right but the North Korean invasion might be the beginning of a global communist offensive.

Consonant with this assessment, President Truman suggested on the 27th that Taiwan might be declared a part of Japan, in effect renewing its colonial status, and hence within the U.S. Far Eastern command. Persuaded by Acheson that this would be a terrible idea, Truman did authorize more military aid to the Philippines and support for the French in Indochina. The next day Truman informed congressional leaders of his decision, emphasizing correctly that the Soviets had played a part in the invasion. He suggested further that the Soviets might be on their way to aggression in multiple areas of the world. To what extent Truman was seeking to undercut political criticism in the United States flowing from both responsible members of the Republican Party, who chastised his inability to thwart communist expansion, and the venomous spew of Senator Joseph McCarthy of Wisconsin, who had his own cynical purposes, is an open question. There is no doubt, however, that Truman saw a U.S. response in Korea as necessary to maintain the credibility of containment, to prove that the United States would not appease aggression as it had done prior to WWII.[4]

The question of MacArthur's command in Korea remained unsettled until July, but the general's assigned responsibilities, not to say his actions, were rapidly determining his authority. Deciding to see for himself what was happening in Korea, particularly if South Korean forces could put up effective resistance to the North Korean onslaught, the general on June 29 flew to an airstrip at Suwon about thirty miles south of Seoul. What he found there was disheartening. The airfield on which his plane landed had been partially damaged by North Korean bombing just hours before, and the South Korean army was disintegrating before his very eyes. As he ventured forth to the Han River, mortar shells landed within one hundred yards of where he stood, and remnants of South Korea's forces, now numbering about 25,000, were rapidly retreating. The other 70,000–80,000 had either been killed or captured or had fled in the face of the enemy. When he returned to Tokyo later that day, he determined that only American ground forces from Japan could save South Korea, and he conveyed his views to Washington.[5]

On June 30, MacArthur received authorization from President Truman not only to continue air strikes against North Korean targets in South Korea but also to utilize ground forces to hold the area around Pusan. In addition he was authorized to conduct air attacks north of the 38th parallel, an authorization that he had once again anticipated. A day before receiving the directive from the Joint Chiefs of Staff he had ordered General George Stratemeyer to conduct air raids in the North. Once again, as when he had approved the shipment of arms to the South without Pentagon endorsement, he could be accused of either arrogant independence or exceptional foresight. As biographer D. Clayton James has observed, he ran considerable risk with the second anticipation of orders because officials in Washington were greatly concerned that the United States do nothing in Korea to provoke war with either the Soviet Union or China. Whatever one's opinion of MacArthur, there is no mistaking the fact that decisions in Washington on June 30 to carry the air war to the North and utilize U.S. ground forces in the South represented the point of no return for the United States in the Korean conflict. MacArthur's strong recommendations in favor of ground forces affected that decision.[6]

Since the United States had taken the Korean crisis to the United Nations on June 25 and since the UN had condemned the North Korean attack and urged member states to repel the invader, the question of President Truman's responsibility to the U.S. Congress quickly arose. Was that responsibility superseded by loyalty to the United Nations, and what sort of military command should be established? Truman, to the detriment of the U.S. Constitution and against the wishes of congressional leaders, abjured a congressional vote. He claimed authority as commander in chief to act in an emergency capacity.

As historian Arthur Schlesinger points out in his introduction to *General MacArthur and President Truman*, the president was neither a constitutional scholar nor a legal expert. He relied on Secretary of State Acheson, a distinguished attorney and former law clerk for U.S. Supreme Court Justice Louis Brandeis, for advice on this point. Acheson advised not going to Congress, but instead relying on the president's inherent executive powers as well as the United Nations resolutions. Acheson's reasoning was as flawed as was a State Department cataloging of instances in which U.S. presidents had in the past undertaken military interventions without congressional authorization. The latter list identified U.S. actions against private, revolutionary bands, terrorists, and other extranational groups, but cited no instance of warfare against a sovereign state. Truman's avoidance of congressional authority unfortunately set an unhappy precedent for the war-making behavior of subsequent American presidents who assumed virtually unchecked powers.[7]

When President Truman on June 30 gave MacArthur "full authority to use the ground forces under his command" in Korea, he tacitly settled the issue of who would be the commander of American and United Nation forces. He formally settled the matter a week later. During the first week of July, the UN Security Council directed that member states wishing to join in the effort to halt the North Koreans' advance should contribute troops to a unified command under the auspices of the United States. The latter was to designate the commander. Although Truman had "little regard or respect" for MacArthur, he believed he had no choice in making the appointment. The Joint Chiefs of Staff submitted only MacArthur's name; MacArthur was already acting in the capacity of a commander; and the president, like Roosevelt before him, worried that the general, through his longtime Republican friends, could create complications for American policy. Despite personal reservations and MacArthur's advanced age (he was then seventy) Truman endorsed the Joint Chiefs' nomination. MacArthur was ecstatic as he responded to the president: "I can only repeat the pledge of my complete personal loyalty to you as well as an absolute devotion to your monumental struggle for peace and good will throughout the world." The general also expressed gratitude to Truman for his earlier assignment as supreme commander in Japan.[8]

Whether or not MacArthur was already overburdened by other duties and slowed by age, as his preeminent biographer has suggested, there can be little doubt that other officers might have been better suited to the assignment. Though MacArthur's claims to special knowledge of Asia might have been partially true, surely someone with a broader worldview, a general officer with a greater concern about American policy toward Eurasia and not just Asia, would have been a better choice. Generals J. Lawton Collins, Matthew Ridgway, and Maxwell Taylor were not only younger but had a greater sense of Washington's global strategies than MacArthur. Truman thus created a problem for himself with the initial decision in the command assignment.[9]

MacArthur began his command in Korea with distinct liabilities, some but not all of which were of his own making. American forces in Japan had spent more service in idleness, frequenting bars and prostitutes and simply biding their time, than in training. MacArthur may be faulted for failure to bring these forces to fighting status. The Eighth Army was an army mainly in name at the start of the war. The air forces under the general's command were no better, but this was less of an issue, given the paucity of planes on the North Korean side. Washington shared in the blame, indeed deserved a greater share of the blame than MacArthur, owing to severe cutbacks in military staffing and focusing U.S. military strength, particularly the B-29 long-range bomber capable of delivering the atomic bomb and other new equipment, on Europe and the Soviet Union.

Never shy about expressing his needs or his strategic and tactical preferences, MacArthur proceeded along two lines in July. Given the North Koreans' strong drive southward, he recognized the urgent need for more American troops. So almost simultaneously with his formal appointment as commander, he asked his superiors in Washington for four additional divisions on July 8. One day later he doubled the previous day's request, calling this time for eight divisions. These requests created a quandary at home where military planners worried that sending so many troops to Korea would deplete National Guard and Reserve units and weaken the American response capability not only elsewhere in the world but within the United States should an emergency occur. MacArthur's hope was to stop the North Korean offensive and hold the line near Pusan on the southeast coast of the Korean peninsula.

If MacArthur could not justly say that he received insufficient troop and supply support during WWII, he certainly could not make the claim in Korea—at least not for long. Before he moved forward with the Inchon landing he possessed nearly 200,000 troops, and, by the end of September, he had approximately 300,000. They did not arrive as rapidly as he would have wished; by the end of July Washington had sent him only about 45,000. But an important point to remember is that during the fierce defense at Pusan and subsequent breakout northward, his forces outnumbered the North Koreans. Moreover, Congress at the same time approved roughly a fourfold increase in military spending for everything from airplanes to tanks, trucks, and munitions.

To assess MacArthur's requests and actual needs, President Truman in mid-July directed the Joint Chiefs of Staff to send representatives to Tokyo to meet with the Far Eastern commander. During these conferences with MacArthur, the representatives, Generals Lawton Collins and Hoyt Vandenberg along with several staff officers, learned that the commander had come to appreciate, far more than he had done at the start of the war, the strength and toughness of the North Korean army. They also learned, not surprisingly given the general's myopic worldview, that he thought everything available in military support should be used to stop communism in Asia. MacArthur revealed for the first time his plan for an invasion behind enemy lines at Inchon, twenty miles to the west of Seoul. Collins questioned this plan owing to the area's high tides, craggy sea wall, and marshy terrain.

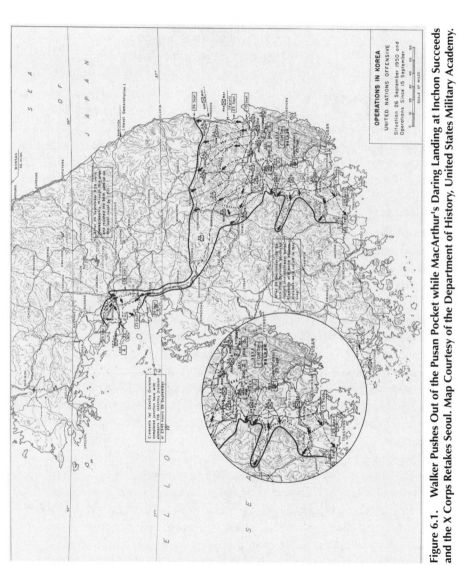

Figure 6.1.   Walker Pushes Out of the Pusan Pocket while MacArthur's Daring Landing at Inchon Succeeds and the X Corps Retakes Seoul. Map Courtesy of the Department of History, United States Military Academy.

The final decision on the matter awaited a considerable debate, in which MacArthur eventually prevailed—to his credit, given the operation's striking success, but also to his debit because the ultimate American military triumph there reinforced the overweening hubris that ultimately contributed to his downfall.

Contributing as well to MacArthur's fall from power was his ongoing alliance with Chiang Kai-shek on Taiwan. While the general agreed in the summer of 1950 with Truman and Acheson that the United States should not accept Chiang's offer of troops for the Korean conflict (they would be "an albatross," MacArthur said), he did believe that a buildup of Chiang's military would prevent the Chinese communists on the mainland from transferring troops from the area of the Taiwan Strait northward for possible use in Korea. And, as MacArthur informed Collins while the latter was in Tokyo, he would soon make a visit to Taipei. Since the generalissimo is "anticommunist," he said, "we should support him." The State Department, he further opined, should "forget its vendetta," forget, in other words, its continuing effort to depose Chiang.[10]

With the approval or at least indulgence of the Joint Chiefs, MacArthur flew to Taiwan on July 31 to confer with Chiang. Though they did not move to stop it, the visit made Truman and Acheson, as well as a number of State Department officials, uneasy. The substance of the MacArthur-Chiang discussions alarmed them even more. MacArthur did not hide from the press his desire to build up the generalissimo's military, and, after meeting with Chiang, he stated that "arrangements have been completed for effective coordination between American forces under my command and those of the Chinese Government."[11] Jointly, the United States and Chiang would resist any attack by the People's Republic of China. MacArthur had not moved at this point to the "unleashing" of Chiang's military to attack the mainland, a position he adopted after Chinese intervention in Korea. But he seemed close to endorsing the opinions of Truman's Republican critics who remained enamored with the anticommunist Chiang and who blamed Truman's administration for the communist accession to power in China—for the alleged "loss of China."

Given MacArthur's bold excursion into foreign policy and his seeming disregard for President Truman's commitment to the "neutralization" of Taiwan, the president felt compelled to respond. He did not want war with China. He did not want a war with the Soviet Union that the Sino-Soviet Pact of February 1950 could trigger in the event of a U.S.-backed Nationalist attack on the mainland. Truman and Acheson agreed with U.S. military leaders that there was no alternative to stopping the North Korean aggression, but Korea was not the occasion or the interest for which the United States should consider a war with its main communist adversaries.

Truman's concern came to a head when General MacArthur announced upon returning to Tokyo that the United States should dispatch jet fighter planes to Taiwan. Fearing that possession of such planes could embolden Chiang to try a return to the mainland, Truman warned that only he possessed the authority to authorize action against the Chinese mainland, a statement that led MacArthur to acknowledge limitations on his authority. Despite this dustup with the Far Eastern commander, President Truman did soon authorize a nearly $300 million military aid commitment to Taiwan.

But the president did not forget easily. Indeed, he tucked away in his mind the indiscretions MacArthur committed while serving as U.S./UN commander. Among his memories was a comment made to him by his assistant press secretary, Eben Ayers, that John Foster Dulles had come to the conclusion the general should be "hauled" back to Washington, an assessment Dulles had made upon dealing with MacArthur on the Japanese peace treaty. That Ayers probably misrepresented what Dulles actually said is beside the point; President Truman believed him, and Truman's opinion of the general did not improve. When MacArthur attacked Truman's policy toward China, as he did during a visit to Tokyo by Truman's adviser Averell Harriman and General Matthew Ridgway in the summer of 1950, the president was not comforted about his general's attitude toward Taiwan. Nor was Harriman convinced at MacArthur's insistence that he would fully abide by the president's directives toward the island. MacArthur, Harriman said, did not agree "on the way he believed things should be handled on Formosa and with the Generalissimo." The general objected to the State Department's negative opinion of Chiang and suggested that it could be good for the United States if Chiang attacked the mainland.[12]

Either out of certitude in his own assessments or contempt for his superiors, MacArthur often compounded his indiscretions. He quickly did so on the Taiwan matter. Drawing upon his earlier, and still classified, statement about Taiwan's strategic value, that the island was in effect on an "unsinkable aircraft carrier," on August 20 the general accepted an invitation from the Veterans of Foreign Wars (VFW) to forward a message to their Chicago convention. His message, which he sent quickly and enthusiastically, reiterated his belief in Chiang Kai-shek as an important ally and the great value to the United States in denying Taiwan to the Communists: the argument, he said, one rooted in appeasement, "that if we defend Formosa we alienate continental Asia," was deeply flawed.[13]

When Truman, Acheson, Harriman, and the Joint Chiefs of Staff learned from a *U.S. News and World Report* article of the VFW message on August 25, they were incensed. The JCS saw the general's revelation of classified material as an unacceptable breach of military conduct. The president and his civilian advisers worried that MacArthur's comment would be seen as signaling a new American policy on Taiwan—to Chiang, to the People's Republic of China, and to allies around the world—that we were embracing the generalissimo, that we might use Taiwan as a base for invading China, or that we were giving Chiang a green light to take military action against the mainland. How could the commander of UN and U.S. troops in the Korean conflict speak in such a manner and not have his remarks interpreted as official American policy? Truman quickly directed that MacArthur withdraw his statement and the general complied, but it was too late; news of the general's views spread internationally, to the detriment of coherence of Truman's policy toward China and the Soviet Union and to the president's strongly avowed desire that the Korean War remain limited and confined to Korea. The president later said to anyone who would listen that he should have fired MacArthur then and there. What he did do then and there was dismiss his secretary of defense, Louis Johnson, whose deference to MacArthur and overall erratic behavior had become intolerable, and replace him with General Marshall, a man Truman had long admired.

American policy toward the Nationalist Chinese on Taiwan would repeatedly reemerge, but, before that issue intensified, the U.S. fortunes of war in Korea also turned repeatedly. The first turn was highly favorable to the U.S. side, including, as it did, a major offensive behind enemy lines and a highly effective pincer movement that severely crippled North Korean forces. By the end of August U.S. air forces, virtually unimpeded in their strikes in North Korea, had destroyed most of the military and industrial sites of value beyond the 38th parallel. American air and infantry power meanwhile had so battered the North Korean army that U.S. commanders were surprised at the ferocity of an attack the enemy was able to launch on the perimeter around Pusan. Over a ten-day period of difficult fighting U.S./UN forces inflicted over 10,000 casualties on the North Koreans. This was possible because the United States had supplied the Eighth Army with vastly superior equipment to that of North Korea, both in quantity and quality.

In July, MacArthur had begun planning an amphibious landing at Inchon twenty miles west of Seoul and the city's port, which he hoped to launch on September 15. As noted earlier, Generals Omar Bradley and Lawton Collins were dubious of the plan, as were many other top officers. They thought it too risky; tides were too high at Inchon and the terrain there terribly inhospitable to an invading force. They also thought that, even if the landing succeeded, a linkup with General Walton Walker's Eighth Army far to the southeast would be extremely difficult. They counseled instead a landing twenty miles or more south of Inchon. General MacArthur would have none of the naysaying. At a military conference in Tokyo on August 23 he extolled the great virtue of surprise in warfare and indicated that an Inchon landing would result in his own "Plains of Abraham"—a reference to the attack on Quebec by British General James Wolfe in 1759 during the French and Indian War. "We shall land at Inchon and I shall crush them," he told the other military officers. The general ultimately overwhelmed the opposition with his confidence. The Joint Chiefs on August 28 gave their tepid approval of the plan.

As MacArthur began putting the pieces in place for the landing (called "Chromite"), officials in Washington developed second thoughts. The general's plan to use a force of 71,000 troops might diminish the resistance in the perimeter near Pusan, and it was terribly risky; the Joint Chiefs asked on September 7 for MacArthur's reconsideration. He responded annoyingly but effusively: "There is no question in my mind as to the feasibility of the operation and I regard its chance of success as excellent." Then he reassured the Joint Chiefs of Staff about Pusan: "There is not the slightest possibility . . . of our forces being ejected from the Pusan beachhead."[14]

MacArthur's landing at Inchon succeeded brilliantly, but not without considerable risk. Had the North Koreans taken time to fortify the area or to plant mines, or had they not weakened themselves so severely in their drive southward, the invasion could have been a disaster. Instead, the landing proved such a stunning success that MacArthur, never one to submit pliantly to authority, seemed thereafter not only beyond reproach but immune to criticism. His offensive at Inchon and the eventual linking up with the Eighth Army resulted in the capture of 130,000 North Korean troops and over 200,000 North Korean causalities. The North Korean defeat subsequent to Inchon eliminated the North Korean army as an independent fighting force. MacArthur's participation in a ceremony restoring President Syngman Rhee to the capital in Seoul on September 29 (where the American rather than a UN flag flew atop the capitol building along side the Korean banner) symbolized the success and the general's wisdom. The operation enhanced his sense of infallibility.

For years after the hard, bitter stalemate that resulted in Korea after the Chinese intervention in November 1950, critics on the Left in American politics blamed MacArthur for the decision, following the Inchon success, to push beyond the 38th parallel. MacArthur favored that move but the decision was a much more complicated one than the critics alleged. Since unifi-cation of Korea was not the major purpose of United States intervention at the beginning of the war, the evolution of American objectives requires elu-cidation. The main responsibility for the invasion of North Korea resides with several State and Defense Department officials and a set of military cir-cumstances that effectively neutralized all opposition. John Allison, director of the Office of Northeast Asian Affairs, appears to have been the first Amer-ican policymaker to question the assumption that the United States should seek only the restoration of the status quo ante bellum. On July 1, as South Korean and United Nations forces were reeling under North Korean blows on the southern part of the peninsula, Allison wrote a memorandum to Dean Rusk arguing that the United States should not recognize the "artificial divi-sion" of the 38th parallel and should, if possible, pursue North Korean troops to the Yalu River. Certainly, he averred, American officials should make no premature announcement of an intention to stop at the 38th parallel.[15]

Allison did not rest with his July 1 memo to Rusk. On July 13, again for Rusk's benefit, he criticized the public statement of a United States military official who had said that the United States sought only to force North Ko-rea out of South Korea. Rusk agreed with Allison and urged Secretary of State Acheson and President Truman to postpone any announcements or decisions about the 38th parallel. John Foster Dulles provided immediate support for Allison and Rusk. If it possessed the power to do so, he said, the United States should destroy the North Korean army and "obliterate the line as a political division."[16]

The State Department Policy Planning Staff opposed the Allison, Rusk, Dulles position. George Kennan and his associates on the Planning Staff be-lieved that American military action in North Korea would incur the risk of Soviet or Chinese intervention; for strategic reasons these communist coun-tries would view with alarm the potential overthrow of North Korea's com-munist regime. This risk of inciting conflict with Russia or China outweighed any possible benefit in the crossing of the 38th parallel; consequently the United States should announce to the world its limited intention of restor-ing the status quo. Staff member Herbert Feis urged that the United States "publicly disassociate" itself from the contemporary notion that North Ko-rea's invasion had nullified the meaning of the 38th parallel. Kennan be-lieved that the United States should repel aggression in the South and then "terminate its involvement on the mainland of Asia."[17]

The Policy Planning Staff's argument did not dissuade Allison and Rusk, and, at the end of July, Allison succeeded in gaining a modification of the Planning Staff's position. Allison stressed that aggression must not go unpunished and that true security could come to South Korea only by invading the North. The Planning Staff subsequently recommended deferral of any decision on the 38th parallel "until military and political developments provide additional information."[18] Though not yet a clear-cut victory for Allison, deferral did represent a setback for those who desired a statement of intent to stop at the 38th parallel.

Events and decisions over the following two months decreased the likelihood of stopping at the 38th parallel. In early August, despite concern about Soviet and Chinese reaction, officials in the Defense Department declared in favor of unifying the peninsula by defeating the North Korean forces and occupying all of Korea. They believed this action would have an exhilarating effect throughout Asia. Meanwhile, General MacArthur, whose recommendations carried great weight in Washington, expressed his desire to destroy North Korean armies without regard for political boundaries. From mid-July when he conferred with General Collins and Vandenberg in Tokyo, MacArthur declared that U.S./UN forces could wipe out all North Korean forces in both the South and the North. In late August the general repeated that he thought it would be necessary to cross the 38th parallel and occupy the North—at least for a time. On August 25 the State Department achieved consensus regarding the erasing of the 38th parallel and agreed that, in the absence of Chinese Communist or Soviet participation, "we should not stop" the northward thrust. Later, after MacArthur's tremendous military success at Inchon, a sense of euphoria suffused the Korean involvement, blurring the vision of United States policymakers. Despite reports the Chinese might intervene and a disquieting CIA assessment warning that such reports should not be treated lightly, Secretary of Defense Marshall, with the approval of the president, informed MacArthur on September 29: "We want you to feel unhampered tactically and strategically to proceed north of 38th parallel."[19] On September 30, MacArthur began sending South Korean forces across the 38th parallel, and on October 7 he dispatched American troops into North Korea.

Documents reveal several combined factors that were responsible for the move north. As mentioned, the excitement created by MacArthur's defeat of North Korean forces south of the parallel played a part. So, too, did the desire to punish the North Koreans and prove to the world that aggression did not pay. Related to the latter was the belief that stopping at the 38th parallel would allow the Communists to regroup and renew their aggression at some later date and would do nothing for South Korean security. If, on the other hand, the United States took the opportunity to unify Korea, it could solve the Korean problem once and for all, it could force a crack in the Soviet empire, and it could impress the rest of Asia with its firmness in the face of military pressure. Militarily, United States officials believed there was no logic in attempting to stop at a latitudinal line because the North Koreans had fought both north and south of the 38th parallel. Moreover, the Communists held large numbers of military and civilian prisoners whom they would not surrender unless forced to do so by total defeat; if negotiations were attempted, these prisoners would be used as hostages. Finally, warnings of Chinese intervention did not deter United States policymakers because they convinced themselves that such intervention would be limited in scope and would be a mere extension of the Chinese involvement apparent from the beginning of the war. American officials had proof that the North Korean invasion had been spearheaded by 20,000 to 30,000 Chinese Communist troops of Korean ethnicity who had been transferred to Korea since 1949, and that China was already providing considerable military and logistical assistance to North Korea.[20]

If United States officials were unafraid of Chinese intervention, they were also dubious about the credibility of the threat. They repeatedly reassured one another that if either the Soviets or Chinese had contemplated intervention they would have come in when South Korean forces faced imminent defeat at Pusan. Since the Chinese had failed to take advantage of that opportunity, United States officials reasoned curiously that they would not enter upon the American crossing of the 38th parallel. Of more importance, however, was the questioned reliability of K. M. Panikkar, the Indian ambassador to Peking and source of much of the information on Chinese intentions. Panikkar was thought to be emotionally and intellectually unstable and a warm sympathizer with the Maoist regime, the People's Republic of China, led by Mao Zedong. American policymakers generally saw his messages as motivated by self-glorification and a desire to blunt the United Nations' offensive in Peking's interest.[21]

With the crossing of the 38th parallel the United States created an entirely new war. It is difficult to assess Sino-Soviet policy during the critical days of August and September, but the evidence suggests that the communist allies began considering contingency plans early in the war. Soviet Foreign Minister Vyacheslav Molotov attended an eleven-day conference of Communist Party of China (CCP) leaders in August, when the Soviets and Chinese discussed their response should United Nations forces invade North Korea.[22] Moscow was fearful of direct conflict with the United States, and Peking dreaded the prospect of heavy military losses; yet neither country believed it could allow the defeat of North Korea. The communist leaders at that point apparently reached some tentative conclusions: the Chinese would watch the situation closely and would warn the United States that they could not stand by idly while United Nations forces crossed the 38th parallel; at the same time, China would indirectly inform the United States that it would not intervene if only South Korean troops crossed the parallel. Meanwhile, the communist side would hold out hope of negotiations. The Chinese thereafter issued several warnings in September and October.[23]

Despite the fact that as early as July the Chinese Communists began moving troops from the area of the Taiwan Strait to Manchuria and aggregated over 300,000 in that region, Mao and his subordinates did not make a firm decision to enter the war in Korea until after Inchon. When the firm decision finally came, the Soviet Union played a role. Kim Il Sung pleaded with Stalin on September 29 for help to save his regime from total destruction. Stalin agreed to logistical support including more arms, ammunition, and airplanes, but told Kim that soldiers must come from China. Kim turned to Mao on October 1. The Chinese Communists made their decision, following intense debate within the party leadership, on October 2. Those who opposed intervention, including Zhou En-lai and Lin Biao, said the United States, armed with nuclear weapons, was too dangerous an adversary to take on at that stage of the People's Republic of China's development. Mao's counterargument was that there was no more suitable or favorable border area in which to confront the United States than Korea.[24]

On October 2 Mao sent Stalin a telegram in which he stated his plan to intervene. On October 3 Zhou told Panikkar of China's intention, but Chinese intentions were as yet tentative, given Chinese officials' statements that they might not come in if only South Korean troops crossed the 38th parallel. Stalin, who had encouraged Chinese intervention since September 15, promised the necessary military hardware if China furnished the troops. To what extent Stalin envisioned the benefits for the Soviet Union of a Sino-American war is unclear, as is the issue of whether the two communist powers considered invoking the Sino-Soviet treaty of February 1950. The latter could have come into play in the event of an American attack on the territory of the People's Republic. It is important to note that in the Sino-Soviet discussions of early October Stalin stressed to his Chinese allies that, although the Soviets were not prepared for WWIII, the time was favorable for a confrontation with the United States, particularly in an area so disadvantageous to the United States as Korea. No other capitalist nation, Stalin said, could provide much help for American objectives. This diplomatic dialogue finally resulted in the initial Chinese Communist troop movement into Korea on October 19, where they would bide their time until MacArthur's divided forces were in their most vulnerable position near the Yalu River.[25]

American officials did not totally disregard Chinese warnings, and it was in part to discuss the question of Chinese intentions that President Truman arranged a meeting with General MacArthur at Wake Island on October 15. This meeting has engendered controversy among historians and contemporary critics of both Truman and MacArthur. The idea for a Truman/MacArthur meeting apparently originated with White House advisors who believed that the president could bask in MacArthur's glory and the Democratic Party could benefit, in the November elections, from the headlines generated by Truman's journey to a Pacific island for discussions with his major military commander. As it turned out, the meeting was genial enough, though decidedly superficial, passing over in a mere ninety minutes some of the most important contemporary foreign/military policy matters.

Truman left Washington with four planeloads of advisors, secret service officials, and members of the press. But, interestingly, the party did not include Secretary of State Acheson, who looked upon the meeting as "distasteful," or General Marshall or General Collins, the latter chairman of the Joint Chiefs of Staff. It did include Assistant Secretary of State Dean Rusk and presidential advisor Averell Harriman. The president did not permit MacArthur, who wished to bring along his own press corps, to show up with all of his major camp followers. But Truman did allow the general to set the venue of the meeting. The president wished to meet at Pearl Harbor; MacArthur favored Wake Island, and Truman agreed.

MacArthur, who disliked flying and particularly disliked flying over stretches of ocean where the air was likely to be choppy and create air sickness, groused about being summoned to a political meeting. He told aides that the president did not seem to realize he had a war to fight and had no time for political stunts. But contrary to reports of conflicts between the two men and disrespect of MacArthur for his commander in chief, the two men and their staffs were cordial to one another. And they came away from Wake with at least temperate feelings.

The most important substantive issue addressed was whether in MacArthur's view the Chinese would intervene in Korea and how to go about creating a unified Korean government once the war was successfully concluded. MacArthur did not foresee a Chinese intervention, and no substantive thoughts were exchanged regarding the form of a unified Korea. Other than on these issues, the discussions jumped about from one subject to another with such rapidity and with such inadequate attention to transition that they appeared only marginally coherent. Though cordiality prevailed between the two men, their basic attitudes toward one another had not changed. MacArthur did not like or admire any president under whom he

Figure 6.2. MacArthur Meets Truman at Wake Island, October 15th 1950. Reprinted Courtesy of the General Douglas MacArthur Foundation.

served—though he tolerated Hoover and considered him a "friend" of sorts. Truman, for his part, later referred sarcastically to the general as "God's right-hand man" in letters to family members.[26]

The meeting satisfied the president on a number of military matters, including Peking's threat, but it surely exacerbated fears on the communist side. With American forces pushing into North Korea, Soviet and Chinese leaders must have concluded the meeting presaged new military moves by the United States, perhaps an attempt along with Chiang Kai-shek's forces to invade the People's Republic of China. As MacArthur, thereafter, pushed on to the Yalu River, and as American planes accidentally bombed Chinese territory in Manchuria, the worst Chinese fears were confirmed. Chinese "volunteers" entered the war first in a limited way in late October and en masse at the end of the month.[27]

Even after entering, however, the Chinese seemed to mask their intentions. Beginning on October 25 Chinese troops (by that date as many as 180,000 of them were south of the Yalu River, a number that MacArthur's in-

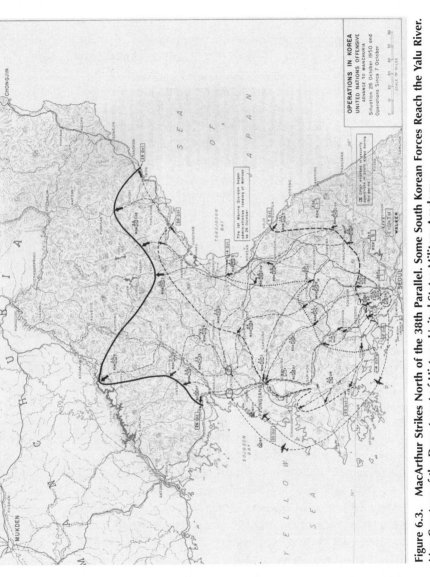

Figure 6.3. MacArthur Strikes North of the 38th Parallel. Some South Korean Forces Reach the Yalu River. Map Courtesy of the Department of History, United States Military Academy.

telligence chief General Willoughby misestimated by over 150,000) struck hard against South Korean troops on the western side of the peninsula. After vicious fighting in which the South Koreans were badly bloodied and in turn they, with help from the U.S. marines, mauled the Chinese, Chinese forces broke contact and retreated into the mountains. Those Chinese troops who were captured, about forty of them, readily admitted the existence of thousands of their "volunteer" countrymen waiting near the Yalu. The reason for their frankness remains an open question; it may have derived from their leaders' desire to warn South Korean and American troops to stop their northward offensive. On November 3, Chinese forces surrounded and captured a part of the First U.S. Cavalry Division. After interrogating the men, the Chinese transported them to the vicinity of the United Nations lines and released them with a felicitous sendoff, a move apparently agreed upon by high-level Chinese officials. The generous and conciliatory treatment accorded these American prisoners puzzled United States observers still further and may have been a signal that the Chinese might have still desired a negotiated settlement. The release came three days before MacArthur's offensive that took him to the border of Manchuria.[28]

The initial contact with Chinese forces and reports that Chinese were massing for a large-scale intervention impelled intensive review of American options in Korea during November. Determined to avoid conflict with the Soviets and Chinese, American officials had earlier decided that if either communist nation entered the war the United States would break contact and stop the United Nations offensive. Now that Chinese entry had begun, however, the question was how extensive it would be and whether the United States should pull back in the face of it. To retreat if the Chinese were bluffing could be disastrous to United States prestige. General MacArthur wanted to go ahead, and his recommendations that he be permitted to bomb bridges over the Yalu to interdict supplies and men and that he go on with plans for his offensive were indicative of his thinking. Washington was more tentative but, in a National Security Council meeting of November 9, decided to support MacArthur's "basic mission," while at the same time trying to achieve a political solution on the matter of Chinese involvement. This meant that, in view of the unattractiveness of the other options, the United States would essentially continue the same course it was then following. All of Truman's civilian and military advisers agreed that this was best, though Dean Acheson has said that he was greatly troubled because he knew that something was badly wrong. Acheson favored stopping and creating a United Nations buffer zone short of the Yalu in accord with a proposal suggested by Ambassador-at-Large Philip Jessup.[29]

As a result of deliberations in Washington it was agreed that, as a way of reassuring the Chinese, the buffer zone idea would be combined with the "continue the present policy" approach. That is to say, officials in Washington would urge MacArthur to complete his military mission and then pull back while securing the approaches to the Yalu River valley. MacArthur strongly opposed the buffer proposal as militarily infeasible and potentially embarrassing because it would signal United States weakness to the rest of Asia. Again, MacArthur's determination to go ahead tended to counter the tentativeness of Washington, but this time the matter became moot when the Chinese entered in great numbers.[30]

Viewed in retrospect, it is regrettable that the United States did not stop at the 38th parallel; it is also regrettable that, having crossed, American and United Nations forces did not arrange to stop at some intermediate line between the 38th parallel and the Yalu River. MacArthur should not bear the brunt of criticism for the decision to move into North Korea, for this was a decision made mainly in Washington; but he must be faulted for the full-scale offensive that followed. His unrestrained enthusiasm for the destruction of North Korean forces and his expressed desire for completion of his mission of unifying Korea led Washington to support his drive to the borders of Manchuria despite fears that the Chinese would increase their involvement. Stopping at defensive positions well south of the Yalu River might not have prevented war with China, but it certainly should have been tried in view of subsequent events.

In his move northward, MacArthur made serious blunders. The commander's battle plan involved taking General Ned Almond's troops from the Seoul area around the peninsula by sea for a landing at Wonsan, roughly a hundred miles north of the 38th parallel. Almond was one of MacArthur's favorite generals, primarily because of his loyalty. General Walton Walker's Eighth Army, which had driven up from the southeast, would move northwest to capture the North Korean capital of Pyongyang. All of this seemed convoluted, but the Joint Chiefs quickly gave approval since MacArthur's clout was now too great to counter. It also seemed convoluted and misguided to General Walker, who tried to convince MacArthur to place the X corps from the Inchon area under his command for a coordinated drive northward; it made little sense to Walker to split U.S. forces for the offensive: Walker in the West, Almond in the East, and Republic of Korea (ROK) forces, which had crossed the 38th parallel on October 1, already in possession of Wonsan. Others, including Admirals C. Turner Joy and Arthur Struble and Generals Doyle Hickey, Edwin "Pinky" Wright and George Eberle, also opposed MacArthur's split forces plan.[31]

Prior to October 8 only ROK troops had crossed the 38th parallel, an important fact, since the Chinese had begun intimating that their intervention would occur only upon U.S. troops also crossing into North Korea. But on October 8 General Walker moved north and despite heavy resistance captured Pyongyang on the 19th. Meanwhile, under MacArthur's plan U.S. marine divisions along with two South Korean divisions advanced northward along the east coast; neither Walker's army, which had supply problems, nor the forces in the east maintained contact with each other. The spine of rugged mountains running down the center of the country made communication extremely difficult, raising additional questions about MacArthur's strategy. Despite misgivings about MacArthur's tactics, twice during this period Washington officials authorized MacArthur's call for unconditional surrender by the North Koreans.

In addition to splitting his forces, against the better judgment and some consternation among the Joint Chiefs of Staff and other solid military minds, MacArthur also made decisions about the extent of his advance toward the Yalu River that clearly stretched the authority that Washington had given him. On October 17 he authorized an offensive line considerably north of the line beyond which only South Korean forces were originally to operate, a move clearly not sanctioned a priori by the Joint Chiefs of Staff. Then on October 24 MacArthur abolished altogether any restraint on non-ROK, U.S./UN forces in the drive to the border of China. This action finally evoked a rebuke from the Joint Chiefs. He responded, in the words of his preeminent biographer, in an amazingly arrogant and illogical way: "The instructions contained in my [message to UN Commanders] were a matter of military necessity." Moreover, he said, the order did not conflict with General Marshall's directive of September 30, stating: "We want you to feel unhampered tactically and strategically to proceed north of the 38th parallel." What MacArthur did not cite were the concerns Washington officials, including the secretary of defense, had expressed about possible contact with Chinese or Soviet forces.[32]

Meanwhile, MacArthur's ego was tolerated in Washington and fed in Korea. Syngman Rhee praised him as the savior of Korea. General Stratemeyer awarded him the Distinguished Flying Cross for "outstanding heroism" in making four flights to Korea, an honor he should have been ashamed to accept and one that elicited the contempt of veteran officers. It was all part of the mood of October. Kim Il Sung had fled his capital for the mountains near the Yalu. General Walker's troops ripped down the statues of Lenin and Stalin in Pyongyang as they also did the portraits of young Kim, the Korean communist leader. Walker set himself up in Kim's office. MacArthur not only issued unconditional surrender demands to North Korea but also planned a reduction of American troops with the stated hope of having them home by Christmas. Civilian American and UN officials began plotting out the unification of Korea as a noncommunist state.

When Chinese entry into the war dashed these hopes and destroyed October's euphoria and optimism, American policymakers faced a bleak time with unhappy choices. General MacArthur advocated a different war, not only to compensate for his failures but also to advance his particular strategic vision. Chinese intervention highlighted his myopia, which in turn provoked his dismissal.

Notes

1. D. Clayton James, *The Years of MacArthur, Volume 3, 1945–1964* (Boston: Houghton Mifflin, 1985), 413–18.

2. James, *The Years of MacArthur, Volume 3*, 419–20; Michael Schaller, *Douglas MacArthur: The Far Eastern General* (New York: Oxford University Press, 1989), 184.

3. James, *The Years of MacArthur, Volume 3*, 423–24; Russell D. Buhite, *Soviet-American Relations in Asia, 1945–1954* (Norman: University of Oklahoma Press, 1981), 170.

4. Schaller, *Douglas MacArthur*, 186–87.

5. James, *The Years of MacArthur, Volume 3*, 426.

6. James, *The Years of MacArthur, Volume 3*, 428, 433.

7. Richard Rovere and Arthur Schlesinger, *General MacArthur and President Truman: The Struggle for Control of American Foreign Policy* (New Brunswick, N.J. and London, U.K.: Transaction, 1992), xiv–xv (with new introduction by Schlesinger). Also see Russell D. Buhite, ed., *Calls To Arms: Presidential Speeches, Messages, and Declarations of War* (Wilmington: Scholarly Resources, 2003), xi–xlii.

8. Quoted in James, *The Years of MacArthur, Volume 3*, 433, 436. Also see Schaller, *Douglas MacArthur*, 190.

9. James, *The Years of MacArthur, Volume 3*, 438.

10. Quoted in Schaller, *Douglas MacArthur*, 194.

11. Schaller, *Douglas MacArthur*, 194.

12. For an assessment of the Ayers-Dulles exchange see James, *The Years of MacArthur, Volume 3*, 43. The quotation by Harrison is in Schaller, *Douglas MacArthur*, 195.

13. Schaller, *Douglas MacArthur*, 196.

14. The best discussion of the issue is in James, *The Years of MacArthur, Volume 3*, 468–69, 472–73.

15. Department of State, *Foreign Relations of the United States* (hereafter cited as *FRUS*), *1950*, vol. 7, 272. Also see James Matray, "Truman's Plan for Victory: National Self Determination and the Thirty-Eighth Parallel Decision in Korea," *Journal of American History* (September 1979): 314–33.

16. *FRUS*, vol. 8, 373, 386.

17. *FRUS*, vol. 8, 624, 450–53, 393; Buhite, *Soviet-American Relations in Asia*, 172–73.

18. *FRUS, 1950*, vol. 7, 473. Quoted in Buhite, *Soviet-American Relations in Asia*, 173.

19. *FRUS, 1950*, vol. 7, 826, 647, 707. This statement was in accord with N.S.C. 81/1 which Truman approved on September 11.

20. *FRUS, 1950*, vol. 7, 874–75. Buhite, *Soviet-American Relations in Asia*, 175.

21. *FRUS, 1950*, vol. 7, 822; Buhite, *Soviet-American Relations in Asia*, 176

22. *FRUS, 1950*, vol. 7, 1019–20.

23. Buhite, *Soviet-American Relations in Asia*, 177.

24. William Stueck, *The Korean War: An International History* (Princeton, N.J.: Princeton University Press, 1995), 98.

25. Stueck, *The Korean War*, 101, 114, 119.

26. John E Wiltz, "Truman and MacArthur: The Wake Island Meeting," *Military Affairs* 42 (Dec. 1978): 169–76; Robert J. Donovan, *Tumultuous Years: The Presidency of Harry S. Truman, 1949–1953* (New York: Norton, 1982), 284; James, *The Years of MacArthur, Volume 3*, 500–517.

27. *FRUS, 1950*, vol. 7, 1019–20. Buhite, *Soviet-American Relations in Asia*, 177.

28. *FRUS, 1950*, vol. 7, 1216–18.

29. *FRUS, 1950*, vol. 7, 1150, 1195–96. Also see Dean Acheson, *Present at the Creation: My Years in the State Department* (New York: Norton, 1969), 602.

30. *FRUS, 1950*, vol. 7, 1222–23.

31. James, *The Years of MacArthur, Volume 3*, 488–89, 492–93.

32. James, *The Years of MacArthur, Volume 3*, 493, 499.

CHAPTER SEVEN

~

Strategic Myopia

After Chinese entry into the war, General MacArthur behaved both shamefully and understandably. His recommendations were clearly at odds with Truman administration policy, but his thoughts about Sino-Soviet relations were marginally prescient. Where he behaved shamefully was in allowing his humiliation at the hands of Chinese generals to cause his public, petulant disputation of the president's specific orders. Where he behaved understandably, in view of his prior experience, was in his insistence that combating communist power in Asia should not be held hostage to containment in Europe and in his disdain for limited war. Moreover, his belief that Soviet interests would take precedence over Chinese interests and that the two communist nations would not necessarily find common ground in the event of an American escalation of the war may well have been correct. Unfortunately, he had no hard evidence to support this belief and Truman administration officials, responsible for addressing worldwide issues, had to consider worst case scenarios.

Among those worst case scenarios were three in particular: MacArthur's advice could lead to the invoking of the Sino-Soviet Alliance of February 1950, which might in turn result in Soviet military aggression in Central and Western Europe; the Soviets and Chinese could attack the virtually undefended U.S. airfields in South Korea; and the two communist countries might attack Japanese ports as a prelude to an invasion of one or more of the home islands. MacArthur's mere dismissal of these prospects was not sufficient to convince his superiors that they were unlikely to occur.

The months of December 1950 and January 1951 constituted an extremely trying time for American officials. As early as November 28 the issue of what to do about the new war was joined between Truman, Acheson, Marshall, and the Joint Chiefs on one side, and MacArthur on the other. Within a few days of entering the war the Chinese had poured at least 300,000 men onto the Korean peninsula, while a reconstituted North Korean force of about 65,000 added to the number on the communist side. These communist forces inflicted heavy casualties on UN troops—killing or wounding nearly 12,000 of them and leading to a dramatic reassessment by Washington of goals in Korea. No longer would the United States hope to unify the country; it would seek instead to stabilize the military situation at a determined, defensible line and negotiate a settlement with the other side. This could mean a division at the narrow waist of the peninsula, which had previously been mentioned as a stopping point for MacArthur's offensive. It could mean a settlement once again at the 38th parallel. It could mean, depending on the effectiveness of the Chinese-North Korean offensive, holding once again at the Pusan perimeter.

Truman and his advisers held a meeting on November 28 to make several key decisions, a gathering that coincided with recommendations coming in from MacArthur. In April 1950 the National Security Council put its imprimatur on a document thereafter known as NSC#68, which envisioned a huge increase in U.S. defense expenditures to confront the perceived worldwide Soviet threat and in effect to embrace and pay for the globalization of containment. The participants in the November 28 meeting agreed that NSC#68 had to become policy. They also agreed that it was necessary to strengthen the North Atlantic Alliance (NATO) and that the United States would need to proceed with great caution in Korea to avoid a war with the Soviet Union and China. Chinese entry en masse, they agreed, raised the possibility of world war. But to fight China and the Soviet Union from the Korean peninsula or elsewhere on the mainland of Asia made no sense to the president and his chief advisers. In any case, the Soviet Union was the main enemy, not China. They decided to work toward an armistice, avoid a further augmentation of MacArthur's force, forswear help from the Nationalists on Taiwan, and do as much as possible to blunt the Chinese communist offensive while preserving American lives and prestige. In other words, policymakers acknowledged at this meeting that it might be hard to stay in Korea, but it would be equally difficult to leave.

MacArthur's opinions were far less complicated or nuanced. He quickly advanced his plan to fight "an entirely new war," which included a dramatic increase in U.S. forces, acceptance of a Chinese Nationalist offer to send troops to China, bombing Chinese territory in Manchuria, and blockading the China coast. There has been debate whether he also recommended that the United States use atomic weapons. Evidence strongly suggests that he did wish to use the bomb and he made his wishes clear to Washington. As early as July 1950, though he denied it later, he had urged using the bomb against the North Koreans, and in February and March 1951 suggested that the United States lay a belt of radioactive waste across enemy supply lines. Prior to that, in late December, as he considered what to do in the event Chinese and North Korean troops threatened to push the United States off the peninsula, he envisioned that key targets in Korea would require as many as thirty-four atomic bombs, with perhaps others to be used in Manchuria. This certainly indicates his interest in the idea. In the period after his dismissal, he spoke even more graphically of how atomic weapons might be used.[1]

Truman's advisers wanted people to believe that the president not only summarily rejected MacArthur's military advice but that Truman quickly took a firm position against use of the atomic bomb. The former is not entirely true and the latter certainly is not. In a November 30 news conference Truman informed reporters that the United States was indeed considering the bomb, a statement that reflected ongoing deliberations, but one that aides hastened to identify as a "misstatement." They were worried about the anguished response the remarks evoked from the British and French. Beyond that, during the week of December 4–8, Truman received strong public encouragement to use the bomb. Bernard Baruch, admittedly not Truman's favorite "adviser to presidents," wrote him citing this public sentiment and added his own opinion: "It ought to be used if it can be used effectively."[2]

During January 1951 the president and his advisers began studying NSC#100, which espoused all of the ideas that MacArthur promoted publicly before his dismissal: a blockade of China by naval and air forces, the bombing of Manchuria, backing of the Nationalists on Taiwan, and "the extension of fullest possible support to all anticommunist elements in the Far East, including Southeast Asia, so they can renew open war and increase guerrilla activities against the Chinese Communists in central and south China." Any further Soviet aggression, in areas to be spelled out, the document went on, "would result in the atomic bombardment of Soviet Russia itself."[3]

Truman, to his credit, did not commit to the proposals of NSC#100, nor, decisions of the November 28 meeting aside, did he have an easy time committing to any specific course of action during December 1950 and January 1951. He had multiple concerns. He did not want U.S. armies to suffer extensive casualties. He did not want a wider war. He did not want the United

States driven off the peninsula. Indeed, Acheson and his State Department colleagues made the argument that American credibility would suffer severely if the United States failed to remain in Korea. Even leaving prematurely of its own volition, the State Department contended, could be equally damaging to the United States. The Republican Party, which had made serious gains in the November elections, and especially its most extreme faction energized by the venomous Senator Joseph McCarthy, pummeled Truman for not being tough enough on communism. The president's public opinion rating slid dramatically over the five months after Chinese entry into the war. At the same time, America's primary allies in Europe were pressuring the administration to seek a negotiated settlement to reduce the risk of a wider war; the British in particular became worried about talk of the atomic bomb. Meanwhile, both the Defense Department and the military establishment, generally, revived the prewar argument that Korea was not a military asset or a high strategic priority.

Truman had his work cut out for him, and MacArthur did not make it any easier. The general offered his opinions so often over the next several months they became a mantra to Washington: use Chinese Nationalist troops; blockade the China coast; pursue Chinese planes into Manchuria; bomb targets in Manchuria. To him it was an entirely new war that was important to win rather than to redefine American goals downward. He would take the war to China even if it led to a major conflict with the Soviet Union. He did not think it would go that far, but, even if it did, he would remain committed to his recommendations—a confounding assessment to some because the general had earlier strongly opposed a land war on the Asian continent and had often spoken of Korea as strategically expendable.

Several factors informed MacArthur's views. It was his war in an area of the world he, like his father before him, always considered most important. Monumentally self-possessed, he had to prevail. Moreover, he deemed it crucial to show no weakness because stopping communist aggression in Asia was as important as, if not more so than, stopping it in Europe. He believed further that he could destroy China's war making power with relative impunity and without evoking a Soviet response on China's behalf. Finally, he was supremely embarrassed if not humiliated by Chinese successes in the early stages of their entrance. Chinese strategists had capitalized on his colossal blunders in separating his armies, advancing to the Yalu without proper logistics or communication, and making his armies so vulnerable to attack. With a ragtag, ill-equipped force, the Chinese routed UN troops. Though large in number, the Chinese army was poorly armed with captured WWII weapons. It possessed no heavy artillery and wore canvas shoes, uniforms ill-suited to the extreme cold, and either makeshift, poorly fitting or no gloves, and each man had a food supply sufficient for approximately four days, after which he had to live off the land. Communication beneath the battalion level bore all the earmarks of an 18th century force.[4]

The general's exculpatory remarks are legendary. He spoke of his ill-fated offensive to the Yalu as "a reconnaissance in force" designed to flush out the Chinese. He blamed British spies in Washington for passing information to the Chinese. He blamed softness on the part of policymakers for the reluctance to take on the Chinese, for in effect emboldening the enemy. He cited his opponents in Washington for wanting him personally to fail. In early December he told the editors of U.S. News and World Report that his offensive had been not only proper but that it could have resulted in victory if he had been, or were yet, permitted to pursue enemy forces beyond the Yalu. Civilian superiors in denying him that right imposed "an enormous handicap, without precedent in military history."[5]

Meanwhile, the Chinese military offensive continued. The South Korean forces on the right flank of the Eighth Army fled, leaving much of their equipment and weaponry behind. The Chinese then routed the Eighth Army, driving it southward in rapid retreat and forcing it within a week to abandon the North Korean capital and continue its withdrawal until it reached the vicinity of the Imgin River. The X Corps battled for its life against a Chinese flanking movement at the Chosin Reservoir in the north central region of the country, while taking heavy casualties and struggling with extreme cold that sometimes dropped the temperature to minus twenty degrees. Only in mid-December did the various American units manage to assemble at Hungnam on the east coast, where they boarded U.S. vessels for a sea borne evacuation to the southern part of the peninsula. By early January the Chinese began crossing the 38th parallel, forcing the abandonment of Seoul and U.S./UN attempts once again to defend the south.

Either out of egotism or desperation, or both, MacArthur began a concerted attempt to leverage Washington to provide more troops and expand the war. In message after message, the general predicted wholesale slaughter of his forces and eviction from the peninsula unless he received more help and his strategic recommendations were followed. Concerned that MacArthur had been indiscreet in his projection of defeat and annoyed at the general's public utterances, President Truman thought about firing the general. He hesitated out of fear that it would appear he was scapegoating in the face of a military setback. Instead, he issued an order on December 6 declaring that military and civilian authorities make no policy pronouncements

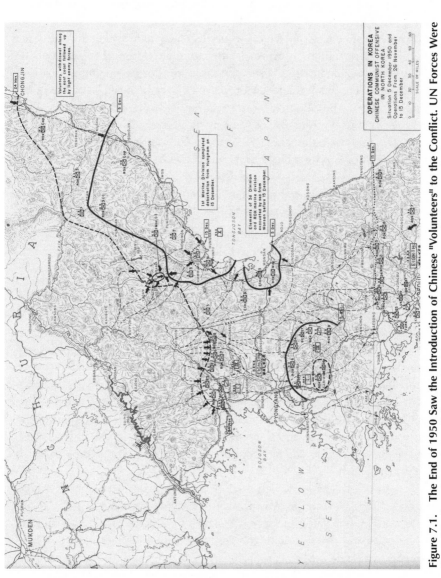

Figure 7.1.   The End of 1950 Saw the Introduction of Chinese "Volunteers" to the Conflict. UN Forces Were Forced Back to the 38th Parallel. Map Courtesy of the Department of History, United States Military Academy.

not previously cleared by the State and Defense Departments and that everyone abjure public statements.

Two developments then occurred that served to mitigate MacArthur's assertiveness and his authority. Truman sent General J. Lawton Collins to Korea and Japan to gain an independent assessment. Collins's judgment not only contradicted General MacArthur's, it also indicated to the president that UN forces could hold on indefinitely at a defensible position in the southern part of the country and that no significant additional troops would be necessary. MacArthur had been using the specter of catastrophe to get his way. Collins made clear that catastrophe was not imminent or even likely. Although there would be difficult days ahead, MacArthur's predictions were overblown. While Collins was in East Asia, British Prime Minister Clement Atlee visited Washington to urge restraint. Korea, he asserted repeatedly, was not the place for a wider war, or the territory over which to initiate one, either by pursuing MacArthur's recommendations or using the atomic bomb. He had been deeply alarmed at Truman's comment on November 30 about possible use of the bomb.[6]

Another decision soon led to the further overshadowing of MacArthur. General Walton Walker was killed in a highway accident in Korea, and General Matthew Ridgway assumed command of the Eighth Army on December 25. Ridgway rallied the forces under his command, improved morale, and proved that he could hold against the Chinese and North Koreans. To his credit, MacArthur did not interfere. These developments rendered MacArthur increasingly irrelevant to events on the ground, a factor that may well have fueled greater indiscretion on his part. Whatever the case, the Chinese offensive south of the 38th parallel, while successful in battering UN armies and gaining territory, also exposed severe weakness. Chinese supply lines became overextended and subject to fierce U.S. bombing attacks. Poorly clothed Chinese troops suffered severe frostbite. They possessed virtually no medical corps and experienced extreme food shortages. Chinese forces had proven themselves against UN armies but they had also revealed serious vulnerabilities.

December proved a critical month in the Korean conflict. Member states of the UN General Assembly not involved in the war called for a cease-fire, hoping to capitalize on China's seemingly stalled offensive and need for a respite. Various proposals surfaced, most of them advocating an armistice followed by discussions of issues such as the withdrawal of foreign troops from Korea, Chinese representation at the United Nations, and control over Taiwan. Such an arrangement would have been acceptable to the United States, especially a cease-fire, provided there was a prisoner exchange and some way of enforcing the cease fire near the 38th parallel. The Chinese refused a cease-fire that did not envision an a priori settlement of their UN representation and the Taiwan question, as well as U.S. withdrawal from Korea. Hence, the Chinese diplomat temporarily assigned to the United Nations picked up his papers and went home. Despite military difficulties, the Chinese believed they could obliterate the 38th parallel and unify the country; they faced decisions not too dissimilar from those of U.S. policymakers in September and October of 1950.[7]

The other matter of great consequence in December was how Truman would address concern in the United States about the war. The president declared a state of national emergency, increased the defense budget dramatically from less than $20 million to well over $50 million, and imposed a trade embargo on China. To appease his European allies, Truman provided greater support for NATO, a move that did not endear him, as though anything could have, to his Republican critics, who favored an Asia-first over a Europe-first approach to foreign/military policy.

That Chinese communist forces developed severe logistical problems in December did not mean they were incapable of further offensive action. Indeed with the beginning of the new year they launched an attack that contributed not only to a serious reevaluation in Washington of the overall mission in Korea but also to another exchange between U.S civilian/military policymakers and MacArthur. Ridgway remained positive in his outlook despite an onslaught of about 500,000 enemy troops that, by the first week of January, pushed UN troops roughly seventy miles south of the 38th parallel. The Joint Chiefs of Staff gloomily considered total withdrawal from the peninsula, as MacArthur himself seemed to be doing. Communication back and forth in January reflected the dilemma in Washington and both misapprehension and contention by MacArthur.

With the approval of the president, Marshall, and Acheson, the Joint Chiefs informed MacArthur that, if the Chinese massed forces sufficient to defeat his armies, he should prepare to withdraw to Japan. The Chiefs repeated their belief and the president's that Korea was not the place to engage in a major war, that no reinforcements could be expected, and that preserving the troops in his command and protecting Japan should be the general's priorities. In the meantime, he should hold succeeding defensive lines and inflict as many casualties as possible on the Chinese and North Koreans. MacArthur replied with a recitation of his mantra: blockade the China coast, use Nationalist troops, bomb Manchuria. The Chiefs' rejoinder reminded him that those steps would be dangerous and extremely difficult to implement. He should follow his orders as given. While Ridgway grew increasingly optimistic, MacArthur kept warning either adopt his recommendations or face annihilation. The Joint Chiefs and their civilian superiors were clearly worried, but they were not prepared to follow the UN commander's ideas unless they had to do so either to effect evacuation or to contain an aggressive Chinese force threatening to destroy U.S. troops in Korea. Their contingency planning went forward but it concluded that only in the event of a military crisis in Korea or obvious Chinese military expansion outside the peninsula would they agree to MacArthur's recommendations.[8]

By the end of January the worst-case-scenario planning was put aside. General Ridgway began a major offensive that drove the Chinese northward, killing and capturing them by the thousands. Generals Collins and Vandenberg then made a trip to Tokyo and Korea where they found not only the new spirit infused by Ridgway but also the falsity of the UN commander's my-way-or-annihilation assessment. In a blatant fabrication, MacArthur later said in his memoirs that he had held a positive attitude all along and had "ordered Ridgway to start north again." He had done no such thing. Moreover, events in Korea and the Collins-Vandenberg report caused such a loss of confidence in MacArthur that policymakers thereafter took his advice far less seriously. As reported in the official history of the Joint Chiefs of Staff: "General MacArthur's counsels no longer commanded the respect they once enjoyed. Washington now exerted a closer and more direct control over the course of operations in Korea. Moreover, the misunderstanding between the general and his superiors was widening and his dismissal had moved a step closer." Chairman of the Joint Chiefs of Staff, General Omar Bradley, opined, none too flatteringly to MacArthur, that the latter wanted a wider war against China primarily to assuage his hatred for the "Red Chinese generals who had made a fool out of him . . . and his infallible military genius."[9]

Neither Truman's policy toward Korea nor his dealings with the UN commander were conducted in a vacuum. He had many critics in the United States who disagreed with his attention to Europe, his alleged appeasement of communist foes, and his failure to go far enough in punishing China for its intrusion into Korea. These critics blamed Truman's policies for the accession of the communists to power in China in the first place. Among the critics were Republican partisans such as Senator Robert Taft of Ohio, Senator Kenneth Wherry of Nebraska, publisher Robert McCormick, and, though not so much a conventional Republican as a drunken demagogue, Senator Joseph McCarthy of Wisconsin. Others joined the chorus, and in mid-January both the House and the Senate passed resolutions pressing the president to secure UN condemnation of China as an aggressor in Korea. Truman administration officials twisted the arms of America's allies, especially the British and French, but also the so-called nonaligned nations and secured the condemnation on February 1. That China had been aggressive in Korea, both by encouraging the North Korean invasion and intervening militarily, hardly justified this U.S. initiative, which certainly complicated relations between the People's Republic and the United States.

As war in Korea dragged on into February and March, UN/U.S. prospects improved and MacArthur was marginalized. If there were anything he could not abide it was to be irrelevant. Hence, he tried to present himself as the author of Ridgeway's successes, sought to be present for the major campaigns, and attempted to have his picture taken, as in WWII, with frontline troops—all to cultivate his image back home. Ridgway did not want him in Korea and on at least one occasion urged him not to come. Ridgway, in fact, one of the true military statesmen of the twentieth century and in so many ways the opposite of the glory-seeking MacArthur, did very well without the UN commander. By the first weeks of February the Eighth Army was advancing toward the 38th parallel, achieving striking successes in punishing Chinese armies. By March, the question arose of once again crossing the 38th parallel and clearing the enemy from North Korea. This time U.S. policymakers recognized they still confronted an enemy the United States could not defeat or occupy and that enemy had an alliance with a nuclear power capable of initiating WWIII.

Against MacArthur's wishes, indeed to his disgust, officials in Washington with encouragement from European allies, decided in March to explore a negotiated conclusion of the conflict. MacArthur began to speak out. He opposed positional warfare at the 38th parallel or any new partition of Korea. He again recommended air attacks on China and a blockade; if the Soviets came in, so be it. As noted earlier, he talked of laying radioactive waste across communist supply lines. To deal with a possible Soviet reaction he wanted the atomic bomb at his disposal. Ridgway thought MacArthur actually sought a full-blown showdown with world communism, staged within his command. The UN commander argued strongly for a UN advance to the Yalu River and for moving the 7th Fleet close to the China coast.[10]

On March 20, the Joint Chiefs of Staff informed MacArthur that the State Department favored a peace initiative in Korea and talks that could include the status of Taiwan and Chinese representation in the United Nations. Four days later MacArthur announced his disdain for Washington's thinking. In a public statement deliberately phrased to infuriate the Chinese and undercut his superiors' move toward negotiations, he declared: "We have now substantially cleared South Korea of organized Communist forces. . . . Red China . . . lacks the industrial capacity to provide adequately many critical items necessary to the conduct of modern war. . . . The enemy, therefore, must by now be painfully aware that a decision of the United Nations to depart from its tolerant effort to contain the war to the area of Korea, through an expansion of our military operation to its coastal areas and internal bases, would doom Red China to the risk of imminent military collapse. . . . I stand ready at any time to confer in the field with the commander in chief of the enemy forces."[11] He did not say he was ready to accept Chinese surrender, but that is what he meant. Since the Chinese were then planning a new military offensive, they would not have then accepted a U.S. peace initiative in any event, but there can be little doubt that the Chinese were upset at the general's statement. So, too, were U.S. allies and MacArthur's superiors. Barely containing his fury, President Truman at that moment decided to fire his insubordinate general.

Dismissal may have been MacArthur's objective. With his thumb on the pulse of American opinion and hoping that he could energize his base of long-term supporters, he must have given serious thought to how a return to the United States would play, how it might enhance his chances in a run for the presidency in 1952. The least it could do was initiate an intense debate over the fundamentals of American foreign policy, a national discussion that would finally give East Asia its just due.[12]

In two nearly simultaneous steps that could not have been better calculated to engineer his dismissal, MacArthur publicly bearded the Truman administration. On February 12, the House minority leader, Joseph Martin of Massachusetts, gave a speech in Brooklyn in which he decried U.S. refusal to use Chinese Nationalist troops on the mainland as a counter to Chinese communist action in Korea, and he argued strongly against the American buildup of forces in Europe, which he interpreted as diminishing U.S. effectiveness in Asia. He sent a copy of the speech to General MacArthur on March 8, asking for his comments. As part of his effort to undercut the administration's peace initiative, MacArthur replied to Martin on March 20. He agreed with the minority leader's call for the use of nationalist troops and then stated: "It seems strangely difficult for some to realize that here in Asia is where the communist conspirators have elected to make their play for global conquest . . . that here we fight Europe's war with arms while the diplomats there still fight it with words; that if we lose this war to communism in Asia the fall of Europe is inevitable. . . . As you pointed out, we must win. There is no substitute for victory."[13] Martin read MacArthur's statement to the U.S. House of Representatives on April 5, thus making the general's remarks public, something that MacArthur, notably, had not forbidden.

On the very day of Martin's release of MacArthur's remarks, the *Daily Telegraph* in London published an interview in which the general lamented the lack of an American objective in Korea and the political constraints under which UN forces operated. The right-wing magazine the *Freeman* also published on April 5 a statement by the general criticizing U.S. policymakers for their unwillingness, despite his recommendation, to enlarge the South Korean military. This recreation of the general's position was utterly false; on January 6, MacArthur had opposed increasing the size of this force, a point officials in Washington hastened to make.

Truman immediately called his main advisers, Acheson, Marshall, Bradley, and Harriman, together to determine how to deal with MacArthur. (Or better put, how best to fire him.) Acheson and Averell Harriman joined Truman in the opinion that the president must dismiss the general at once, that, in fact, such action was long overdue. Marshall and Bradley suggested at least three possible steps short of outright dismissal: to send Marshall to Tokyo to bring MacArthur into line; to rebuke him in writing; or to call him to Washington for a severe dressing down. Knowing of Truman's predilections and those of Acheson and Harriman, as well as the president's consultation with other members of his cabinet and both Vice President Alban Barkley and Speaker of the House Sam Rayburn, Marshall, Bradley, and the other Joint Chiefs came to agree that there were very good reasons to relieve MacArthur. Neither Marshall nor Bradley was decisive on the matter, probably out of fear of complications arising with a new command arrangement and concern over the public response, but they finally were willing to state: "If it should be the President's decision to relieve MacArthur, the JCS concurs."[14] On April 9, Truman made his final decision based on the (somewhat contrived) unanimity of his advisers.

The decision to relieve MacArthur occurred in the context of what appeared to be an emerging crisis in East Asia, a development that may well have influenced the Chiefs' timidity about firing him. On the other hand, this same crisis may have impelled the others toward dismissal. Intelligence reports indicated a large buildup of Chinese troops and aircraft in Manchuria as well as the positioning of over seventy Soviet submarines in the vicinity of Vladivostok and Sakhalin Island. This increased enemy force suggested a new, aggressive offensive, perhaps even against Japan, and led the Joint Chiefs and ultimately President Truman to authorize the transfer of nine atomic bombs to the air force, which would hold them near the Asian mainland. The president also authorized attacks on China, should a major joint Soviet-Chinese offensive begin, but the decision to act would be the responsibility of the UN commander. To Truman and his civilian advisers the availability of atomic bombs was further reason to remove a recalcitrant general who wanted war with China and might trigger the use of this weapon prematurely.[15] Understandably, the military people in Truman's circle also worried about a change in command at the time of a looming crisis.

President Truman announced MacArthur's dismissal on April 11, at 1:00 a.m. Washington time. Much has been made of the discourtesy in the way the news reached the general, but the president had heard rumors that MacArthur was preparing to announce his resignation. Truman was not about to let a general who deserved the ignominy of dismissal resign on him. General Bradley signed the dismissal order requiring that MacArthur turn over all of his commands to General Ridgway. Truman informed the American people: "With deep regret I have concluded that General of the Army Douglas MacArthur is unable to give his wholehearted support to the policies of the United States Government and the United Nations in matters pertaining to his official duties. . . . I have, therefore, relieved General MacArthur of his command and have designated Lieutenant General Matthew B. Ridgway as his successor."[16] MacArthur was not shocked, magnanimous, or pleased with the announcement or how he received it. It came via a whispered comment by his wife Jean, who interrupted the general's luncheon with a corporate executive and a U.S. senator; she had gotten the news from Sid Huff, who had heard it on the radio. He recalled in his memoirs published in 1964 that "no office boy, no charwoman, no servant of any sort would have been dismissed with such callous disregard for the ordinary decencies."[17] Despite his public display of equanimity at the time of the dismissal, the general harbored bitter feeling toward Truman and others in Washington, telling diplomat William Sebald that he would have been pleased to resign if asked and that his firing was part of a plot to sell out Taiwan. He also told General Ridgway that a prominent medical person had told him that the president was a sick man, unstable mentally, with malignant hypertension, who "wouldn't live six months."[18]

Encomiums quickly poured in for MacArthur and vitriol for Truman. Within the first twenty-four to forty-eight hours almost 40,000 pieces of hate mail arrived at the White House. In contrast, the general received an invitation to speak to a joint session of the U.S. Congress on April 19, resolutions of praise from the National Assembly in Korea and Diet in Japan, a massive outpouring of affection from the Japanese people, and promises of street demonstrations in San Francisco and New York when he arrived in the United States. He was especially pleased to receive the invitation from Congress and eagerly looked forward to addressing that body. His departure from Tokyo could not have been staged better. It was typical MacArthur theater:

a nineteen-gun salute together with a formation of jet fighters and bombers that flew over the airport just before he and his family took off.

MacArthur returned to the United States as a hero and a comparatively wealthy man. He retained his five star general's rank for life, his $18,000 yearly salary (which was increased to keep pace with inflation), an airplane, a staff of sycophants, and the $500,000 "honorarium" he had received while in the Philippines. Soon after his return he was given a suite in the Waldorf Towers in New York, where he paid $450 per month for the rest of his life. He then became chairman of the board of Remington Rand Corporation, a position that did not indulge his fabulist self-perception but gave him significant income. Truman, by contrast, was pilloried far and wide, though as president he possessed the means and the will to fight back.

Congressional Republicans were especially hard on the president. Senator McCarthy set the standard, calling Truman a "son-of-a-bitch" "who was probably drunk on bourbon and benedictine" when he fired the heroic general. Representative Martin called him a bungler. Senator William Jenner of Indiana demanded his impeachment. Senator Taft joined in the appeasement-of-communism cry. Some congressmen insisted that the *Congressional Record* reflect the views of letter-writers labeling Truman "a little ward politician," "a Judas," and an "imbecile."

Public opinion, though mixed, temporarily favored MacArthur. A Gallup poll showed the general with a 66 percent approval rating, while only 25 percent favored the president's action. Truman was hanged in effigy. Several state legislatures, responding to outrage from constituents, passed resolutions condemning the president and others invited MacArthur to address their chambers. The Scripps-Howard, Hearst, and McCormick newspaper chains practically deified MacArthur while vilifying Truman. The *Chicago Tribune* declared he was "unfit to be president." The 500,000 people who greeted the general's arrival in San Francisco and the 7.5 million who celebrated him in New York following his address to Congress provided a measure of public feeling.[19] But Truman had some cards to play. His party controlled both houses of Congress; and Democratic congressmen could press the martyred general on his worldview and political allies could speak up for the president's policies.

MacArthur's address to the joint session of Congress on April 19 represented high drama. It was an impressive speech delivered to a packed house, with Mrs. MacArthur and their thirteen-year-old son, Arthur, as well as long-time aides, in the gallery. Millions of people watched the performance on the new medium of television or listened on the radio. He received thunderous applause as he walked in, thunderous interruptions along the way, and even more thunderous acclaim at the conclusion. One wag suggested there was not a dry eye in the place, or a dry seat among Republicans.[20] He began with an expression of pride and humility, then denied partisanship or bitterness, said how much he hated war, condemned appeasement, especially of Communist China, praised the South Koreans for their bravery, indicated there was no substitute for victory, repeated his mantra on how to win, claimed the Joint Chiefs supported his ideas, and closed with a reference to the old soldiers' barracks ballad: "Old soldiers never die; they just fade away. And like the old soldier of that ballad, I now close my military career and just fade away—an old soldier who tried to do his duty as God gave him the light to see that duty. Good-bye." It was a well-delivered expression of his views and often seen as one of the great speeches of his time. It makes a favorable technical impression to the casual and informed listener even today. But his "old soldiers never die" line was shopworn; he had used it several times over the years, a fact of which his listeners seemed unaware.

Truman thought it was "nothing but a bunch of bullshit." And he quickly set his administration people and his supporters to work discrediting the general.

Figure 7.2.   MacArthur Speaks Before a Joint Session of Congress, 1951. Reprinted Courtesy of the General Douglas MacArthur Foundation.

One of his first points was to indicate that he and Acheson had been very busy and had not heard the address (though he had read an advance copy). Acheson referred to the speech as "demagogic," which in a sense it was. The Joint Chiefs immediately stated publicly that MacArthur had been wrong in claiming their support; they declared their unanimous agreement with the president on policy as well as his decision to relieve the general. Key Democratic senators spoke up in favor of Truman. The president's domestic advisers began digging up information on the general's sexual behavior in the 1930s and indiscretions by his major congressional defenders. American correspondents, assigned to Japan and Korea, made their negative views of MacArthur available to the press, and nearly 76 percent of them held the general in contempt and supported Truman. A survey released by Elmo Roper Associates showed that a vast majority of the working press thought that the general's incompetence as a military commander in Korea fully justified his relief.[21]

None of this immediately turned public opinion. Former President Herbert Hoover spoke of MacArthur as "the reincarnation of Saint Paul into a great general of the Army." Representative Dewey Short of Missouri referred to the general, immediately after his speech to Congress, as "a great hunk of God in the flesh, and we heard the voice of God." On the afternoon of April 19, 250,000 people saluted his car as it drove down Pennsylvania Avenue. He received a key to the city of Washington, D.C. Then that evening he went on to New York, where the next day he was feted with a huge celebration in which an estimated 7.5 million people turned out and showered his motorcade with over two thousand tons of confetti and ticker tape. Even Charles Lindbergh had not done as well. Over the next couple of weeks he gave speeches attacking American foreign policy to enthusiastic audiences in Milwaukee and Chicago.[22]

But his star began to fade with the Senate hearings that began on May 3. Called formally "Hearings into the Military Situation in the Far East" and conducted jointly by the Senate Foreign Relations and Armed Services Committees, this inquiry, controlled by the majority Democratic Party (eight to seven on each committee), put MacArthur on the spot in a most uncomfortable manner and often made him look foolish. Senator Richard Russell of Georgia chaired the hearings, but Lyndon Johnson of Texas proved the genius behind the inquiry. Historian Michael Schaller succinctly delineates the strategy that Johnson, his staff, and fellow Democratic senators devised. Their idea was to let MacArthur speak, on and on and on, knowing that he would relish the opportunity, knowing also that he would eventually discredit himself. Democratic senators would listen respectfully, not interrupting the general. Then, equally respectfully, they would begin asking key questions: How could he as a military commander without full intelligence information know how the Soviet Union and China would react to an escalation of the war in Korea? Did he have better information than others in the government? Did he know how America's allies would react to an attack on China? Did the United States need allies to contain communism in Europe and Asia? How wide a war was he willing to provoke? Would he bomb China's cities? Could the United States defend Japan from Chinese and Soviet attack? What would Chinese Nationalist troops really contribute? What logistic support would he offer Chinese Nationalist troops? And what if we had to bail them out on the mainland?[23]

The hearings provide a window on the thinking of Truman's advisers as well as on MacArthur's worldview and psychology. Two conflicting approaches to foreign policy came to the fore in these sessions. The administration's belief that in confronting the Soviet Union, which the United States could not hope to defeat militarily, occupy, or change politically, and the People's Republic of China, which would prove equally impossible to defeat and occupy, containment of communist power was the only logical policy. Containment meant restraint, compromise, and acceptance of solutions short of victory. Anything else was simply too risky. The Soviets had the atomic bomb, and the Chinese boasted vast territory and a huge population. Moreover, containment meant eschewing unilateralism and working with allies. It meant nuanced diplomacy, sometimes the use of force but seldom any final solutions. MacArthur and his Republican defenders, not to mention many Democrats, believed that if communism were evil, if the communist nation-states could truly be equated with the fascist powers of the thirties and forties, as most officials thought they could, compromise was impossible, even immoral. Containment itself thus became immoral. That partially explains the outpouring of emotion on the occasion of MacArthur's dismissal. It also helps explain the contretemps in the hearings. In matters of war and peace MacArthur did not embrace nuance.

MacArthur led off in these sessions, which went on for the better part of two months and generated extensive documentation, not all of which appeared in print until 1973. The general requested long, marathon meetings, foregoing lunch and going late into the afternoon, partly, one suspects, to show he was up to the task. With his aide, General Courtney Whitney, he commuted back and forth from New York each of his three days before the committee. As Truman and the Democratic members assumed and as anyone who knew the general's mind well knew, he admitted no mistakes during his command in Korea. He split his forces, he said, largely because of the rugged mountain terrain, and he advanced as he did to gauge Chinese intentions. If he misjudged the Chinese, it was because he did not receive adequate intelligence information from his superiors in Washington. He argued strongly that, if he had been permitted to hit the privileged Chinese sanctuaries in Manchuria, he could have won the war and completed the process of unifying Korea. Pursuit into Manchuria would have dealt the People's Republic a crippling blow, especially if combined with a sustained Chinese Nationalist invasion of South China.

He could have done all this, he said, without the risk of a wider war, without an escalation of military activity by the Soviet Union. The latter would not have honored fully the Sino-Soviet treaty, and would have protected its own interests. He firmly believed the Soviets would have refrained from risking a world war over an issue of such marginal importance to them as the Korean peninsula. In any event, he argued that the Soviets would almost certainly grow suspicious of Chinese communist power and its rivalry within the communist movement. The action he recommended, in other words, could have precipitated a Sino-Soviet split. In view of later developments, this comment showed insight, but to contemporary observers it also reflected the general's grasping at straws in defense of his position. He offered no firm evidence of a Sino-Soviet schism, and he seemed ignorant of the debate that played out in U.S. policy circles in 1949–1950 on the very matter of how close the two communist countries would remain over the short term. The debate had concluded that for the foreseeable future China would remain in the Soviet camp.

He dismissed the charge that he had been insubordinate with two statements, neither of them true. In what stands out as one of his most outrageous falsehoods in a career filled with them, one that raised eyebrows among both friends and foes, he said: "No more subordinate officer has ever worn the American uniform." He then argued that the Joint Chiefs, as evidenced in their directive of January 12, had agreed with his military recommendations—not acknowledging that the January 12 plans reflected a contingency, only to be implemented if the Chinese and Soviets widened the war, threatened to attack Japan and Taiwan, or seemed poised to drive U.S./UN troops totally out of Korea. When given the opportunity to testify, the Chiefs made this point unanimously.

MacArthur fell victim to several gaffes in his testimony. He rambled on about Chinese history, making some serious factual errors along the way. In discussing Asian psychology, which he always claimed to know better than anyone, he referred condescendingly to Japanese immaturity and the twentieth-century transformation of the Chinese personality. His most serious mistake came in his statement that, had his recommendation to widen the war received approval and had the Soviets responded aggressively, he bore no responsibility for the consequences: "That doesn't happen to be my responsibility," he stated.[24] It may not have been his responsibility to form policy, but, to the senators quizzing him in the hearings, his sudden willingness to distance himself from the possible results of a course he recommended bore all the marks of a non sequitur at best and evasion of responsibility at worst.

The testimony that followed did not do the general's cause much good, or that of his Republican backers. In turn, General Marshall and members of the Joint Chiefs of Staff made many telling points, nearly all of which seriously undermined MacArthur. It was possible, the Chiefs and Marshall stated, for the Soviets and Chinese acting in concert to concentrate enough air and sea power to drive the United States out of Korea and seriously threaten Japan. This information was not made public at the time for obvious reasons. General Vandenberg noted that the airfields in Manchuria were so heavily fortified that the enemy could and surely would inflict heavy casualties on an attacking American air force. The latter, in any event, was not very powerful, he testified, and could not sustain a major campaign. A surprising bit of information came with General Bradley's disposal of the privileged sanctuary argument. The other side, he said, was also fighting a limited war, one marked by considerable restraint. It had not chosen to unleash the full force of its air power on UN airfields, communication lines, or ports in South Korea or Japan. The United States, in other words, derived some real advantage from the limited war concept.

As for the unleashing of Chinese Nationalist forces in South China, the Chiefs cited serious problems. If those forces were taken from Taiwan, the island would become more not less vulnerable to attack. And the United States, in the event of a Chinese communist invasion of Taiwan, would then be honor-bound to assume major responsibility for the island's defense. Moreover, if Nationalist troops landed in China and were soon threatened with defeat, as they surely would be (given they were, after all, driven off the mainland despite large-scale American support less than two years before), the United States would have to save them. This would draw the United States into a land war on the Asian continent itself, a prospect even MacArthur said he abhorred.[25]

Despite Republican pleas to the contrary, the Democratic majority on the committee insisted on hearing all of the military testimony, because it enhanced Truman's case and derogated MacArthur's. The Republicans responded by shifting the line of questioning to the canard about Democratic softness on communism and Truman's alleged "sellout" of Chiang Kai-shek. This message had gained political traction in the United States and would continue to do so for a long time to come. Over nine days the Republicans hammered Secretary of State Acheson about the China issue and appeasement of communism. They called several other witnesses, including General Albert Wedemeyer, whose testimony backfired on them. Wedemeyer, former commander of U.S. forces in China during WWII, delivered his opinion that neither China nor Korea was a strategically vital area and that indeed a U.S. withdrawal from Korea was preferable to a stalemated, resource-draining war. Former Secretary of Defense Louis Johnson dismissed as unsound the idea of using Nationalist troops and did not, despite his great admiration for MacArthur, question the general's removal. Only Patrick J. Hurley bolstered the Republican cause. Hurley, President Roosevelt's envoy, then ambassador, in China in 1944 and 1945 had been sent there to reconcile differences between General Joseph Stilwell and Chiang Kai-shek and to arrange unification of the Chinese communists with Chiang's government. Hurley repeated before the committee his by then all too familiar refrain that he had been undermined in his efforts in China by a State Department that favored the communists while going along with British imperialism, and by a group of U.S. Foreign Service officers in China who sympathized with the communist position. Owing to confrontations with these officers, Hurley also bore a personal animus toward them.[26]

Altogether, the hearings took the glitter off MacArthur's standing. Public acclaim soon began to diminish. People listened to his three days of testimony; after that they lost interest. Those who followed on could not fail to be influenced by the strategic myopia reflected in his repeated recommendations and by the testimony of the Joint Chiefs who pointed out forcefully that the general had been insubordinate, multiple times, had violated direct orders, and had disregarded the president's directive of December 6, 1950, prohibiting public pronouncements. Even many of those who admired him came to see that he deserved dismissal.

The general, however, did not slink away in silence. He entertained visitors, or supplicants, in his ten-room suite at the Waldorf Towers, with its guarded entrance, overlooking Park Avenue. He lived richly, the beneficiary of a handsome salary, good "investments," and gifts from friends. When he moved from Tokyo, he brought forty-nine tons of personal effects, including large quantities of oriental art, jade, ivory, ebony, and silver. Under law, he retained the right to a staff and to wear his uniform, as he continued to do while fulfilling his many speaking engagements. For the year following his dismissal there were many audiences awaiting his appearance.

From mid-June 1951 through the Republican convention of 1952, MacArthur worked hard to deliver his message and to salve his ego though bitter, vituperative attacks on President Truman. Although always insisting that he was motivated by a dedicated love of country and unwavering patriotism rather than political ambition, he envisioned a run for the presidency in 1952. Financed largely through the generosity of Texas millionaires H. L. Hunt and Clint Murchison, he traveled the country, first in several cities in Texas, then in Massachusetts, Pennsylvania, Ohio, Washington state, Florida, and wherever he could turn out a large audience to hear his message.

That message had several parts. One was that the Yalu rather than the Rhine or the Elbe represented America's first line of defense. It was possible to save Europe only by stopping communism in Asia. He also asserted that the United States under the Democrats—Roosevelt and Truman—had allowed government to grow to enormous proportions, financed by excessive taxes (a favorite Hunt/right-wing Republican theme), and had endorsed a form of socialism that would destroy the country from within. MacArthur, who had spent his entire life from birth in a socialist system, a welfare state in which public money had met all of his personal needs, both in the U.S. army and in the Philippines, seemed oblivious to the irony of such contentions. Like so many military officers after him, he became a great advocate of rugged individualism, capitalism, and free enterprise and a leading proponent of the Republican domestic agenda.

Criticism of Truman pervaded his speeches. The president and his advisers, he stated ad nauseam, had allowed a rot to infest American foreign, as well as domestic, policy, with the result that communism was spreading throughout the world. He would deal with that contagion, first in Asia. The president, he said, had not only failed to listen to his opinion but tried to silence him. In a particularly outrageous oration in Boston, he crossed the line, raising once again the specter of insubordination. In the words of his outstanding biographer, he showed "how distorted was his own interpretation of an American military officer's oath." "I find in existence," railed the general, "a new and heretofore unknown and dangerous concept that the members of our armed forces owe primary allegiance and loyalty to those who temporarily exercise the authority of the executive branch of Government, rather than to the country and its Constitution which they are sworn to defend."[27] MacArthur's insubordinate father could not have enunciated any better the opinion of this "most subordinate officer."

During the 1951–1952 political maneuvering MacArthur and Senator Taft performed a kind of mating dance. Taft desperately wanted the Republican nomination and asked the general for his support. MacArthur extended his support, all the while desiring the nod himself. Both men worried they would have to stop Eisenhower who became the top choice of many leading figures in the party. MacArthur, Hunt, and right-wing Republicans hoped for a Taft-Eisenhower deadlock, at which point the party would turn to MacArthur. The general, as earlier, would not put his ego on the line with an open declaration for the nomination. When Eisenhower won out, MacArthur was sorely disappointed and refused to campaign for him.

Meanwhile, the Truman administration's attempt to achieve a negotiated end to the war in Korea went forward. The domestic commotion following MacArthur's dismissal did not seriously deter that effort. For a while, both before and after the general's recall, neither the Chinese nor the Soviets proved willing to engage in serious talks. The Chinese mobilized their forces for a major offensive that they hoped would either drive the United States out of Korea or make it more willing to negotiate on Chinese terms. Those terms always included Chinese seating in the United Nations and U.S. withdrawal of support for Taiwan. Those were not compelling issues to the Soviets, who came to question the costs and benefits of continuing the war in Korea. A breakthrough occurred early in 1951 after General Ridgway and his new commander in Korea, General James Van Fleet, rallied UN troops to defeat the Chinese spring offensive. Ill-equipped and poorly nourished Chinese troops surrendered in great numbers, after which UN forces advanced rapidly to the 38th parallel. There they stopped, as policymakers in Washington and from the Soviet Union began working toward a settlement of the war. The risks of recrossing the 38th parallel seemed too high and the likely cost of a longer war excessive in view of limited American interests.

Aware of a desire for an early end to the war, George Kennan, who had had his differences with Acheson and had left his post at the Policy Planning Staff of the State Department and moved to an appointment at Princeton University, suggested to the State Department that he might unofficially sound out the Soviet UN Representative, Jacob Malik, on the prospects for an armistice. Kennan subsequently drove out to Malik's residence on Long Island, where the Soviet envoy cordially but nervously greeted him. Malik agreed to consult his government, which, less than a week later, authorized him to tell Kennan of its interest in crafting a truce "as rapidly as possible." In a June 23 radio address, Malik made public the Soviet desire for peace.[28]

The Kennan-Malik exchange marked the third attempt on the part of the Soviets to limit the consequences of the war. The first had come in July 1950 when the Soviets, recognizing that the North Korean offensive was about spent, gave tentative approval to an Indian suggestion in which the belligerents would return to the status-quo ante bellum in return for Chinese representation in the United Nations The United States rejected this proposal because it included no guarantee against another North Korean invasion of the

South. The second came in October 1950 as UN troops began their rapid advance into North Korea. The Soviets this time proposed an all-Korea election supervised by a UN commission in which the Chinese communists would participate. The United States, at that time of great military success, saw no advantage or justification in accepting the Soviet plan. Now in late spring and early summer of 1951, the United States and the Soviets, joined by their respective allies, agreed to proceed with discussions, and on July 10 truce negotiations began at Kaesong and later continued at Panmunjom. The discussions dragged on for over two years, as the fighting continued, before the parties signed an armistice on July 27, 1953.[29]

In the negotiations both sides focused on issues other than those that dominated the conflict in 1950. No longer did the adversaries envision unification. Nor did the Chinese insist that armistice preconditions include their seating in the United Nations, the withdrawal of America forces from Korea, or the abandonment of U.S. support for Taiwan. The negotiations focused on the repatriation of prisoners of war, which the communists wanted done unconditionally, while the UN command insisted on returning only those men who wished to be repatriated. The drawing of the cease-fire line and the method of enforcing the armistice were also central concerns.[30]

The timing of the breakthrough in July 1953 after bitter recrimination and interruption in the talks warrants attention, especially in view of MacArthur's recommendations to president-elect Eisenhower in the fall of 1952 and claims by Secretary of State Dulles that the Eisenhower administration broke the impasse with a threat to use nuclear weapons to end the war. MacArthur met with Eisenhower and Dulles in New York on December 17, 1952 to discuss a memo he had drafted laying out a plan to end the war. The general proposed that the president-elect call a conference with Stalin that would deal with Korea within the larger world context. Eisenhower should then lay out the following plan: Germany, Japan, Austria, and Korea (he and Kennan had come to similar views about Korea prior to the Korean War) would be neutralized under guarantee by the United States and the Soviet Union; Germany and Korea should be unified by popular vote; all foreign troops should be removed from Germany and Austria and from Japan and Korea (again a view not far removed from Kennan's); the United States and the Soviet Union would outlaw war in their constitutions; finally, if the aforementioned terms were not accepted, the United States would unilaterally clear Korea of enemy troops, if necessary using atomic weapons and laying down fields of radioactive materials. Beyond that, MacArthur said, Eisenhower should follow the plan he had recommended to President Truman to attack Manchuria and unleash Chinese Nationalist troops.[31]

If Dulles were right about what broke the impasse, then MacArthur might deserve vindication. But several caveats are in order. Quite apart from Dulles's claims, there is evidence that the United States had been prepared for some time to "get tough" with the Chinese and Soviets if armistice talks broke down. In any case, policymakers talked tough among themselves. Acheson told Churchill and Eden in January 1952 a message that, in view of Soviet agents' penetration of the British foreign policy apparatus, surely became known to Stalin, that, if the talks eventually proved unavailing, the United States was prepared to bomb Chinese targets and impose a tight blockade on China. And Truman, in a fit of emotion, vented his frustration with the talks, stating that continued Chinese and Soviet obstructionism could mean "all-out war."[32]

It is also true that Eisenhower after assuming the presidency took some threatening steps. He increased the size of the Korean army, announced that the 7th Fleet would no longer keep Chiang Kai-shek's armies from crossing the Taiwan Strait, authorized the bombing of irrigation dams in North Korea, had Secretary Dulles convey to Prime Minister Jawaharial Nehru of India the possibility of American expansion of the war, and indirectly hinted that if talks broke down the United States would not restrict its use of weapons or the areas in which it would fight. Neither the Chinese nor the Soviet archives have revealed the effects of these steps.

In any event, restraints on the new administration probably offset these threats. The restraints were significant. America's European allies remained steadfastly opposed to a widening of the war. Moreover, there was always the danger of a world war in which the Soviet Union could attack Japan and specific sites in Korea, such as Pusan and Inchon. But most important to Eisenhower was the knowledge that, in the event of a major war with the Soviets, their bombers could hit the United States with atomic bombs, thereby reducing the effectiveness of the Strategic Air Command and killing millions of American civilians.[33]

Evidence suggests, quite apart from American threats, that the North Korean regime needed peace and Stalin's successors (Stalin died on March 5, 1953) realized the war had become too costly for Soviet interests. The war had brought almost unbelievable hardship to North Korea: by 1953 income had decreased by more than a third; inflation was rampant; and confiscation of farm produce and animals destroyed any residual goodwill in the countryside, with hoarding and tax evasion pervasive. Life had become nearly unbearable in North Korea and the "morale of the North Korean people . . . came dangerously close to the breaking point." The Chinese, moreover, had suffered enormous losses in Korea, in the process learning that they could not, at any acceptable human cost, drive UN forces off the peninsula. In addition, monetary costs were so staggering that continued war might threaten the stability of the new communist regime.

For the new Soviet leaders the war spelled nothing but trouble. It had resulted in the reassertion of American power around the world and the solidification of an anti-Soviet bloc in Western Europe. In two years the United States increased its defense budget from $13 billion to over $60 billion, tripled U.S. air forces in Great Britain, stepped up aid to Southeast Asian nations, arranged for permanent bases in Japan, and strengthened NATO. Stalin's heirs realized that, although North Korea and China had borne the major burden in the fighting, the Soviet Union paid a heavy price for negligible benefit. Without the Soviets, the war could not go on. The Soviets saw the need to conclude the war. Therein lies the main reason for the armistice, not threats of greater offensive action as suggested by MacArthur.[34]

Notes

1. Michael Schaller, *Douglas MacArthur: The Far Eastern General* (New York: Oxford University Press, 1989), 216–17, 225, 230–31.

2. Quoted in Russell D. Buhite, *Soviet-American Relations in Asia, 1945–1954* (Norman: University of Oklahoma Press, 1981), 181n.

3. NSC#100 Jan. 11, 1951, Modern Military Records, National Archives. Buhite, *Soviet-American Relations in Asia*, 180–81.

4. William Stueck, *The Korean War: An International History* (Princeton, N.J.: Princeton University Press, 1995), 127–30.

5. Quoted in Stueck, *The Korean War*, 131.

6. Schaller, *Douglas MacArthur*, 218, 221.

7. Stueck, *The Korean War*, 130, 143.

8. D. Clayton James, *The Years of MacArthur, Volume 3, 1945–1964* (Boston: Houghton Mifflin, 1985), 549–54.

9. Quoted in James, *The Years of MacArthur, Volume 3*, 559.

10. Schaller, *Douglas MacArthur*, 230–31.

11. Quoted in James, *The Years of MacArthur, Volume 3*, 586–87.

12. James, *The Years of MacArthur, Volume 3*, 589.

13. Quoted in James, *The Years of MacArthur, Volume 3*, 590.

14. Quoted in James, *The Years of MacArthur, Volume 3*, 594. See also James, *The Years of MacArthur, Volume 3*, 590–96.

15. Schaller, *Douglas MacArthur*, 236–37.

16. Quoted in James, *The Years of MacArthur, Volume 3*, 598.

17. Douglas MacArthur, *Reminiscences* (New York: Fawcett World Library and Time Inc., 1965), 394–95.

18. Quoted in Schaller, *Douglas MacArthur*, 240.

19. See Schaller, *Douglas MacArthur*, 241–43; James, *The Years of MacArthur, Volume 3*, 607–9.

20. Quoted in Schaller, *Douglas MacArthur*, 243.

21. James, *The Years of MacArthur, Volume 3*, 608–16.

22. James, *The Years of MacArthur, Volume 3*, 617.

23. Schaller, *Douglas MacArthur*, 246.

24. *Military Situation in the Far East* (Washington, D.C.: Government Printing Office, 1951), 76. For the full extent of MacArthur's testimony, see *Military Situation in the Far East*, 2–320.

25. *Military Situation in the Far East*, 730–45.

26. Russell D. Buhite, *Patrick J. Hurley and American Foreign Policy* (Ithaca, N.Y.: Cornell University Press, 1973), 134–238, 239–52.

27. Quoted in James, *The Years of MacArthur, Volume 3*, 644. See also James, *The Years of MacArthur, Volume 3*, 642–46.

28. Buhite, *Soviet-American Relations in Asia*, 181–82.

29. Buhite, *Soviet-American Relations in Asia*, 182–83.

30. Buhite, *Soviet-American Relations in Asia*, 183–85.

31. James, *The Years of MacArthur, Volume 3*, 654.

32. Buhite, *Soviet-American Relations in Asia*, 183–84.

33. Stueck, *The Korean War*, 329, 324, 322–24.

34. Robert Scalapino and Chang-sik Lee, *Communism in Korea* (Berkeley: University of California Press, 1972), 422; Buhite, *Soviet-American Relations in Asia*, 184–85.

CHAPTER EIGHT

~

An Appraisal

Of the several themes that dominated MacArthur's life after the election of 1952, four in particular stand out: his unrelenting hostility to President Truman and of course the latter's hostility to him; his reaping and relishing of awards in unseemly number; his work for the Remington-Rand Corporation wherein he embraced the military-industrial complex; his inconsistency during his declining years as he seemed to change his worldview, his attitude toward war, and some of his opinions about domestic politics.

The Truman-MacArthur controversy lived on as long as each man. MacArthur's speeches not only prior to the Republican Convention of 1952, but afterward as well, were filled with unflattering references to the president; his most cutting comment always held that he could have won the war in Korea within weeks but for the meddling, small-minded man in the White House. Truman responded in kind in his memoirs where he pointedly cited the general's insubordination. MacArthur in turn dismissed Truman as a "vulgar little clown." Truman retorted that he had punctured MacArthur's ego and the result was lots of whistling noise from the escaping air. The two men publicly debated whether the general had ever advocated the use of atomic weapons, and at one point in 1954 MacArthur gave an interview to *U.S. News and World Report* (released to the public after his death in 1964) in which he referred to the "fools" in Washington who had mismanaged the Korean War. Truman refused to invite MacArthur to the ceremony marking the signing of the Japanese Peace Treaty, a slap in the face to the general that bordered on pettiness. If MacArthur ever mellowed toward Truman, as biographer William Manchester claims, the general may have agreed only grudgingly that "the little bastard had guts to fire me." Or that Truman was "a man of raw courage."[1]

The nation's ongoing desire for a hero in a media age that had begun making mere mortals out of everyone led during the 1950s to undue adulation of MacArthur. Streets, schools, bridges, buildings of various types, parks, and airports received the MacArthur name. He gained awards from civic organizations, resolutions of praise from Congress, top honors from the Boy Scouts, and six honorary doctorates. Representative Joseph Martin introduced legislation to make him a six-star general, a rank higher than anyone other than John J. Pershing had ever achieved. Neither President Eisenhower nor other members of the general officer rank were particularly thrilled with the idea. That honor did not materialize, probably because of Eisenhower's opposition. Truman, for his part said if he had remained in the White House he would have busted MacArthur to "four star."[2]

At Remington Rand, later called Sperry Rand, MacArthur's main duties as chairman of the board were to make speeches on behalf of the firm, calling attention to its activities and to maintaining its high profile. The firm specialized in electronic products, many of them designed for military use, and the general made no secret of his endorsement of the military-industrial connection. For his work he received handsome reward. Four times a week a chauffeur picked him up at the Waldorf Towers and drove him and General Courtney Whitney, who also had a position at the company, to Stamford, Connecticut, site of the firm's offices, for fancy luncheons and business meetings. At the outset, James Rand, founder of the company, paid him $45,000 a year for his services, a figure soon raised to $68,800 (comparable to over $500,000 in early twenty-first-century dollars). By the time of his death in 1964 his estate had a value of over $2 million, which would translate to between $15 and $20 million—far more than any modern general officer would normally accumulate.

For a while in the mid and late 1950s, the general and his wife attended Broadway plays and continued to enjoy movies, always a pleasant form of entertainment for MacArthur. Most evenings, however, he spent quietly at home watching sports on television, especially baseball games. The pair did some entertaining, though less and less as he aged. They usually confined their socializing to friends in the Waldorf, including former President Hoover who had a suite below the general's. Others occasionally came calling. One of them was Earl "Red" Blaik, the Military Academy football coach who brought films of games and showed the general many of his newly designed plays.

Although President Eisenhower possessed a healthy disdain for MacArthur's persona and his talents, he indulged the general with invitations to the White House, thinking it politically wise at least to appear his friend and confidant. Vice President Richard M. Nixon, who saw MacArthur more often, knew better than to bring up the general's name in Eisenhower's presence. The president did not seek MacArthur's advice, nor did he act on his memorandum of December 1952.

Eisenhower's indifference and that of Secretary of State Dulles engendered MacArthur's enmity and prompted him to begin staking out points of difference with the administration. By the late fifties he frequently decried war, pointing out how technology as it had evolved in his lifetime had made warfare impossible to justify. He deemed the Eisenhower/Dulles doctrine of massive retaliation not only an unworkable way to settle disputes but also a threat to the existence of civilization. But he never thought much good could come from the flexible response military doctrine emerging during that same period either. What he saw as most logical was to outlaw war entirely, writing this prohibition into the constitutions of the major players on the world stage and in effect reviving the outlawry movement of the 1920s. No key figure in the Eisenhower administration considered this idea viable.

MacArthur's response to presidents John F. Kennedy and Lyndon Johnson was fascinating. Kennedy, probably because he saw it as politically expedient, reached out to the old general. In so doing, he endowed MacArthur with elder statesman status. Whatever Kennedy's initial motivation, he and the old general became friends of sorts. Kennedy invited him to the White House, provided an airplane to fly the general and his family to the Philippines, and asked him to mediate a dispute between the National Collegiate Athletic Association and the Amateur Athletic Union that threatened to disrupt U.S. participation in the 1964 Olympics. By all accounts, the general handled the assignment with skill, helping resolve the differences. Lyndon Johnson nurtured the general during and prior to his final illness. MacArthur, to his credit, strongly warned both men against involvement in Vietnam or in any land war on the Asian continent because such a war would be unwinnable.

Among his most pleasurable activities during his declining years were trips to the Philippines and to West Point in 1961 and 1962, respectively. In the Philippines he found a red carpet, receiving treatment accorded to the greatest of heroes. He toured the islands, gave several speeches, including one to a combined session of the Filipino House and Senate, and generally enjoyed what he knew would be his last visit to a country he had considered home for so many years. His other visit of note, one in which he reveled, was to address the cadets at the Military Academy in the spring of 1962. His speech there, considered one of his finest, was filled with typical MacArthur flourish and plenty of Duty, Honor, Country, God, and July 4th patriotism. His audience was entranced and teary eyed as they listened to the old general and perceived hero.

For a man who throughout most of his long career never exercised, never played golf, bowled, or engaged in any physical activity, MacArthur remained in remarkably good health until he reached his eightieth year. This good health was also extraordinary because he avoided doctors, either out of contempt for their profession, an arrogant assumption that he would never need help, or a fatalistic view that what was going to happen would eventually happen. He became ill in January 1960. In March of that year he entered the hospital where he was treated for a severe kidney infection and had a tumor removed from his prostate. Public information indicated that the tumor was benign, but as his condition began to worsen in 1962 and as various organs began to fail over the next year and a half, particularly his liver, intestines, spleen, and lungs, metastasized cancer appears to have been the cause of his decline. In March 1964, President Johnson convinced him to enter Walter Reed Army Medical Center in Washington. He died in the hospital on April 5, at age 84.

One measure of his huge ego to the very end was his insistence that the Defense Department's plan for military funerals be altered in his case. Instead of the four days of lying in state in the capitol, after which burial would occur at the Arlington National Cemetery, he insisted on seven days, with proper honors to be accorded in New York and in Norfolk as well. He requested burial at the MacArthur Memorial Museum in Norfolk. Another measure was his frantic work during the last year of his life to complete his memoirs, an effort in which he labored hard but also had considerable assistance from Whitney. The work was important to him as a way of recording his version of his story and correcting or augmenting previous publications, some of which were decidedly unflattering.[3]

No explanation of MacArthur, or his worldview, at any stage of his life makes sense without reference to his overweening ego, an issue that nearly all biographers, journalists, and contemporary observers strongly emphasize. But it is necessary to go beyond mere ego in understanding what motivated him—to see him, in fact, within the context of a personality disorder referred to by psychologists as narcissism of the most malignant sort, or as "narcissistic personality disorder."

Psychobiography may or may not be good history. To take the theories or postulates of Sigmund Freud or some other psychologist and apply them to a figure long since deceased, or in any event unobserved by the author, may lead to distortion of the most egregious sort. On the other hand, it may be useful to offer a psychological explanation when other explanations fail, or when the personality of the individual under study is so directly intertwined with his policy views. MacArthur deserves the attention of a psychologist trained in history or an historian trained in psychology. Because this biographer is neither, what seems most appropriate here is to advance a model that suits the subject, show how MacArthur seemed to manifest the pathology depicted in that model, and to demonstrate cautiously its connection to his worldview.

The term narcissism comes from Greek mythology wherein a handsome young man named Narcissus rejected the advances of the nymph Echo, who had fallen in love—or lust—with him. Owing to his nonresponsiveness to Echo, Narcissus was doomed to fall in love with himself, or rather his reflection in a pool of water. Over time, as he could not consummate his love, Narcissus turned into a flower bearing his name. The idea received scholarly attention when in 1915 Freud examined the pathology of narcissism in an essay entitled, "On Narcissism." Over the years a number of other scholars have written on the topic, including Robert Hare, Karen Horney, Otto Kernberg, Franz Kohut, and Elsa Roningstam.

Most recently, Sam Vaknin, in his book *Malignant Self-Love: Narcissism Revisited*, has taken the *Diagnostic and Statistical Manual of Mental Disorders*, 4th edition, published by the American Psychiatric Association, and used it with some modification as the basis of his study. Vaknin repeats the manual's definition and then extracts the nine diagnostic criteria for the disorder from the manual and revises each of them in a way that not only makes them more complete but more comprehensible. The manual defines narcissistic personality disorder (NPD) as "an all-pervasive pattern of grandiosity (in fantasy or behavior), need for admiration or adulation and lack of empathy, usually beginning by early adulthood and present in various contexts."

The nine criteria as amended by Vaknin, only five of which are require for a diagnosis of NPD, are as follows:

1. Feels grandiose and self-important (e.g., exaggerates accomplishments, talents, skills, contacts, and personality traits to the point of lying), demands to be recognized as superior without commensurate achievements.
2. Is obsessed with fantasies of unlimited success, fame, fearsome power or omnipotence, unequalled brilliance, bodily beauty or sexual performance, or ideal everlasting, all-conquering love or passion.

3. Firmly convinced that he or she is unique and, being special, can only be understood by, or associate with, other special or unique or high status people (or institutions).
4. Requires excessive admiration, adulation, attention, and affirmation—or failing that, wishes to be feared and be notorious.
5. Feels entitled. Demands automatic and full compliance with his or her unreasonable expectations for special and favorable priority treatment.
6. Is interpersonally exploitative (i.e., uses others to achieve his or her ends).
7. Devoid of empathy. Is unable or unwilling to identify with, acknowledge, or accept the feelings, needs, preferences, priorities, and choices of others.
8. Constantly envious of others and seeks to hurt or destroy the objects of his or her frustration. Suffers from persecutory (paranoid) delusions as he or she believes that they feel the same about him or her and are likely to act similarly.
9. Behaves arrogantly and haughtily. Feels superior, omnipotent, omniscient, invincible, immune, above the law, and omnipresent. Rages when frustrated, contradicted, or confronted by people he or she considers inferior to him or her and unworthy.

In addition to the nine points noted above, scholars have identified several other common characteristics of narcissistic personality disorder. One of them holds that an individual with the disorder often grew up in a dysfunctional family or had a mother who displayed controlling behavior and unreasonably high expectations for the child. Often the mother continued as a dominant presence in the person's life until the child was well past middle age. The mother's approval was extremely hard to get, but it was always necessary.

The narcissistic person does not love himself or herself so much as the reflection of self. This means that the individual in question must project an image or have someone else project it, but that image has to be consistent with the self-image. If another person does well in supporting the narcissist's self-image, then that person will be valued. If not, that person will be discarded. Others are valued less as people than as instruments, important only for their utility. In the narcissistic worldview, in other words, it is easy for the subordinate to become insubordinate.

The narcissistic individual is also often reclusive, using other people to convey his wishes or state his opinions. He may withdraw for long periods or make himself inaccessible on the pretense of preoccupation with his work or on larger questions than normal mortals would confront. He may defy social mores on the expectation that they are not required of him; he is too important for mundane matters.

Although the narcissist is very often a high achiever occupying transcendent positions of power or authority, he frequently sees himself as terribly persecuted. He may perceive himself as the target of unjust attack from higher authority because only someone as talented as he could possibly be singled out for rebuke by a superior. Often the narcissist will bait or provoke a superior into dismissing him because this is a natural way to enhance a delusional self-image. Such provocative behavior is a common feature of the narcissist.

Finally, among the more identifiable narcissistic traits is a firm belief in one's triumphal nature. The narcissist may demonstrate this nature through acts of foolish fearlessness. He may feel himself invisible to enemies or may act God-like and in possession of divine or cosmic immunity to danger. He may feel impervious to evil, or forces he defines as evil.[4]

How the foregoing applies to MacArthur may or may not seem evident. Some things, however, seem to stand out as unexplainable except through the narcissistic model. He courted danger throughout his long military life and obviously got away with it: in the Philippines and Mexico as a young man; during WWI; on Corregidor; on the South Pacific Islands during WWII; in Japan, which he entered unarmed and with minimal military escort; and in Korea. There may have been a practical motive (to avoid criticism at Corregidor, as he later explained his actions there to Faubion Bowers), but that hardly seems to provide an adequate explanation for a career filled with such recklessness.

The list goes on. His strutting, preening, popinjay manner and dress; his attempts to seem taller than he actually was; his grandiosity; his publicity-seeking; his sweeping grandiloquent language—"for a thousand years," "to the end of time," and "throughout history"; his lying about the readiness of the Philippine army; his proclamations about throwing the Japanese back at Filipino beaches; his blatant falsification of success in the Southwest Pacific; his portrayal of himself as the frontline leader in every military success even though much of the time he was in Australia; his God-like behavior toward the Japanese people; his reclusiveness (he never had a phone in his office, never traveled about Japan, and only briefly visited Korea); his exaggeration of the "communist" threat posed by the Bonus Marchers and draconian measures to subdue this alleged danger; the sense of entitlement that allowed him to accept a huge illegal gift of $500,000 from the Philippine government; the same sense that later led him to live in a posh and spacious apartment in the

Waldorf Towers virtually rent-free; his attitude toward U.S. presidents; his defiance or baiting of President Truman; his desire to become president but not actually run for the office. All these things convey relevance of the narcissistic personality disorder model (how else these things could be explained remains a mystery).

Most telling, perhaps, was his relationship with his mother and his sexual history. His mother's expectations for him, which she hammered home relentlessly, were inordinately high. She managed not only his early life, but much of his career. He remained unable to achieve separation until her death and not even then could he escape her overpowering presence. He worried about living up to the standard set by his hero-father, a specter his mother kept alive to the end of her days. His sexual relationships did not begin until his forties; then he frequented prostitutes and a Eurasian mistress he could temporarily dominate. Early attempts at intimacy with his first wife ended in inadequacy, failure, and divorce. His second wife indulged his control and his "heroism."

On matters of foreign policy his inconsistencies were legion, his recommendations nearly always personal. East Asia held the greatest strategic value for the United States because this was the area of the world to which his father had been assigned. Later it would be his area. That Europe received highest priority during WWII offended him deeply; his war was of greater importance; his enemies within the U.S. military gained too much attention, too many of the resources, too much glory for winning the war. The European war, he believed in his heart, was defined as of the highest priority to deny him his rightful honor. His war, he said, required the retaking of the Philippines regardless of the questionable strategic wisdom of that move; "he" had promised to return. Some of the time he argued for bringing the Soviet Union into the Asian-Pacific war; later, complying with the Republican line and attacking the Yalta Accords, he portrayed it as a mistake. His perspectives depended on what he was pursuing at the moment rather than on careful strategic analysis. Korea, he argued repeatedly prior to June 1950, was peripheral to American interests. After his command assignment Korea became vital, a country over which he would risk WWIII. He counseled avoidance of a land war in Asia, yet he was willing to risk such a war by attacking China. He opted for a less militarized foreign policy in the late fifties as a way to distance himself from his old rival, Eisenhower, one of those subordinates who had failed impertinently to advance the MacArthur ethos.

His inconsistencies aside, with one major exception MacArthur's overall tangible impact on American foreign policy proved largely negative. Along with Secretary of War Patrick J. Hurley and Secretary of State Henry L.

Stimson he worked to slow the drive toward Philippine independence in the early 1930s. Despite his warning not to become engaged in Vietnam, his insistence on the priority of East Asia in U.S. foreign relations became dogma with his Republican friends, complicating policy formulation for the Truman administration and contributing to the subsequent globalization of containment. His emphasis on the merits of Chiang Kai-shek's regime on Taiwan reinforced the myth of America's "loss of China," influenced public opinion in the United States, and encouraged the so-called China lobby, which for over twenty years helped prevent a flexible approach to the People's Republic of China. Although most of the critical decisions on Japan were made in Washington, in fairness MacArthur compiled a strong, positive record in directing the occupation of that country. Indeed, it is difficult to think of any of his contemporary officers who could have done better in that assignment; and if his work is compared to that done in a more recent occupation, his efforts seem superb.

Following the Gulf War of 1991, then Secretary of Defense Dick Cheney argued against the overthrow of Saddam Hussein and occupation of Iraq: "Once you've got Baghdad, it's not clear what you do with it. It's not clear what kind of government you would put in place of the one that's currently there now. Is it going to be a Shia regime, a Sunni regime or a Kurdish regime? Or one that tilts toward the Baathists, or one that tilts toward the Islamic fundamentalists? How much credibility is that government going to have if it's set up by the United States military when it's there? How long does the United States military have to stay to protect the people that sign on for that government, and what happens to it once we leave?"[5] Cheney's change of heart in 2003 and afterward may or may not have derived from the terrorist attacks on the World Trade Center and Pentagon on September 11, 2001, but there can be little doubt that he was more prophetic about the occupation of Iraq on the former occasion than on the latter.

The failure to occupy Iraq successfully following the short, decisive, military defeat of Saddam Hussein's regime in the spring of 2003 begs comparison to the American experience in Japan in 1945, following a long, bitter, total war. Why did one occupation succeed and the other fail? The answer lies in part with the planning, the preparation, and, more especially, with indigenous differences. Iraq was an artificial entity held together by a tyrant, a country rife with ethnic and sectarian differences—just as Cheney indicated in 1991. Japan, by contrast, was a comparatively homogeneous society with a long history, a country comprised of a people susceptible to situational ethics and new authority—one that possessed incipient democratic institutions prior to the advent of twentieth-century militarism. Part of the answer, however, lies in the choice of commanders. General MacArthur, for all of his faults and personality flaws, proved an ideal choice for Japan, and for reasons noted in chapter 4, the Japanese came to revere him as they had revered no other Westerner. It was in Japan that the general made his most significant contribution to American foreign policy.

As a military figure, he had both successes and failures. Because he succeeded so brilliantly at Inchon, his daring invasion plan stands as a stroke of genius. He deserves credit for an accurate assessment of the risks and rewards of the operation. He also pushed the plan against strong opposition from some of his fellow general officers and superiors. That he was at the same time extremely lucky does not measurably detract from his accomplishment. Though the foreign policy decisions that followed the landing were disastrous, he should bear only part of the blame for them. Policymakers in Washington escalated their goals for Korea and did little to restrain the imperious general. If he may be absolved of some of the responsibility for Washington's tragic judgments, his military decisions in Korea following Inchon were fatally flawed. Moreover, his heroic record in WWII was a product of his relentless propaganda machine, for the most part fabricated by his press releases. His performance in the Philippines, especially in the immediate hours after Pearl Harbor, was stunningly abysmal—bad enough to warrant dismissal. But his record as commander in chief of the Philippine armed forces was little better. Though a man of above average competence, he was hardly a military or any other kind of genius. He was not an American Caesar nor even an Eisenhower or a Grant. Despite his self-image of greatness, he was in the end as much thespian as statesman, as much facade as substance.

Notes

1. William Manchester, *American Caesar: Douglas MacArthur, 1880–1946* (Boston: Little, Brown, 1978), 690.

2. Quoted in D. Clayton James, *The Years of MacArthur, Volume 3, 1945–1964* (Boston: Houghton Mifflin, 1985), 675.

3. Nearly everyone who in recent years has written on the last phase of MacArthur's life has utilized the narrative provided in James, *The Years of MacArthur, Volume 3*, 641–90.

4. *The Diagnostic and Statistical Manual of Mental Disorders*, 4th ed. (Washington, D.C.: American Psychiatric Association, 2000), 714–17; Sam Vaknin, *Malignant Self Love: Narcissism Revisited* (Skopje, Macedonia: Narcissism Publication, 2004), chap. 1, 2, 3, 4, 6, 9. See also Carolyne C. Morf and Frederick Rhodewalt, "Unraveling the Paradoxes of Narcissism: A Dynamic Self-Regulatory Processing Model," *Psychological Inquiry* 12, no. 4 (2001): 177–96. Morf and Rhodewalt observe on page 185 that:

"When directly confronted with failure . . . narcissists find ways of undoing it. They respond to negative feedback for example, by derogating the evaluator or the evaluation technique. . . . Alternatively, they might even distort and restructure past events to soften the blow."

5. Cheney quoted in George Will, "Inoculated for Exuberance," *Washington* Post, Nov. 10, 2006, A31.

~

Bibliographical Essay

The work available on General Douglas MacArthur and the issues with which he became involved over his long career is voluminous. There are over twenty-five biographies, some of them scholarly, balanced and well written— some not. Among the biographies, the most definitive, the most complete, the most objective, and the most scholarly is the three volume study by D. Clayton James, *The Years of MacArthur, vol. I, 1880–1941* (Boston: Houghton Mifflin, 1970); *vol. II, 1941–1945* (Boston: Houghton Mifflin, 1975); *vol. III, 1945–1964* (Boston: Houghton Mifflin, 1985). A more negative but equally scholarly assessment is Michael Schaller, *Douglas MacArthur: The Far Eastern General* (New York: Oxford University Press, 1989). Carol Petillo, *Douglas MacArthur: The Philippine Years* (Bloomington: Indiana University Press, 1981), provides an excellent psychological portrait of the young MacArthur with primary focus on his experience in the Philippines. The best-selling popular biography, one that is generally favorable but not uncritical, is William Manchester, *American Caesar: Douglas MacArthur 1880–1964* (Boston: Little Brown, 1978). A recent, critical, highly readable study of MacArthur in Korea is Stanley Weintraub, *MacArthur's War: Korea and the Undoing of an American Hero* (New York: Free Press, 2000). Another recent study that is engagingly written and emphasizes "will power" as MacArthur's motivating force is Geoffrey Perret, *Old Soldiers Never Die: The Life of Douglas MacArthur* (New York: Random House, 1996). For a superb study of MacArthur as rhetorician, see Bernard K. Duffy, *Douglas MacArthur: Warrior as Wordsmith* (Westport, Conn.: Greenwood, 1997). Richard Connaughton, *MacArthur and Defeat in the Philippines* (Woodstock, N.Y.: Overlook Press, 2001), is a work that is favorable to MacArthur in his early years but critical on the Philippine defeat.

Going back to an earlier era, the studies are of mixed utility. In 1943, John Hersey published *Men on Bataan* (New York: Knopf, 1943), a useful and well-crafted look at MacArthur within the context of the Bataan campaign. Francis T. Miller's hagiographic book is much less useful: *General Douglas MacArthur: Fighter for Freedom* (Chicago: Winston, 1942).

In the 1950s six biographical books of note appeared: John Gunther, *The Riddle of MacArthur: Japan, Korea and the Far East* (New York: Harper, 1951), which focused on the general's activities in Japan; Clark Lee and Richard Henschel, *Douglas MacArthur* (New York: Holt, Rinehart and Winston, 1952), which is filled with interesting pictures but little else except some material on the general's family; Frazier Hunt, *The Untold Story of Douglas MacArthur* (New York: The Devin Adair Company, 1954), an anticommunist rant authorized by MacArthur himself; Charles Willoughby and John Chamberlain, *MacArthur, 1941-1951* (New York: McGraw-Hill, 1954), a paean to the general that should have made him blush but probably did not; Courtney Whitney, *MacArthur: His Rendezvous with History* (New York: Knopf, 1955), also an authorized work intended to blunt criticism of the insubordinate general. The last two books were inspired at least in part by Richard Rovere and Arthur M. Schlesinger Jr., *The General and the President, and the Future of American Foreign Policy* (New York: Farrar, Straus & Young, 1951), a sprightly, humorous, and sharp critique of MacArthur's behavior before and after his dismissal. It is a biographical essay but not a biography per se.

During the 1960s and the 1970s four noteworthy biographies appeared including the aforementioned book by William Manchester: Gavin Long, *MacArthur as Military Commander* (London: Batsford, 1969), a fairly balanced and sometimes critical study that deals not only with the general's WWII experience but his activities before and after from a partially Australian slant; Sidney L Mayer, *MacArthur* (New York: Ballantine, 1971), which is properly critical; and William S. Phillips Jr., *Douglas MacArthur: A Modern Knight Errant* (Philadelphia: Dorrance Publishing Co., 1978), which treats the general's rhetorical flourishes.

A great many memoirs by and biographies of key contemporaries of MacArthur from WWI through WWII and Korea provide valuable insight into the general's character and his worldview. Dean Acheson, *Present at the Creation: My Years in the State Department* (New York: Norton, 1969), reflects Acheson's contempt; Omar Bradley and Clay Blair, *A General's Life: An Autobiography* (New York: Simon & Schuster, 1983), is more objective than MacArthur had a right to expect; Mark Clark, *From the Danube to the Yalu*

(New York: TAB Books, 1954), is a useful account by another general officer; J. Lawton Collins, *Lightning Joe: An Autobiography* (Baton Rouge: Louisiana State University Press, 1979), offers insight that only a chairman of the Joint Chiefs of Staff could provide. Robert L. Eichelberger, *Our Jungle Road to Tokyo* (New York: Viking, 1950), shows that Eichelberger always had an awareness of MacArthur's ego; he often referred to MacArthur as "Sarah" for the actress, Sarah Bernhardt. Dwight D. Eisenhower, *At Ease: Stories I Tell to Friends* (Garden City, N.Y.: Doubleday, 1967), shows Eisenhower's dislike for his former superior; Sidney Huff, *My Fifteen Years with General MacArthur* (New York: Hunt Frazier, 1964), is by an aide to MacArthur and is uncritical; Marguerite Higgins, *War in Korea: The Report of a Woman Combat Correspondent* (Garden City, N.Y.: Doubleday, 1951), contains a firsthand look at the war in Korea. George F. Kennan, *Memoirs*, vols. *I, II* (Boston: Little, Brown, 1967–1972), depicts the difficulty in working with MacArthur in Japan. Douglas MacArthur, *Reminiscences* (New York: McGraw Hill, 1964), is unapologetic and self-glorifying. Matthew R. Ridgway, *The Korean War* (Garden City, N.Y.: Doubleday, 1967), is an interesting memoir by the officer who replaced MacArthur. William Sebold, *With MacArthur in Japan: A Personal History of the Occupation* (New York: Norton, 1965), tells of the frustrations of a foreign service officer during the occupation. Harry S. Truman, *Memoirs*, 2 vols. (Garden City, N.Y.: Doubleday, 1955–1956), shows little sympathy for MacArthur.

The most noteworthy and, for this study, useful biographies of MacArthur's contemporaries are the following: Alonzo Hamby, *Man of the People: A Life of Harry S. Truman* (New York: Oxford University Press, 1995); Robert Ferrell, *Harry S. Truman: A Life* (Columbia: University of Missouri Press, 1994); Robert Donovan, *Conflict and Crisis: The Presidency of Harry S. Truman 1945–1948* (New York: Norton, 1977); Robert Donovan, *Tumultuous Years: The Presidency of Harry S. Truman 1949–1953* (New York: Norton, 1982); Bert Cochran, *Harry Truman and the Crisis Presidency* (New York: Funk and Wagnalls, 1973); David McCullough, *Truman* (New York: Simon and Schuster, 1992); Robert L. Beisner, *Dean Acheson: A Life in the Cold War* (New York: Oxford University Press, 2006); Douglas Brinkley, *Dean Acheson and the Making of U.S. Foreign Policy* (London: Macmillan, 1993); David S. McLellan, *Dean Acheson: The State Department Years* (New York: Dodd Mead & Co, 1976); Stephen Ambrose, *Eisenhower: Soldier, General of the Army, President-Elect, 1890–1952* (New York: Simon and Schuster, 1983); Richard Immerman, *John Foster Dulles: Piety, Pragmatism and Power in U.S. Foreign Policy* (Wilmington, Del.: Scholarly Resources, 1999); Louis Gerson, *John Foster Dulles* (New York: Cooper Square, 1967); Townsend

Hoopes, *The Devil and John Foster Dulles* (Boston: Little, Brown, 1973); and Herbert S. Parmet, *Eisenhower and The American Crusades* (New York: Macmillan, 1972).

Moving backward in time, a number of biographies and memoirs from the Roosevelt era are essential. Robert Dallek, *Franklin D. Roosevelt and American Foreign Policy, 1932–1945* (New York: Oxford University Press, 1978), is a balanced overview. Harold Ickes, *The Secret Diary of Harold Ickes*, 3 vols. (New York: Simon & Schuster, 1953–1954), reveals Ickes's dislike of MacArthur. Eric Larrabee, *Commander in Chief: Franklin D. Roosevelt, His Lieutenants, and Their War* (New York: Simon & Schuster, 1987), treats FDR's management of WWII. William Leahy, *I Was There* (New York: Whittlesey House, 1950). Jay Luvaas, ed., *Dear Miss Em* (Westport, Conn: Greenwood, 1972), provides a candid look at General Robert Eichelberger's thoughts about MacArthur. Forrest Pogue, *George C. Marshall*, 4 vols. (New York: Viking, 1964–1987), is the definitive work on Marshall; James M. Burns, *Roosevelt: The Soldier of Freedom, 1940–1945* (New York: Harcourt Brace Jovanovich, 1970) is a well-written account of FDR's wartime policies. Elting E. Morrison, *Turmoil and Tradition: A Study of the Life and Times of Henry L. Stimson* (Boston: Houghton Mifflin, 1960), is a solid study of the venerable statesman who served as FDR's secretary of war. David F. Schmitz, *Henry L. Stimson: The First Wise Man* (Wilmington, Del.: Scholarly Resources, 2001), is an excellent short biography in this series. Clarence Cramer, *Newton Baker: A Biography* (Cleveland: World Publishing Company, 1961), and Burke Davis, *The Billy Mitchell Affair* (New York: Random House, 1967), are useful works on episodes in MacArthur's early career. Biographical studies on Herbert Hoover include: Joseph Brandes, *Herbert Hoover and Economic Diplomacy: Department of Commerce Policy, 1921–1928* (Pittsburgh: University of Pittsburgh Press, 1962); Martin Fausold, *The Presidency of Herbert Hoover* (Lawrence: University Press of Kansas, 1985); and Joan Hoff Wilson, *Herbert Hoover: Forgotten Progressive* (Boston: Little, Brown, 1975).

The nonbiographical secondary literature on the years of MacArthur's involvement in international affairs is so extensive that only a portion of it may be mentioned in this essay. Starting with the Korean conflict, the books and articles are so numerous as to belie the "forgotten-war" appellation often used in reference to the Korean War. The following works on the war were the most useful in the study. Roy Appleman, *East of Chosin: Entrapment and Breakout in Korea, 1950* (College Station: Texas A&M University Press, 1987); Clay Blair, *The Forgotten War: America in Korea 1950–1953* (New York: Times Books, 1987); Ronald Caridi, *The Korean War and American Pol-*

itics: The Republican Party as a Case Study (Philadelphia: University of Pennsylvania Press, 1968); Gordan Chang, *Friends and Enemies: The United States, China and the Soviet Union 1948–1972* (Stanford: Stanford University Press, 1990); Jian Chen, "China's Changing Aims During the Korean War, 1950–1951," *The Journal of American East Asian Relations* 1 (Spring 1992): 8–41; Bruce Cumings, *The Origins of the Korean War, vols. I and II* (Princeton: Princeton University Press, 1981, 1990); Rosemary Foot, *The Wrong War: American Policy and Dimensions of the Korean Conflict, 1950–1953* (Ithaca: Cornell University Press, 1985); Sergei Goncharov, John W. Lewis, and Xue Litai, *Uncertain Partner: Stalin, Mao, and the Korean War* (Stanford: Stanford University Press, 1993); Joseph Goulden, *Korea: The Untold Story of the War* (New York: Times Books, 1982); David Halberstam, *The Coldest Winter: America and the Korean War.* (New York: Hyperion 2007). Yufan Hao and Zhai Zhihai, "China's Decision to Enter the Korean War: History Revisted," *China Quarterly* 121 (March 1990): 94–115; Max Hastings, *The Korean War* (New York: Simon & Schuster, 1987); Michael Hunt, "Beijing and the Korean Crisis, June 1950–June 1951," *Political Science Quarterly* 107 (Fall 1992): 453–78. Burton Kaufman, *The Korean War: Challenges in Crisis, Credibility and Command* (Philadelphia: Temple University Press, 1986); Edward Keefer, "President Dwight D. Eisenhower and the End of the Korean War," *Diplomatic History* 10 (Summer 1986): 267–89; James Matray, *The Reluctant Crusade: American Foreign Policy in Korea 1941–1950* (Honolulu: University of Hawaii Press, 1985); Allan R. Millett, *The War For Korea, 1945–1950* (Lawrence: University Press of Kansas, 2005); Glen Paige, *The Korean Decision* (New York: Free Press, 1968); David Rees, *The Limited War* (New York: Free Press, 1968); Dean Rusk, *As I Saw It* (New York: Norton, 1990); William Stueck, *The Korean War: An International History* (Princeton: Princeton University Press, 1995); Kathryn Weathersby, "New Findings on the Korean War," *Bulletin of the Cold War International History Project,* Woodrow Wilson Center for Scholars, Washington, D.C., no. 3 (Fall 1993): 99, 14–18. Allen Whiting, *China Crosses the Yalu: The Decision to Enter the Korean War* (New York: Macmillan, 1960); D. Clayton James, with Anne Sharp Wells, *Refighting the Last War: Command and Crisis in Korea, 1950–1953* (New York: Free Press, 1993); Russell D. Buhite, *Soviet American Relations in Asia 1945–1954* (Norman: University of Okalahoma Press, 1981), contains a chapter on Korea. A recent work is Dennis D. Wainstock, *Truman, MacArthur and the Korean War* (Westport, Conn.: Greenwood, 1999). Of the aforementioned books, the work by Stueck stands out as an example of balanced up-to-date scholarship, but the others make excellent contributions as well.

The occupation of Japan is covered in a number of specialized accounts, all or most of which deal with MacArthur's role in some fashion. Among the best and most useful for this study are: Thomas Bisson, *Zaibatsu Dissolution in Japan* (Berkeley: University of California Press 1954); William Borden, *The Pacific Alliance: United States Foreign Economic Policy and Japanese Trade Recovery, 1947–1955* (Madison: University of Wisconsin Press, 1984); Hugh Barton, *American Presurrender Planning for Post War Japan* (New York: Columbia University, Occasional Papers of the East Asian Institute, 1967); Roger Buckley, *Occupation Diplomacy: Britain, the United States and Japan, 1942–1949* (Cambridge, U.K.: Cambridge University Press, 1982); Thomas Burkman, ed., *The Occupation of Japan: The International Context* (Norfolk: MacArthur Memorial Press, 1984); Theodore Cohen, *Remaking Japan: The American Occupation as New Deal* (New York: Free Press, 1987); William Coughlin, *Conquered Press: The MacArthur Era in Japanese Journalism* (Palo Alto: Stanford University Press, 1952); John Dower, *Empire and Aftermath: Yoshida Shigeru and the Japanese Experience, 1878–1954* (Cambridge: Harvard University Press, 1979); Miriam Farley, *Aspects of Japan's Labor Problems* (New York: J. Day Co., 1950); Herbert Feis, *Contest Over Japan* (New York: Norton, 1967); Eleanor Hadley, *Anti Trust in Japan* (Princeton: Princeton University Press, 1974); Joe Moore, *Japanese Workers and the Struggle for Power* (Madison: University of Wisconsin Press, 1983); Michael Schaller, *The American Occupation of Japan: The Origins of the Cold War in Asia* (New York: Oxford University Press, 1985); Howard Schonberger, *Aftermath of War: Americans and the Remaking of Japan* (Kent, Ohio: Kent State University Press, 1988); Richard B. Finn, *Winners in Peace: MacArthur, Yoshida and Postwar Japan* (Berkeley: University of California Press, 1992); Harry Wildes, *Typhoon in Tokyo: The Occupation and Its Aftermath* (New York: Macmillan, 1954); Robert Wolf, ed., *Americans as Proconsuls: The United States Military Government in Germany and Japan* (Carbondale, Ill.: Southern Illinois University Press, 1984); William Woodard, *The Allied Occupation of Japan, 1945–1952, and Japanese Religions* (Leiden, The Netherlands: Brill, 1972); Rinjiro Sodei, *Dear General MacArthur: Letters From the Japanese During the American Occupation* (Lanham, Md.: Rowman & Littlefield, 2001)

WWII scholarship is huge and always growing. Among the works dealing with the military history of the war the following are noteworthy and were useful: Roy Appleman, et al., *Okinawa: the Last Battle* (Washington: Office of the Chief of Military History, 1948); Daniel Barbey, *MacArthur's Amphibious Navy: Seventh Amphibious Force Operations, 1943–1945* (Annapolis: Naval Institute Press, 1969); Clair Blair, *Silent Victory: The U.S. Submarine War Against Japan* (Philadelphia: Lippincott, 1975); Conrad Crane, *Bombs, Cities and Civilians: American Airpower Strategy in World War II* (Lawrence: University Press of Kansas, 1993); John Dower, *War Without Mercy: Race and Power in the Pacific War* (New York: Pantheon Books, 1986); Edward Drea, *MacArthur's Ultra: Codebreaking in the War Against Japan 1942–1945* (Lawrence: University Press of Kansas, 1992); Robert Eichelberger, *Our Jungle Road to Tokyo* (New York: Viking Press, 1950); Thomas E. Griffith Jr., *MacArthur's Airman: General George E. Kenney and the War in the Southwest Pacific* (Lawrence: University Press of Kansas, 1998); Robert R. Smith, *The Approach to the Philippines* (Washington: Office of the Chief of Military History, 1953); Robert Smith, *Triumph in the Philippines* (Washington: Office of the Chief of the Military History, 1963); Ronald Spector, *Eagle Against the Sun: The War with Japan* (New York: Free Press, 1985); Stephen R. Taffe, *MacArthur's Jungle War: The 1944 New Guinea Campaign* (Lawrence: University Press of Kansas, 1998).

Wartime diplomacy has attracted a great deal of attention from scholars as well. The following are a few of the books consulted in this study. Wesley M. Bagby, *The Eagle-Dragon Alliance: America's Relations With China in World War II* (Newark: University of Delaware Press, 1992); Russell D. Buhite, *Decisions at Yalta* (Wilmington, Del.: Scholarly Resources, 1986); Diane Clemens, *Yalta* (New York: Oxford University Press, 1970); John Dower, *Embracing Defeat: Japan in the Wake of World War II* (New York: Norton, 1999); Akira Iriye, *Power and Culture: The Japanese American War, 1941–1945* (Cambridge: Harvard University Press, 1981); Warren Kimball, *The Juggler: Franklin Roosevelt as Wartime Statesman* (Princeton: Princeton University Press, 1991); Walter La Faber, *The Clash: A History of U.S.-Japanese Relations* (New York: Norton, 1997); Edward Miller, *War Plan Orange: The U.S. Strategy to Defeat Japan, 1897–1945* (Annapolis: Naval Institute Press, 1991); Michael Sheng, *Battling Western Imperialism: Mao, Stalin and the United States* (Princeton: Princeton University Press, 1998); Christopher Thorne, *Allies of a Kind: The United States, Britain and the War Against Japan, 1941–1945* (Oxford: Oxford University Press, 1978); Barbara Tuchman, *Stilwell and The American Experience in China 1911–1945* (New York: Macmillan, 1971).

Among the many studies providing background on MacArthur's other assignments over the years are the following. For the Philippines key works are: Teodoro Agoncillo and Milagros Guerrero, *History of the Filipino People*, 5th ed. (Quezon City: R. P. Garcia Publishing Co., 1977); Uldarico Baclagon, *Military History of the Philippines* (Manila: St. Mary's Publishing Co., 1975); David Bernstein, *The Philippine Story* (New York: Farrar, Straus and Co., 1947); John Beck, *MacArthur and Wainwright: Sacrifice of the Philippines* (Albuquerque: University of New Mexico Press, 1974); Graham Cosmas, *An Army for Empire: The United*

States Army in the Spanish-American War (Columbia: University of Missouri Press, 1971); Charles Elliott, *The Philippines to the End of the Military Regime* (Indianapolis: Bobbs-Merrill Co., 1916); James Eyre, *The Roosevelt-MacArthur Conflict* (Chambersburg, Penn.; Croft Press, 1950); John Gates, *Schoolbooks and Krags: The Unites States Army in the Philippines, 1898–1901* (Westport, Conn.: Greenwood, 1973), Garel Grunder and William Livezey, *The Philippines and the United States* (Norman: University of Oklahoma Press, 1951); Federic Marquardt, *Before Bataan and After* (New York: Bobbs-Merrill Co., 1943); Milton Meyer, *A Diplomatic History of the Philippines* (Honolulu: University of Hawaii Press, 1965); Jonathan Wainwright, *General Wainwright's Story* (New York: Doubleday, 1946).

For the Bonus March and MacArthur as Army Chief of Staff, Russell D. Buhite, *Patrick J. Hurley and American Foreign Policy* (Ithaca: Cornell University Press, 1973), is a helpful work, as is the article by Donald Lisio, "A Blunder Becomes Catastrophe: Hoover, the Legion and the Bonus Army," *Wisconsin Magazine of History* 51 (Autumn, 1967): 37–50.

Although this book is based largely on the secondary literature and biographies available on MacArthur and his era, a number of manuscripts and published primary sources were also utilized. The following is a list of items consulted over years of research. In the MacArthur Memorial Archives in Norfolk, Virginia: the Douglas MacArthur Papers; the Richard K. Sutherland Papers; the Charles A Willoughby Papers; and the Faubion Bowers Oral History. In the Dwight D. Eisenhower Presidential Library: the Dwight D. Eisenhower Papers. In the Harry S. Truman Presidential Library: the Harry S. Truman Papers and the Dean Acheson Papers. At Clemson University: the James F. Byrnes Papers. At the Herbert Hoover Presidential Library: the Herbert Hoover Papers. At the University of Oklahoma: the Patrick J. Hurley Papers. At the Franklin D. Roosevelt Presidential Library: the Franklin D. Roosevelt Papers and the Henry Morgenthau Papers and Diaries. The National Archives: Modern Military Records and Department of State Papers.

Among the most important published sources were Department of State, *Foreign Relations of the United States* (Washington, D.C.: Government Printing Office, 1931–1951); U.S. Senate, Committee on Armed Service and Committee on Foreign Relations, *Hearings to Conduct an Inquiry into the Military Situation in the Far East and the Facts Surrounding the Relief of General of the Army Douglas MacArthur From His Assignment in That Area*, 82nd Congress, 1st sess. (Washington, D.C.: Government Printing Office, 1951).

Index

Soviet zone of occupation in Japan, 67; U.S.S.R., 72

Saddam Hussein, 169
Sams, Crawford, 86, 87
Sayre, Francis, 36, 43
Sebald, William, 147
Seven Years War (French and Indian War), 25, 122; Plains of Abraham, 122
Shigeru, Yoshida, 80
Short, Dewey, 150
Sino-American War, 126; Sino-Soviet Alliance of 1950, 90, 119, 126, 135, 152; Sino-Soviet Relations, 119, 135, 152
Southeast Asian region, 52
Southwest Pacific Area (SWPA), 50; SWPA Commander, 52, 55–57, 59, 60, 62, 63; SWPA Forces, 53
Spain, 4, 5, 24, 25; Mestizo class, (Philippines) 25, 26; Spain's East Asian colony, 25; Spanish-Cuban-American War, 5; Spanish Empire, 24; Spanish Mexico and China, 24
Sperry—Rand, 162
Spiritual regeneration of Japan, 25; Buddhists, 86; Christianity, 85, 86; Christianization campaign, 85; Dominicans, 24; Emperor worship, 72; Episcopalians, 85; Shintoism, 86
Stalin, Joseph, 43, 52, 55, 64, 94, 95, 105–7, 110, 113, 126, 132, 157–59
Stassen, Harold, 83, 84
State and War Departments, 78, 82; State Department's Policy Planning Staff, 81, 85, 89, 101, 123, 156; State-War-Coordinating Committee (SWNCC), 68, 69, 78; the War Department, 111, 169
Steinbeck, John, 89
Stimson, Henry, 13, 14, 27, 28, 33, 38, 39, 42, 43, 49, 169

Stratemeyer, George, 115, 132
Struble, Arthur, 131
Summerall, Charles, 6
Supreme Commander of Allied Powers (SCAP), 75; Civil Information and Education Section, 86; SCAP Public Health and Welfare Section, 86; Supreme Commander in Japan, 58, 81, 116; Tribunal sentencing of Homma, 76, 77
Sutherland, Richard, 38, 39, 49, 50, 56, 180

Taft, Robert, 143, 148, 155, 156, 183
Taft, William Howard, 5, 8, 88
Taiwan, 36, 41, 104, 106, 107, 109, 113, 114, 119, 120, 121, 126, 136, 137, 141, 142, 144, 147, 152, 153, 157, 158, 169; Formosa (Taiwan), 41, 56, 58, 59, 109, 120; Nationalists on Taiwan, 136, 137; Taiwan Strait, 114, 119, 126, 158
Taruc, Luis, 62
Taylor, Maxwell, 116
Tench, Charles, 69
Truman, Harry S., 20, 23, 59, 63, 68, 71, 76, 77, 79, 81, 81–85, 89, 90, 105, 107, 112–21, 123, 127, 128, 130, 135–38, 141–51, 153, 155–57, 161, 162, 168, 169
Truman, Doctrine, 79, 83
Tojo, Hideki, 77
Tydings, Millard, 44
Tydings-McDuffie bill, 28

U.N. meetings: Cairo, 56, 93; Casablanca, 56; Lake Success, New York, 113; Quebec, 56, 122; Teheran, 55, 56; Washington, 56
United Nations, 99–102, 107, 113, 115, 116, 123, 125, 126, 130, 131, 141, 142, 144, 145, 147, 156, 157; UN General Assembly, 102, 104,

~

About the Author

Professor **Russell D. Buhite** received his Ph.D. at Michigan State University where he studied with professors Paul A. Varg and Warren I. Cohen. He taught for twenty-five years at the University of Oklahoma, where for ten years he also served as chair of the history department. He subsequently held the position of head of the history department at the University of Tennessee. Since 1997, he has been, respectively, dean of the College of Arts and Sciences and professor of history at the University of Missouri-Rolla. He has published ten previous books and numerous articles on American foreign policy.